Microsoft®

OFFICE

For Windows™

Step by Step

Microsoft Press®

PUBLISHED BY
Microsoft Press
A Division of Microsoft Corporation
One Microsoft Way
Redmond, Washington 98052-6399

Library of Congress Cataloging-in-Publication Data
Microsoft Office for Windows step by step / Catapult, Inc.
          p.   cm.
    Includes index.
    ISBN 1-55615-648-0
    1. Microsoft Windows (Computer file)   2. Microsoft Word for
Windows.   3. Microsoft Excel for Windows.   4. Microsoft PowerPoint
for Windows.   5. Microsoft Mail for Windows.   6. Microsoft Access.
7. Business--Computer programs.
    I. Catapult, Inc.
HF5548.2.M477   1994
650'.0285'5369--dc20   94-31277
                                                                                            CIP

Printed and bound in the United States of America.

  2 3 4 5 6 7 8 9   MLML   9 8 7 6 5 4

Distributed to the book trade in Canada by Macmillan of Canada, a division of Canada Publishing Corporation.

A CIP catalogue record for this book is available from the British Library.

Microsoft Press books are available through booksellers and distributors worldwide. For further information about
international editions, contact your local Microsoft Corporation office. Or contact Microsoft Press International
directly at fax (206) 936-7329.

Pentium is a trademark of Intel Corporation. Microsoft, Microsoft Access, Microsoft Press, MS-DOS, and PowerPoint
are registered trademarks and Windows and Windows NT are trademarks of Microsoft Corporation.

Companies, names, and/or data used in screens and sample output are fictitious unless otherwise noted.

For Catapult, Inc.
Managing Editor: Donald Elman
Writer: Teresa S. Stover
Project Editor: Ann T. Rosenthal
Production/Layout Editors: Nailah Shami and Jeanne K. Hunt
Production Assistant: Joshua Elman

For Microsoft Press
Acquisitions Editor: Casey D. Doyle
Project Editor: Laura Sackerman

Catapult, Inc. & Microsoft Press

Microsoft Office for Windows Step by Step has been created by the professional trainers and writers at Catapult, Inc., to the exacting standards you've come to expect from Microsoft Press. Together, we are pleased to present this self-paced training guide, which you can use individually or as part of a class.

Catapult, Inc. is a software training company with years of experience in PC and Macintosh instruction. Catapult's exclusive Performance-Based Training system is available in Catapult training centers across North America and at customer sites. Based on the principles of adult learning, Performance-Based Training ensures that students leave the classroom with confidence and the ability to apply skills to real-world scenarios. *Microsoft Office for Windows Step by Step* incorporates Catapult's training expertise to ensure that you'll receive the maximum return on your training time. You'll focus on the skills that increase productivity the most while working at your own pace and convenience.

Microsoft Press is the independent—and independent-minded—book publishing division of Microsoft Corporation. The leading publisher of information on Microsoft software, Microsoft Press is dedicated to providing the highest quality end-user training, reference, and technical books that make using Microsoft software easier, more enjoyable, and more productive.

After you've used this *Step by Step* book, please fill out the feedback form in the back of the book and let us know what you think! Incorporating feedback from readers is a key component in continuously improving the books in the *Step by Step* series, and your help ensures that our materials remain as useful to you as possible.

Contents

Appendixes

About This Book

Microsoft Office is an integrated family of popular business applications that you can use together as a single application. Microsoft Office Standard edition (Office version 4.2) includes Microsoft Word, Microsoft Excel, Microsoft PowerPoint, and a Microsoft Mail workstation license. Microsoft Office Professional edition (Office version 4.3) adds Microsoft Access to this package.

Microsoft Office for Windows Step by Step shows you how to use Microsoft Office to produce sophisticated combination documents by integrating data you produce with the Microsoft Office applications. For example, you might want to add a Microsoft Excel chart of sales figures to an annual report you're creating in Word. Then you could distribute the report with a personalized letter that uses information from an Access database. Finally, you could use the report as the basis for a PowerPoint slide presentation for your sales staff.

Microsoft Office for Windows Step by Step is designed as a self-paced tutorial, and it can also be used in a classroom setting. You get hands-on practice using Office by using the practice files on the disk that accompanies this book. More information about the practice files and instructions for copying the practice files to your computer hard disk are in "Getting Ready," the next section in this book.

How to Use This Book

This book is designed for people learning the integration techniques of Microsoft Office for the first time, and for experienced users who want to learn better methods for creating files that use integrated information from more than one application. Either way, *Microsoft Office for Windows Step by Step* will help you get the most out of Microsoft Office.

This book assumes that you know how to use your computer and that you are familiar with using Microsoft Windows and using a mouse. It also assumes that you are familiar with the basics of at least one of the Microsoft Office applications, particularly Microsoft Word or Microsoft Excel. (To gain experience with one or more of the individual Microsoft Office applications, you can use the *Step by Step* book that is available for each application.)

Finding Your Best Path Through the Book

Microsoft Office for Windows Step by Step is divided into five major parts, each containing two or more related lessons. In Part 1, Lessons 1 through 4 provide a foundation for the other lessons in the book. Lesson 1 teaches you how to use the Microsoft Office Manager and the tools that are common to all Microsoft Office applications. Lessons 2 through 4 cover the six basic integration techniques for sharing information between applications: copying and moving, linking and embedding, and importing and exporting. In addition to learning each of these techniques, you also gain an understanding of when it is best to use a particular technique.

Since Parts 2 through 5 build on the knowledge you develop in Part 1, we recommend that you begin with Lessons 1 through 4. If you think you know the information covered in these lessons, you can review the Lesson Summary at the end of each lesson, and then read any sections that are unfamiliar.

With a basic understanding of the integration techniques, you can proceed through Parts 2 through 5 in any order. Each of these parts uses one application as the base into which information and resources from other Microsoft Office applications are integrated. In Part 2, the base application is Word; in Part 3, Microsoft Excel; in Part 4, PowerPoint; and in Part 5, Microsoft Access.

Within Parts 2 through 5, you can pick out those lessons that correspond to your specific needs, just as you might select individual recipes from a cookbook. The modular design of the lessons allows you to go directly to the information you want. To determine which lessons best fit your needs, you can refer to the following table, which describes the type of end product as well as the applications used in each lesson. In addition, the application icons and the integration technique indicators at the start of each lesson provide an instant reference to the applications and techniques covered in that lesson.

End product	Example	Applications	See
A text document containing a numerical table or chart	A marketing status report showing sales performance data	Word, with data from Excel	Lesson 5
A document with quantitative data that is automatically updated	A regular manufacturing report with figures from a workbook that changes weekly	Word, with linked data from Excel	Lesson 6
A document containing all or part of a slide presentation	A handout about a new product presentation	Word, with PowerPoint data	Lesson 7
A set of personalized form letters, including names, addresses, and other information from a database	A form letter to be mailed to potential clients that includes personalized information for each client	Word, with merged data from Access	Lesson 8
A document including a database table or report	A sales report that includes sales figures from a database	Word, with data from Access	Lesson 9

End product	Example	Applications	See
A workbook including a table or formatted text originally created in Word	An Excel workbook containing financial calculations on data from a Word table	Excel, with Word text or a Word table	Lesson 10
A workbook that includes an entire slide presentation, with graphics and transition effects	A manufacturing presentation within a production workbook that you electronically send to others	Excel, with presentation data from PowerPoint	Lesson 11
A workbook including information from a database table	A sales workbook that has information from a database table for complex analysis	Excel, with data exported from Access	Lesson 12
A slide presentation created from an existing Word document	A presentation, based on the company's annual report, to be given at a shareholders meeting	PowerPoint, with data from Word	Lesson 13
A slide presentation containing a calculated table or a chart of figures	A presentation to potential investors that includes calculated worksheets and charts	PowerPoint, with data from Excel	Lesson 14
A database table using tabular information originating in Word	An inventory database table created from an inventory list document	Access, with data from Word	Lesson 15
A database table, form, or report using information from a Microsoft Excel workbook	Product records in a workbook that could be used more effectively in a product database	Access, with data from Excel	Lesson 16

If you are working on a network and are running Microsoft Mail, you can do the optional Microsoft Mail exercises sprinkled throughout the lessons. These exercises cover various methods for sending integrated Microsoft Office files to other users in your workgroup.

Each lesson takes approximately 20 to 45 minutes, including the optional "One Step Further" exercise at the end of the lesson. At the end of each part, you will find a Review & Practice section that gives you the opportunity to practice the skills you learned in that part. Each Review & Practice allows you to test your knowledge and prepare for your own work.

Using This Book As a Classroom Aid

If you're an instructor, you can use *Microsoft Office for Windows Step by Step* for teaching computer users. You might want to select certain lessons that meet your students' particular needs and incorporate your own demonstrations into the lessons.

If you plan to teach the entire contents of this book, you should probably set aside up to three days of classroom time to allow for discussion, questions, and any customized practice you might create.

Conventions Used in This Book

Before you start any of the lessons, it's important that you understand the terms and notational conventions used in this book.

Procedural Conventions

- Hands-on exercises that you are to follow are given in numbered lists of steps (1, 2, and so on). A triangular bullet (▶)indicates an exercise with only one step.

- The word *choose* is used for carrying out a command from a menu or a dialog box.

- The word *select* is used for highlighting directories, filenames, text boxes, and menu bars and options, and for selecting options in a dialog box.

Notational Conventions

- Characters or commands that you type appear in **bold lowercase** type.

- Important terms (where first defined) and titles of books appear in *italic* type.

- Names of files, paths, or directories appear in ALL CAPITALS, except when they are to be directly typed in.

Keyboard Conventions

- Names of keys that you press are in small capital letters—for example, TAB and SHIFT.

- A plus sign (+) between two key names means that you must press those keys at the same time. For example, "Press ALT+TAB" means that you hold down the ALT key while you press TAB.

- You can choose menu commands with the keyboard. Press the ALT key to activate the menu bar, and then sequentially press the keys that correspond to the highlighted or underlined letter of the menu name and of the command name. For some commands, you can also press a key combination listed in the menu.

Mouse Conventions

- *Click* means to point to an object and then press and release the mouse button. For example, "Click the Microsoft PowerPoint button." The word "click" is used for selecting command buttons, option buttons, and check boxes.

- *Drag* means to hold down the mouse button while you move the mouse. For example, "Drag the object frame."

- *Double-click* means to rapidly press and release the mouse button twice. For example, "Double-click the Microsoft Office icon to start Microsoft Office."

Other Features of This Book

- Text in the left margin provides tips, additional useful information, or keyboard alternatives.

- The "One Step Further" exercise at the end of each lesson introduces new options or techniques that build on the commands and skills you used in the lesson.

- Each lesson concludes with a summary list of the skills you learned in the lesson and gives a brief review of how to accomplish particular tasks.

- The optional "Review & Practice" activity at the end of each part provides an opportunity to use the major skills presented in the lessons of that part. These activities reinforce what you have learned and encourage you to recognize new ways that you can use Microsoft Office.

Copy

- You can carry out many commands by clicking a button on a toolbar. If a procedure instructs you to click a button, a picture of the button appears in the left margin, as the Copy button does here.

- In Appendix A, you can review issues and suggestions having to do with installing Microsoft Office on your computer. Refer to this section of the book if you're having difficulty installing all or part of Microsoft Office, or if you're experiencing poor system performance while using Microsoft Office.

Cross-References to Microsoft Office Documentation

References to *Microsoft Office Getting Started* and the Office online Help at the end of each lesson direct you to specific chapters or Help topics for additional information. Use these materials to take full advantage of the features of Microsoft Office.

Online Help

The Help system in Microsoft Office provides a complete online reference to Microsoft Office. You'll learn more about the Help system in "Getting Ready," the next section in this book.

Microsoft Office Getting Started

This manual includes information about setting up and starting Microsoft Office, using the Help system, and working with the family of applications. It also provides explanations and examples of how the Microsoft Office applications work together, and how to share Microsoft Office information across different computers in a network.

Microsoft Word User's Guide

This manual includes detailed information about setting up and starting Microsoft Word, using its Help system, and working with the application. It also provides explanations of Word's unique features, which you can use to format text, design pages, create mail merge documents, customize Word, and create macros.

Microsoft Excel User's Guide

This manual includes detailed information about setting up and starting Microsoft Excel, using its Help system, and working with the application. It also provides explanations of Microsoft Excel's powerful tools, which you can use to create workbooks, generate charts, organize data, analyze information, and create pivot tables.

Microsoft PowerPoint User's Guide

This manual includes detailed information about setting up and starting Microsoft PowerPoint, using its Help system, and working with the application. It also provides explanations of PowerPoint's special capabilities, including working with objects, adding text and visuals, and creating speaker notes and slide shows.

Microsoft Access User's Guide

This manual includes detailed information about setting up and starting Microsoft Access, using its Help system, and working with the application. It also provides explanations of Microsoft Access features, which you can use to design databases, manage database objects, create tables and forms, generate reports, and design macros.

Getting Ready

This section of the book provides instructions for installing and using the *Step by Step* practice files on the disk that accompanies this book. After installing the practice files on your hard disk, you will review how to start Microsoft Office, use the Office online Help, and then quit Office.

You will learn how to:

- Install the *Step by Step* practice files on your computer hard disk.
- Start Microsoft Office.
- Use the online Help system in Microsoft Office.
- Quit Microsoft Office.

Installing the Practice Files from the Floppy Disk

The disk attached to the inside back cover of this book contains 45 practice files that you'll use as you work through the lessons in this book. You'll use the practice files to perform the tasks you learn in each lesson. For example, the lesson that teaches you how to link workbook information to a report instructs you to open two practice files: a Microsoft Excel workbook and a Word report. Then you learn how to link the workbook information to the report. Because the practice files simulate documents, spreadsheets, databases, and presentations that you'll encounter in a typical business setting, you can easily transfer what you learn from this book to your own work. The names, lesson numbers, and descriptions of all practice files are listed in Appendix B.

Install the practice files

Follow these steps to copy the practice files to your computer hard disk so that you can use them with the lessons.

1 If your computer isn't already on, turn it on now.

- If Microsoft Windows starts automatically when you turn on your computer, go to step 2.
- If MS-DOS starts, type **win** and press ENTER to start Windows, and then go to step 2.
- If a menu appears and Windows is one of the choices, select and start Windows.

2   Put the Practice Files disk in drive A or B of your computer.

The disk can be found in the package on the inside back cover of this book.

3   In the Program Manager window, open the File menu and choose Run.

4   In the Run dialog box, type **a:\install** (or **b:\install** if you put the disk in drive B), and then press ENTER. Do not type a space between the drive letter and the slash.

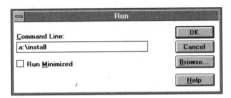

After the installation program begins, a new window appears, asking some questions.

5   Follow the directions on the screen. For best results in using the practice files with this book, accept the recommendations made by the installation program until it finishes.

6   Remove the disk from your computer.

Because the practice files are now on your computer hard disk, you won't need the Practice Files disk again as you work through the lessons unless you want to reinstall some or all of the practice files.

The Step by Step installation program copies the practice files from the floppy disk onto your hard disk in a subdirectory called PRACTICE of the Microsoft Office home directory (usually called MSOFFICE). You'll need to remember the name of the drive and directory where the practice files are stored so you can open the files for each lesson.

Using the Practice Files

The text in each lesson of this book explains when and how to use the practice files for that lesson. Be sure to follow the instructions for saving the files and giving them new names. In general, each practice filename begins with the lesson number, or "P" followed by the part number for Review & Practice files. When you save or create a file, you specify a name that ends with that number. Renaming the practice files allows you to make changes, experiment, and observe results without affecting the original practice files. With the original practice files intact, you can reuse them later if you want to repeat a lesson or try a new option.

Note You will notice a variation to this convention with the Microsoft Access database practice file named SBSDATA.MDB, which is used in several lessons. Instead of saving and renaming the entire database file, you will copy and rename individual tables, forms, or reports within the database.

The practice files are used in the lessons to simulate what you might encounter using Microsoft Office in a typical business setting. For these lessons, imagine that you work for a company called Childs Play. Childs Play is a manufacturer of progressive and educational toys. Throughout these lessons, you use Microsoft Office to create documents, workbooks, and other files for the Human Resources department at Childs Play using resources and information from a combination of Microsoft Office applications.

Starting Microsoft Office

This book assumes that you have Microsoft Windows and Microsoft Office installed on your system. If you have not yet installed Microsoft Office, refer to *Microsoft Office Getting Started,* which came with your Microsoft Office software package, and follow the instructions for a full installation of Microsoft Office. Also refer to Appendix A, toward the end of this book, to learn about issues regarding Microsoft Office installation.

The normal installation of Microsoft Office creates a new group or uses an existing group, and then creates an icon within that group for the Microsoft Office program and its applications. Double-clicking the group icon that contains Microsoft Office opens the program group window that holds the icon for Microsoft Office.

Note The following steps might not be necessary if you have chosen to have Microsoft Office automatically start up as soon as Microsoft Windows starts.

Start Microsoft Office from Program Manager

If you need help starting Microsoft Windows, refer to step 1 under the preceding exercise, "Install the practice files."

Use the following procedures to start Microsoft Office and dock the Office Manager toolbar at the top of your screen. The following illustration might be different from your screen, depending on your particular setup, the applications installed on your computer, and any customizing you might have done. For more information about Microsoft Windows, see *Microsoft Windows User's Guide.*

1   Start Microsoft Windows if it is not already started.

2   In the Program Manager window, double-click the Microsoft Office group icon to open the Microsoft Office program group.

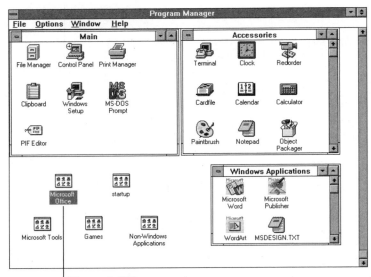

|Microsoft Office group icon

Microsoft Office

Microsoft Office

3 Double-click the Microsoft Office program icon.

The Office Manager toolbar appears on the screen, displaying the program icons for all the Microsoft Office applications.

4 On the Office Manager toolbar, click the Microsoft Office button to open the Office menu, and then choose Customize.

5 Click the View tab, select the Small Buttons option button, and then choose the OK button.

The Office Manager toolbar docks at the top of your screen and appears with small buttons.

Using Online Help

Microsoft Office includes Help, a complete online reference for all of the Office applications. While you are using Office or an Office application, you can refer to online Help to learn how to use the features and tools for that application. You can access Help information in several ways. You can choose the Help command from the Office Manager menu, or you can choose a command from the Help menu in the menu bar of any individual Office application.

To get Help information	Do this
By topic or activity	From the Help menu in Office, choose Contents.
While working in a window or dialog box	Press F1 or choose the Help button in the dialog box.
About a specific command, toolbar button, or other element on the screen	Click the Help button on the toolbar, and then click the command, button, or other screen element.
By keyword	Double-click the Help toolbar button. In the Search dialog box, type a keyword and then select a Help topic.

Display the list of Help topics

Microsoft Office

▶ On the Office Manager toolbar, click the Microsoft Office button to open the menu, and choose Help.

If you are in any Microsoft Office application, you can choose Contents from the Help menu.

The Microsoft Office Help Contents window looks like the following illustration.

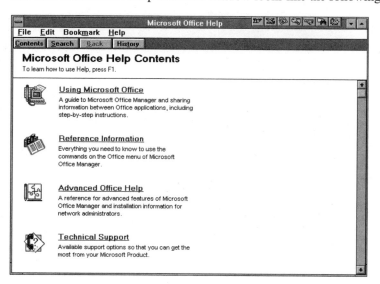

You can size, move, and scroll through a Help window. You can switch between the Help window and the current Microsoft Office application, or you can choose the Always On Top command from the Help menu to keep the Help window on top of other windows so that you can refer to Help while you work.

Getting Help on Help

To learn how you can make best use of all the information in Help, you can read through instructions for using Help.

Learn to use Help

1   With the Microsoft Office Help Contents window still open, press F1.

The Contents For How To Use Help list appears.

2   In the first paragraph, locate the phrase "scroll bar," which has a dotted underline, and click it.

A definition of the term appears in a popup box. Clicking a term that has a dotted underline displays a popup definition in a topic window.

3   Click the phrase again.

The definition popup box closes.

4   Locate the phrase "Help Basics," which has a solid underline, and click it.

A new screen appears with information about Help. Clicking an underlined term "jumps" you to a related topic.

5   Click the term "jumps," which has a dotted underline.

Another popup definition appears.

6   Click the term again.

The definition closes.

Getting Help on a Topic

The Help system allows you to find information on a topic in several ways. First, the Contents list allows you to choose from among a list of functionally organized topics and subtopics. Second, the Search option allows you to quickly locate Help topics by using a key word. If you know the command or term you want help on, you can go directly to the topic. You can also use the Index or the Help button on the Standard toolbar to find Help.

In the next exercises, you look for information using the Contents list and the Search option.

Use the Help Contents list

Microsoft Office

1   On the Office Manager toolbar, click the Microsoft Office button to open the menu, and choose <u>H</u>elp.

The Microsoft Office Help Contents list appears again.

2   Scroll downward in the list, and click any topic that is underlined in green.

A new screen appears with information about the topic.

Search for a topic

1 Click the Search button.

2 In the Search dialog box, type **print**

The printing files topic appears in the list.

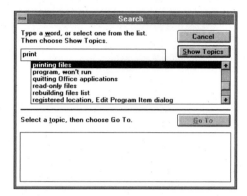

3 In the list of topics, select "printing files," and then choose the Show Topics button.

4 Select a topic from the list at the bottom of the dialog box, and then choose the Go To button.

The Help window displays the selected topic.

5 In the Help window, from the File menu, choose Exit.

The Help window closes.

Quitting Microsoft Office Manager

When you quit Microsoft Office Manager, the Microsoft Office Manager toolbar closes. Quitting Microsoft Office Manager does not close any open Microsoft Office applications. To quit Microsoft Office Manager, do the following.

Quit Microsoft Office Manager

▶ On the Office Manager toolbar, click the Microsoft Office button to open the menu, and choose Exit.

1 Introducing Integration with Microsoft Office

In this part, you'll learn the basics of using Microsoft Office, including how to start up and shut down Microsoft Office and the individual applications. You'll also practice using the various tools and resources available to all Microsoft Office applications. You'll learn the basic techniques for integrating information between the different applications, including copying and moving information, linking and embedding information, and importing and exporting files. This will provide you with the foundation you need to effectively work through the succeeding lessons in this book.

Using Microsoft Office Resources

With Microsoft Office and the Microsoft Office Manager, you can quickly open and switch between Microsoft Excel, Word, PowerPoint, Microsoft Access, and Microsoft Mail. A number of tools, such as ClipArt Gallery, WordArt, and Graph, are available across all the Microsoft Office applications. In this lesson, you'll learn how to use the Microsoft Office Manager to perform a variety of activities across applications, and you'll experiment with the Microsoft Office tools common to these applications.

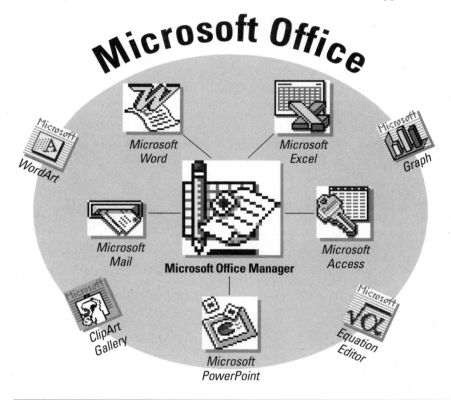

You will learn how to:

- Open, switch between, and close different Microsoft Office applications using the Microsoft Office Manager.

- Use Microsoft Office tools that are common to all Microsoft Office applications, such as the ClipArt Gallery and the WordArt tool.

Estimated lesson time: 40 minutes

Using the Microsoft Office Manager

The *Microsoft Office Manager* is a utility that allows Microsoft Office applications to be used together in an integrated fashion. When the Microsoft Office Manager is open, it displays a toolbar on the Windows desktop, and this toolbar is always visible. The Office Manager toolbar consists of buttons that represent each of the Microsoft Office applications you have installed on your computer. These buttons can vary depending on the applications you have, and how you customize the toolbar.

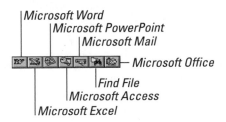

In the following exercises, you'll open existing files in your PRACTICE directory called 01LESSN.DOC, 01LESSN.XLS, and 01LESSN.PPT. You'll use these files throughout this lesson to learn about using Microsoft Office resources. For better system performance, be sure that any other applications are closed.

For information about installing the practice files on your hard disk, see "Getting Ready," earlier in this book.

Starting and Switching Between Applications

You can quickly start an application or switch to an open application with a single click. If needed, you can have all the applications open at once. You can also have the Microsoft Office Manager arrange two different application windows on a single screen. This can be particularly useful when sharing information between applications.

Start Word and open a document file

Start Word with the Office Manager toolbar, and then open the practice file.

1   Be sure that the Microsoft Office Manager is open.

   The Microsoft Office Manager is open if you see the Office Manager toolbar on your desktop. If the Microsoft Office Manager is not open, double-click the Microsoft Office icon in Program Manager.

Microsoft Word

2   On the Office Manager toolbar, click the Microsoft Word button. If the Tip Of The Day dialog box appears, choose the OK button.

3   On the Standard toolbar in Word, click the Open button.

   The Open dialog box appears.

Open

4   In the Directories list, open the PRACTICE subdirectory within the MSOFFICE directory.

5 In the File Name list, select the file 01LESSN.DOC, and then choose the OK button.

The file opens, displaying a letter to new employees of Childs Play. Be sure that both the Word window and the document window are maximized. Your screen should look like the following illustration.

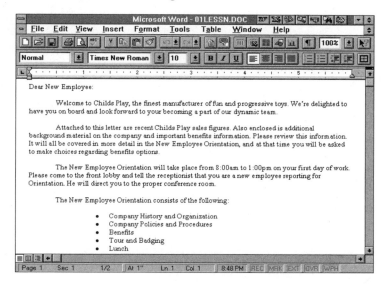

If your Office Manager toolbar does not appear near the upper-right corner as shown here, see the section "Starting Microsoft Office" in "Getting Ready."

6 From the File menu, choose Save As.

The Save As dialog box appears.

7 In the File Name box, type **lessn01** and then choose the OK button. If the Summary Info dialog box appears, choose the OK button.

The document is saved with the filename LESSN01.DOC, which appears in the title bar.

Start Microsoft Excel and open a workbook file

Start Microsoft Excel with the Office Manager toolbar, and then open the practice file.

Microsoft Excel

1 On the Office Manager toolbar, click the Microsoft Excel button.

2 On the Standard toolbar in Microsoft Excel, click the Open button.

The Open dialog box appears.

3 In the Directories list, open the PRACTICE subdirectory within the MSOFFICE directory.

4 In the File Name list, select the file 01LESSN.XLS, and then choose the OK button.

The file opens, displaying a workbook with information about new Childs Play employees in Sheet1. Be sure that both the Microsoft Excel window and the workbook window are maximized. Your screen should look like the following illustration.

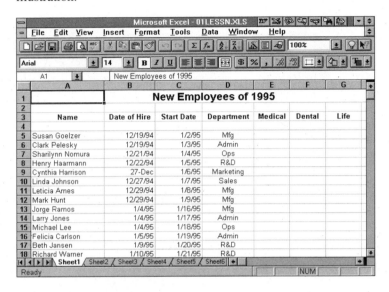

5   From the File menu, choose Save As.

The Save As dialog box appears.

6   In the File Name box, type **lessn01** and then choose the OK button. If the Summary Info box appears, choose the OK button.

The workbook is saved with the filename LESSN01.XLS, which appears in the title bar.

Start PowerPoint and open a presentation file

Start PowerPoint with the Office Manager toolbar, and then open the practice file.

Microsoft PowerPoint

1   On the Office Manager toolbar, click the Microsoft PowerPoint button. If the Tip Of The Day dialog box appears, choose the OK button.

The PowerPoint dialog box appears.

2   Select Open An Existing Presentation, and then choose the OK button.

The Open dialog box appears.

3   In the Directories list, open the PRACTICE subdirectory within the MSOFFICE directory.

Having multiple applications and files open at the same time can cause operations to run slower than usual. Refer to Appendix A to learn strategies for optimizing your system performance.

4 In the File Name list, select the file 01LESSN.PPT and then choose the OK button.

The file 01LESSN.PPT opens, displaying a portion of the new employee orientation presentation. Be sure that both the PowerPoint window and the presentation window are maximized. Your screen should look like the following illustration.

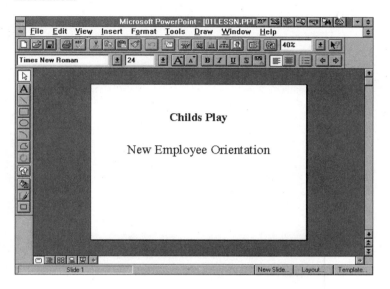

5 From the File menu in PowerPoint, choose Save As.

The Save As dialog box appears.

6 In the File Name box, type **lessn01** and then choose the OK button. If the Summary Info dialog box appears, choose the OK button.

The file is saved with the filename LESSN01.PPT, which appears in the title bar.

You have now opened three Microsoft Office applications using the Office Manager toolbar.

Switch among the open applications

Use the Office Manager toolbar to move among the three open applications.

Microsoft Word

1 On the Office Manager toolbar, click the Microsoft Word button.

The open Word document appears. The PowerPoint document is still open, but it is now running in the background.

Microsoft Excel

2 On the Office Manager toolbar, click the Microsoft Excel button.

The open Microsoft Excel workbook appears.

*Microsoft
PowerPoint*

3   On the Office Manager toolbar, click the Microsoft PowerPoint button.

The open PowerPoint presentation appears.

Arrange two applications on one screen

Use the Office Manager toolbar to tile and view the contents of two files in two
different applications.

Microsoft Word

1   With the PowerPoint presentation still displayed, hold down SHIFT and, on the
Office Manager toolbar, click the Microsoft Word button.

The windows are arranged, or *tiled*, so that you can see PowerPoint and Word at
the same time, as shown in the following illustration.

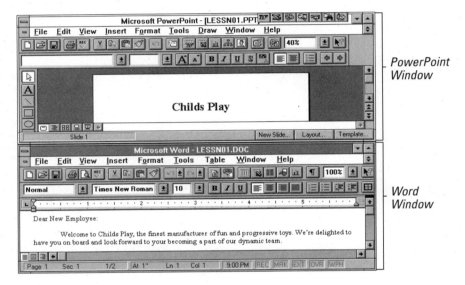

*PowerPoint
Window*

*Word
Window*

2   Click the Maximize button on the Word window to restore it to full size.

3   On the Office Manager toolbar, click the Microsoft PowerPoint button.

4   Click the Maximize button on the PowerPoint window to restore it to full size.

Managing Files, Tools, and Utilities

You can use the Microsoft Office Manager to open and use the Microsoft Windows
tools and utilities in Program Manager and File Manager. This can help you move
between Microsoft Office and Microsoft Windows, providing easy access to Windows
features and commands.

Switch to Program Manager

Use the Microsoft Office menu to switch to Program Manager.

Microsoft Office

The commands on this menu can vary depending on the applications you have and how you customize the menu.

1 On the Office Manager toolbar, click the Microsoft Office button.

The Microsoft Office menu appears.

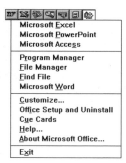

2 From the Microsoft Office menu, choose Program Manager.

The Program Manager appears.

Switch to File Manager

Use the Microsoft Office menu to switch to File Manager.

1 On the Office Manager toolbar, click the Microsoft Office button.

The Microsoft Office menu appears.

2 From the Microsoft Office menu, choose File Manager.

The File Manager appears.

3 From the File menu in File Manager, choose Exit.

Quitting Microsoft Office Applications

There are several ways you can quit Microsoft Office applications. When you choose Exit from the Microsoft Office menu, only Microsoft Office closes, which also closes the Office Manager toolbar. The applications opened by the Office Manager remain open, and must each be closed individually.

The following exercises demonstrate three basic methods for quitting Microsoft Office applications.

Quit PowerPoint

Use PowerPoint's File menu to quit the application.

1 On the Office Manager toolbar, click the Microsoft PowerPoint button.

The current PowerPoint presentation appears.

2 From the File menu in PowerPoint, choose Exit.

3 If you see the Save dialog box, choose Yes.

Quit Microsoft Excel

Use Microsoft Excel's Control-menu box to quit the application.

Microsoft Excel

1   On the Microsoft Office Manager toolbar, click the Microsoft Excel button.

The current Microsoft Excel workbook appears.

2   Double-click the Control-menu box in the far upper-left corner of the Microsoft Excel window.

3   If you see the Save dialog box, choose Yes.

Quit Word

Use the Office Manager toolbar to quit Word.

Microsoft Word

1   Hold down ALT and, on the Office Manager toolbar, click the Microsoft Word button.

This method closes the application directly from the Office Manager toolbar.

2   If you see the Save dialog box, choose Yes.

Using Microsoft Office Tools

Microsoft Office provides a set of powerful tools that are available across all applications. These tools can enhance your files and provide easy interaction between the Microsoft Office applications.

The following table lists several of the shared Microsoft Office tools.

With this tool	You can	For more information
ClipArt Gallery	Access more than 1,000 clip art illustrations from any Microsoft Office application. You can add images from other applications to the ClipArt Gallery, and add images you've created yourself.	In Microsoft Office online Help, search for "previewing pictures."
Equation Editor	Enter correctly and automatically formatted mathematical expressions, such as fractions and exponents, into your file.	In Word online Help, search for "equation editor."

With this tool	You can	For more information
WordArt	Apply creative effects to text in your document. These effects include stretching, shadows, and unusual alignments.	In Word online Help, search for "WordArt."
Graph	Create a variety of charts from tables of numeric data.	Open Graph and press F1 for Help.
Microsoft Organization Chart	Create an organization chart in your file, to show the management structure of a company.	In PowerPoint, open Microsoft Organization Chart, and press F1 for Help.
PowerPoint Viewer	View slide presentations on your computer or on other computers on which PowerPoint is not installed.	In PowerPoint online Help, search for "PowerPoint Viewer."

The following is the general process for including the objects created by these tools.

■ Select the location where the object will be inserted.

■ Open the tool.

■ Create or select the object.

You will learn more about embedding in Lesson 3, "Linking and Embedding Objects."

■ Insert, or *embed*, the object in the selected location.

In the following exercises, you experiment with a few of these Microsoft Office tools.

Including Graphics with the ClipArt Gallery

You can create appeal in your document by using clip art illustrations. The ClipArt Gallery is available in all Microsoft Office applications, and includes more than 1,000 separate clip art images.

You can open the ClipArt Gallery in Word, Microsoft Excel, or PowerPoint by choosing the Object command from the Insert menu. You can open the ClipArt Gallery in Microsoft Mail or Microsoft Access with the Insert Object command from the Edit menu.

Open a Word document

As the Childs Play Human Resources Coordinator, you've written a letter to all newly hired employees. Open the letter and do some minor editing.

Microsoft Word

Open

1   On the Office Manager toolbar, click the Microsoft Word button. If the Tip Of The Day dialog box appears, choose the OK button.

2   On the Standard toolbar, click the Open button.

The Open dialog box appears.

3   In the Directories list, be sure that the MSOFFICE directory and the PRACTICE subdirectory are selected.

4   In the File Name list, select LESSN01.DOC, and then choose the OK button.

The selected document opens. Be sure that both the Word window and the document window are maximized.

Insert clip art into the document

Below your signature, you want to add a decorative flourish. Insert a clip art object in the letter.

Note   If you do not have the full set of Microsoft Office clip art, run the Microsoft Office Setup program again, choose the Complete/Custom installation, and then select Clip Art for installation. The Microsoft Office clip art will be added to any existing clip art in your ClipArt Gallery.

---

1   Scroll to the bottom of the first page, and then place the insertion point in the blank line below "Human Resources Coordinator."

This will be the point where your clip art is inserted.

2   From the Insert menu, choose Object.

The Object dialog box appears.

3   Be sure that the Create New tab is active.

4   In the Object Type list, select Microsoft ClipArt Gallery, and then choose the OK button.

The Microsoft ClipArt Gallery dialog box appears.

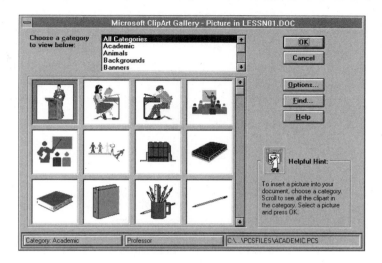

Note If you have recently installed Microsoft Office and have not used the ClipArt Gallery yet, you might see a dialog box asking if you want to add pictures from the ClipArt Gallery. Choose the Yes button. Adding the pictures might take a few minutes.

5 From the category list at the top, select the Dividers and Decorations category.

You might have to scroll through the list to find it. The set of Dividers and Decorations clip art appears in the preview area.

Note If you do not see the Dividers and Decorations category, this might mean that the ClipArt Gallery is using a different set of clip art, from another application. You can choose a comparable category for this exercise.

6 Select the first graphic, called Art Deco Fan.

You can see the name of the clip art at the bottom of the Gallery dialog box.

7 Choose the OK button.

The selected clip art appears in your document at the insertion point.

8 If necessary, adjust the sizing boxes and move the object until it looks similar to the following illustration.

Save

9   On the Standard toolbar, click the Save button.

The ClipArt Gallery is available in the other Microsoft Office applications as well, and can be inserted in the same manner. For more information, from the Office Manager toolbar, click the Microsoft Office button. From the Microsoft Office menu, choose Help. Click the Search button, and then type **previewing pictures** to learn more about using the ClipArt Gallery with different applications.

Note   If you do not see any Help topics for Microsoft Office, run the Microsoft Office Setup program again, and choose the Complete/Custom installation. Select Microsoft Office Help for installation.

Designing Effects with WordArt

By using WordArt, you can create special design effects with your text. The WordArt tool transforms text into a graphic that you can stretch or condense, rotate, add a shadow to, slant up or down, or curve over or under.

You can open WordArt in Word, Microsoft Excel, or PowerPoint with the Object command from the Insert menu. You can open WordArt in Microsoft Mail or Microsoft Access with the Insert Object command from the Edit menu.

Open a PowerPoint presentation

You have begun to create the new employee orientation presentation in PowerPoint. Open the file in order to edit the slides.

*Microsoft
PowerPoint*

1   On the Office Manager toolbar, click the Microsoft PowerPoint button. If the Tip Of The Day dialog box appears, choose the OK button.

The PowerPoint dialog box appears.

2   Select Open An Existing Presentation, and then choose the OK button.

The Open dialog box appears.

3   In the Directories list, be sure that the MSOFFICE directory and the PRACTICE subdirectory are selected.

4   In the File Name list, select LESSN01.PPT, and then choose the OK button.

The selected presentation opens. Be sure that the PowerPoint window and the presentation window are maximized to see all of the information in the windows.

Insert WordArt text

You want to add the company motto, "Where Work Is Play," to the title slide of the employee orientation presentation. Because this is the title slide, you want the motto to look especially appealing. Insert the motto as a WordArt object.

1 Be sure that Slide 1, "Childs Play New Employee Orientation," is the active slide.

2 From the Insert menu, choose Object.

The Insert Object dialog box appears.

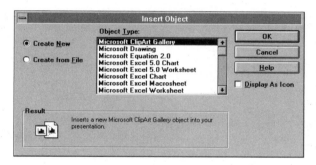

3 In the Object Type list, scroll downward to select Microsoft WordArt 2.0, and then choose the OK button.

A dialog box appears for you to enter the text for which you want to design font effects.

4 Type **Where Work Is Play**, and then double-click the Control-menu box in the upper-left corner of the Enter Your Text Here dialog box.

The dialog box closes, and the words you entered appear as a WordArt object in an object frame on the slide.

Design a font effect for presentation text

Now that the motto is entered as a WordArt object on your slide, specify the font effects for the motto.

1 Click outside the object to redraw the slide.

The WordArt object should now be selected, with the sizing boxes displayed.

Childs Play

'New Employee Orientation'

Where Work Is Play'

2   From the Edit menu, choose WordArt Object, and then choose Open.

The WordArt 2.0 dialog box appears.

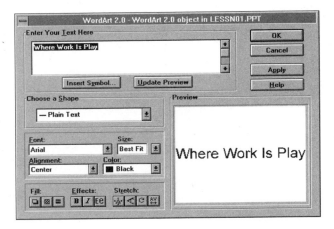

You can also select shapes, fills, fonts, and other WordArt effects from the toolbar that appears with the WordArt Enter Your Text Here dialog box.

3   Under Choose A Shape, click the down arrow and select the shape for Arch Down (Curve). This shape looks like a thin smile.

The shape name appears in the text box after you select the shape. If you select the wrong one, keep trying until Arch Down (Curve) appears in the text box.

4   Under Fill, click the first button, which opens the Shadow dialog box. Select the third shadow type, and then choose the OK button.

5   Under Effects, click the B (Bold) button.

After adding each new effect, the text appears with the specified change in the Preview box.

6   Choose the OK button.

The text appears with the specified effects in your slide.

7 Adjust the sizing boxes so that the object frame is beneath the words "New Employee Orientation," and it is the proper size for the slide, as shown in the following illustration.

Save

8 On the Standard toolbar, click the Save button.

WordArt is available in the other Microsoft Office applications as well, and it can be used in the same manner. For more information about using WordArt, search for "WordArt" in Word online Help.

Charting with the Graph Tool

You can transform your numbers into colorful and easy-to-understand charts using the Graph tool. A variety of chart types and formats are available to help present your information effectively.

You can open Graph in Word, Microsoft Excel, or PowerPoint with the Object command from the Insert menu. You can open Graph in Microsoft Mail or Microsoft Access with the Insert Object command from the Edit menu.

Create a graph in a document

Along with your letter to new employees, you want to include historical sales performance information. Use Graph to enter the sales data in a datasheet from which a chart will be created.

Microsoft Word

1 On the Office Manager toolbar, click the Microsoft Word button.

Word appears again with the LESSN01.DOC document.

2 Go to the second page of the document, and position the insertion point in the blank line below the title "Sales Performance."

This is where the graph will be inserted.

In Word, you can also open Graph by clicking the Insert Chart button on the Standard toolbar.

3 From the Insert menu, choose Object.

The Object dialog box appears.

4 In the Object Type list, select Microsoft Graph 5.0, and then choose the OK button.

The Microsoft Graph datasheet appears.

		A	B	C	D	
		1st Qtr	2nd Qtr	3rd Qtr	4th Qtr	
1	East	20.4	27.4	90	20.4	
2	West	30.6	38.6	34.6	31.6	
3	North	45.9	46.9	45	43.9	
4						

LESSN01.DOC - Datasheet

5 Replace the existing headings and data in the datasheet with the following information. Delete the data in any columns you are not using.

	1993	1994
Toys	**240,000**	**240,300**
Sports	**162,900**	**182,900**
Books	**64,300**	**51,700**

6 Click outside the datasheet window.

The datasheet disappears, and the graph is drawn in your document.

Center

7 On the Formatting toolbar, click the Center button to center the graph horizontally on the page.

You might need to click on some text in the Word document to activate the Word toolbars. Your graph should look similar to the following illustration.

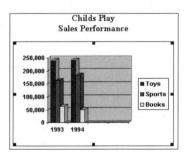

Save

8 On the Standard toolbar, click the Save button.

Graph is available in the other Microsoft Office applications as well, and it can be used in the same manner. For more information about using Graph, open Graph and press F1 for Help.

One Step Further

You can customize the Office Manager toolbar to automate tasks you do frequently in Microsoft Office as well as in Windows. You can add, remove, and rearrange buttons on the Office Manager toolbar. You customize the Office Manager toolbar using the Microsoft Office menu.

Add a button to the Office Manager toolbar

While working in the different Microsoft Office applications, you find that you often use File Manager. So that you'll be able to open File Manager more quickly while you're working, add the File Manager button to the Office Manager toolbar.

Note If you have Microsoft Mail installed on your system, you can use this procedure to add the Microsoft Mail button to the toolbar for easy access to your mail messages.

Microsoft Office

1 On the Office Manager toolbar, click the Microsoft Office button.

2 From the Microsoft Office menu, choose Customize.

3 In the Customize dialog box, click the Toolbar tab to make it active.

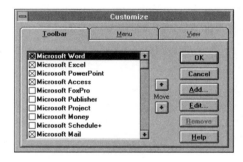

4 In the applications list, select the File Manager check box.

5 Choose the OK button.

The File Manager button, which looks like a filing cabinet, is added to the Office Manager toolbar.

File Manager

File Manager

6 On the Office Manager toolbar, click the File Manager button.

File Manager opens.

7   From the <u>F</u>ile menu in File Manager, choose E<u>x</u>it.

Remove a button from the Office Manager toolbar

Although the Find File button is on the Office Manager toolbar, you have found that you do not use it very often. Remove the Find File button from the Office Manager toolbar.

Microsoft Office

1   On the Office Manager toolbar, click the Microsoft Office button.

2   From the Office Manager menu, choose <u>C</u>ustomize.

3   In the Customize dialog box, click the Toolbar tab.

4   In the applications list, clear the Find File check box.

5   Choose the OK button.

The Find File button is removed from the Office Manager toolbar.

Note   You can use this same process to add or remove commands from the Microsoft Office menu. In the Customize dialog box, instead of clicking the Toolbar tab, click the Menu tab.

End the Lesson

1   To continue to the next lesson, from the <u>F</u>ile menu in Word, choose <u>C</u>lose. To quit for now, from the <u>F</u>ile menu in Word, choose E<u>x</u>it.

If you see the Save dialog box, choose Yes.

Microsoft PowerPoint

2   Hold down ALT and, on the Office Manager toolbar, click the Microsoft PowerPoint button.

If you see the Save dialog box, choose Yes.

Lesson Summary

To	Do this	Button
Open a Microsoft Office application	On the Office Manager toolbar, click the application button, such as the Word button.	
Switch to another open application	On the Office Manager toolbar, click the application button, such as the Microsoft Excel button.	

To	Do this	Button
Tile the windows of two applications	Display the first application by clicking its button on the Office Manager toolbar. Tile the two windows by holding down SHIFT and clicking the button of the second application on the Office Manager toolbar.	
Switch to Program Manager	On the Office Manager toolbar, click the Microsoft Office button. From the Microsoft Office menu, choose Program Manager.	
Switch to File Manager	On the Office Manager toolbar, click the Microsoft Office button, and then choose File Manager.	
Quit a Microsoft Office application	Hold down ALT and, on the Office Manager toolbar, click the application button.	
Insert clip art into a document	Position the insertion point in the document, where you want the clip art to appear. From the Insert menu in Word, Microsoft Excel, or PowerPoint, choose Object. Or, from the Edit menu in Microsoft Mail or Microsoft Access, choose Insert Object. Be sure the Create New tab is active, and then from the Object Type list, choose ClipArt Gallery. Select the clip art, and then choose OK.	
Design font effects with WordArt	Position the insertion point where you want the WordArt to appear. From the Insert menu in Word, Microsoft Excel, or PowerPoint, choose Object. From the Edit menu in Microsoft Mail or Microsoft Access, choose Insert Object. In the Object Type list choose WordArt. In the dialog box, enter the text you want. From the Edit menu, choose WordArt 2.0 Object, and then choose Open. Select the effects you want, and then choose OK.	

To	Do this
Create a chart from a table of numbers	Position the insertion point where you want the chart to appear. From the Insert menu in Word, Microsoft Excel, or PowerPoint, choose Object. From the Edit menu in Microsoft Mail or Microsoft Access, choose Insert Object. In the Object Type list, choose Graph, and then choose OK.

For more information on	See in *Microsoft Office Getting Started*
Opening, switching between, and quitting applications	Chapter 3, "Getting Started with Microsoft Office"
Using Microsoft Office tools	Chapter 3, "Getting Started with Microsoft Office"
Customizing the Microsoft Office Manager	Chapter 3, "Getting Started with Microsoft Office"

For online information about	From
Opening and quitting Office applications, and arranging the application windows	The Microsoft Office menu, choose Help, click the Search button, and then type **arranging Office application windows**
Switching between open applications	The Microsoft Office menu, choose Help, click the Search button, and then type **switching applications**
Switching to applications and utilities not displayed on the Office Manager toolbar	The Microsoft Office menu, choose Help, click the Search button, and then type **menu**
Using the ClipArt Gallery	The Microsoft Office menu, choose Help, click the Search button, and then type **previewing pictures**
Using WordArt	The Microsoft Word Help menu, choose Search, and then type **WordArt**
Using Graph	Graph, press F1

Preview of the Next Lesson

In the next lesson, you'll learn how to copy and move your information between different applications in Microsoft Office. You'll learn how to copy and move information using the menu commands as well as drag-and-drop editing.

Copying and Moving Information

You're probably already familiar with copying and moving information within a single document or file. You can also copy and move information between documents or files in different applications. When you do this, the information you've copied or moved appears as if you typed the information there to begin with.

For example, you might have information in a Microsoft Excel workbook that you want to use in a Word document or a PowerPoint presentation. You can easily transfer information between documents in different applications by copying or moving it.

In this lesson, you'll learn how to copy and move information from one application into another. If you are working on a network and have Microsoft Mail, you'll also learn one method of mailing a file to another user.

You will learn how to:

- Copy information between applications.
- Move information between applications.
- Use drag-and-drop editing to copy and move information.

Estimated lesson time: 20 minutes

Start the lesson

Start Microsoft Excel and open 02LESSN.XLS. Start Word and open 02LESSN.DOC.

1 Be sure that the Microsoft Office Manager is open.

The Microsoft Office Manager is open if the Office Manager toolbar appears on your desktop. If Microsoft Office Manager is not open, double-click the Microsoft Office icon in Program Manager.

Microsoft Excel

2 On the Office Manager toolbar, click the Microsoft Excel button.

3 From your PRACTICE directory, open 02LESSN.XLS.

This workbook contains employee benefits information. Be sure that both the Microsoft Excel window and the workbook window are maximized.

4 Save the document as **lessn02.xls**

Microsoft Word

5 On the Office Manager toolbar, click the Microsoft Word button. If the Tip Of The Day dialog box appears, choose the OK button.

6 From your PRACTICE directory, open 02LESSN.DOC.

This is a document regarding employee benefits information. Be sure that both the Word window and the document window are maximized.

7 Save the document as **lessn02.doc**

Copying Information Between Applications

When you copy information between applications, you make a duplicate of the information from one file (the *source*) and place that duplicate into another file (the *destination*). You therefore end up with the same information in two different places—in both the source and the destination files.

There are two methods for copying. You can copy either with the Copy command and the Paste command, or with drag-and-drop editing.

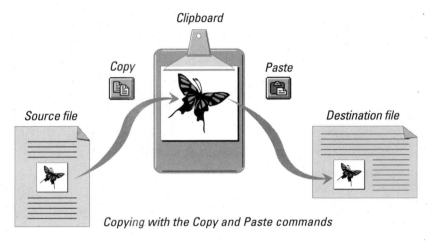

Copying with the Copy and Paste commands

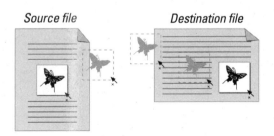

Copying with drag-and-drop editing

Copy information between applications when your project meets all of the following criteria:

■   You have information in one application, and you want to duplicate and use it in another application.

- The information stands alone, and it does not need to be updated if the source file changes.

- The copied information either does not need to be edited, or you're able to edit it within the destination application.

Using Commands to Copy Information

You can use the Copy and Paste commands on the Edit menu, or their equivalent buttons on the Standard toolbar, to copy information between applications. When you select information and choose the Copy command, the selected information is copied onto the *Clipboard*—a temporary holding area in Microsoft Windows that always remembers the last set of information you copied or cut. When you select the destination location and choose the Paste command, the contents of the Clipboard are inserted at that location. Because the information remains on the Clipboard, you can repeat the Paste command to place it in multiple locations.

Copy and paste between applications

Copy employee benefits information from Word and paste it into a Microsoft Excel workbook.

1   In the Word document, select the first paragraph and numbered list, from "Childs Play" through "Stock Option Plan."

Copy

2   On the Standard toolbar in Word, click the Copy button.

3   On the Office Manager toolbar, click the Microsoft Excel button to switch to the open Microsoft Excel workbook.

Microsoft Excel

4   Be sure that Sheet1 is the active sheet.

5   Select cell A3 to make it active.

This is where the copied information from Word will be pasted.

Paste

6   On the Standard toolbar in Microsoft Excel, click the Paste button, and then click in an empty cell.

The Word text appears in the workbook.

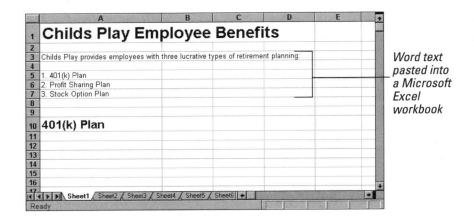

Word text
pasted into
a Microsoft
Excel
workbook

Save

7   On the Standard toolbar in Word, click the Save button.

Using Drag-and-Drop Editing to Copy Data

As an alternative to using the Copy command and the Paste command with the Clipboard, you can use drag-and-drop editing to copy information between applications. With drag-and-drop editing, you bypass the Clipboard and use the mouse to directly copy the information from one location to another. To copy (rather than move) information by dragging, you hold down CTRL while you drag.

To move (rather than copy) with drag-and-drop editing, you simply drag the selection without holding down CTRL or any other key.

When you use drag-and-drop editing to copy, you need to arrange the source and destination files on your screen in such a way that the locations from and to which you're dragging are both visible. Note that only one window can be active at a time.

Copy information with drag-and-drop editing

Drag benefits information from a Word document and drop it into a Microsoft Excel workbook that provides benefits information to new employees.

Microsoft Word

1   With Microsoft Excel as the active application, hold down SHIFT and click the Microsoft Word button on the Office Manager toolbar.

The Microsoft Excel and Word windows are tiled on the screen.

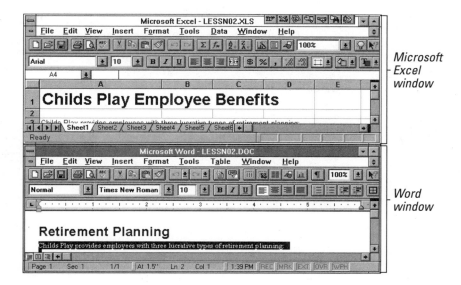

Microsoft Excel window

Word window

2   In the Microsoft Excel workbook, be sure that cell A14 is visible.

3   In the Word document, select the first sentence below the "401(k) Plan" heading.

4   Position the mouse pointer on the selection until the pointer changes to an arrow. While holding down CTRL, drag the selection from Word into cell A14 of the Microsoft Excel workbook. Release the mouse button.

The selected text is copied into cell A14 of the workbook.

5   Click the Maximize button in the Microsoft Excel window so that you'll be able to better view your results.

6   On the Standard toolbar in Microsoft Excel, click the Save button.

Moving Information Between Applications

When you move information, you remove the selected information from the source document and place it in the destination document. You therefore end up with only one copy of the information. It no longer exists in the source—it exists only in the destination.

There are two methods for moving information. You can move either with the Cut command and the Paste command on the Edit menu, or with drag-and-drop editing.

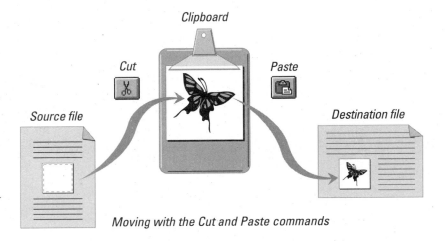

Moving with the Cut and Paste commands

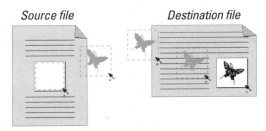

Moving with drag-and-drop editing

Move information between applications when your project meets all of the following criteria:

- You have information in one application, and you want to transfer it to a file in another application.
- The information stands alone, and it does not need to be updated if the original source file changes.
- The moved information either does not need to be edited, or you're able to edit it within the destination application.

Using Commands to Move Information

You can either use the Cut command and the Paste command on the Edit menu, or you can use their equivalent buttons on the Standard toolbar to move information between applications. When you select information and choose the Cut command, the source application removes the selected information from the source document and places it on the Clipboard. When you select the destination location and choose the Paste command, the contents of the Clipboard are inserted at that location.

Cut and paste between applications

Move Childs Play benefits information from a Word document and paste it into a Microsoft Excel workbook.

Microsoft Word

1 On the Office Manager toolbar, click the Microsoft Word button to switch to Word. Click the Maximize button on the Word window.

2 Select the second paragraph under the "401(k) Plan" heading, which begins with "You'll also benefit" and ends with "aggressive investment."

Cut

3 On the Standard toolbar in Word, click the Cut button.

The selected information is removed from the worksheet and copied to the Clipboard.

4 On the Office Manager toolbar, click the Microsoft Excel button to switch to your Microsoft Excel workbook.

Microsoft Excel

5 Select cell A16 to make it active.

This is where the selected copied from Word will be moved to.

Paste

6 On the Standard toolbar, click the Paste button.

The selected information is pasted from the Clipboard into the Microsoft Excel workbook.

Save

7 On the Standard toolbar, click the Save button.

Using Drag-and-Drop Editing to Move Data

To copy (rather than move) information with drag-and-drop editing, hold down CTRL while dragging.

When you select information and then use drag-and-drop editing, you bypass the Clipboard and use the mouse to directly move the information from one location to another. When you use drag-and-drop editing between applications, the information is automatically moved rather than copied.

Move information with drag-and-drop editing

Use drag-and-drop editing to move Childs Play employee benefits information from a Word document into a Microsoft Excel workbook.

1 With Microsoft Excel active, hold down SHIFT and click the Microsoft Word button on the Office Manager toolbar.

The Microsoft Excel and Word windows are tiled on the screen.

2 In the Microsoft Excel workbook, be sure that cell A28 is visible.

3 In the Word document, select the third paragraph below the "401(k) Plan" heading, which begins with "The following table" and ends with "your annual salary."

4 Position the mouse pointer on the selection until the pointer changes to an arrow. Drag the selection from Word into cell A28 of the Microsoft Excel workbook. Release the mouse button.

The selected text is moved into cell A28 of the workbook and it is removed from the Word document.

Save

5 Click the Maximize button in the Microsoft Excel window so that you'll be able to better view your results.

6 On the Standard toolbar, click the Save button.

Microsoft Word

7 On the Office Manager toolbar, click the Microsoft Word button, and then click the Maximize button in Word to view your document after moving the selected text.

One Step Further

If you are working on a network and are running Microsoft Mail, you can stay in your application and mail the current file to other users on your network. To do this, you use the Send command on the File menu in the active application. You might want to do this if you want a co-worker to review a file, or if someone else needs a file that you have.

Note This exercise is optional, and works only if you have installed Microsoft Mail version 3.0 or later on your computer.

Mail the letter to another user

Before mailing the letter to the new employees, you want your manager as well as a colleague in the Sales Department to review it for accuracy. From Word, send the document using Microsoft Mail.

1 From the File menu in Word, choose the Send command.

The Send Note dialog box appears with an icon that represents your document.

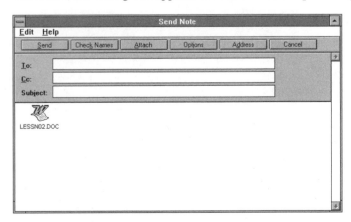

2   In the To box, type the mail user name of another user on your network. Also type your own user name so that you will receive a copy of the document.

You can select user names by choosing the Address button.

Note   If you do not want to send this document to other users, you can just use your own user name to send it to yourself.

---

3   In the Subject box, type **Microsoft Office Test**

4   In the Message Text box, type **This is a test**, or any other message you prefer.

5   Click the Send button.

The Word document and your message are sent to the user you specified, and they will be in your mailbox as well.

End the Lesson

1   Hold down ALT and, on the Office Manager toolbar, click the Microsoft Word button.

If you see the Save dialog box, choose Yes.

2   To continue to the next lesson, from the File menu in Microsoft Excel, choose Close. To quit for now, from the File menu in Microsoft Excel, choose Exit.

If you see the Save dialog box, choose Yes.

Lesson Summary

To	Do this	Button
Copy information from one application to another by using menu commands	Select the information in the source application to be copied. On the Standard toolbar, click the Copy button. Switch to the destination application, and position the insertion point where you want to insert the copied information. On the Standard toolbar, click the Paste button.	

To	Do this	Button
Copy information from one application to another using drag-and-drop editing	Tile the windows for the source and destination applications so that both are visible on the screen. Select the information in the source application to be copied. Position the mouse pointer near the edge of the selection until the pointer changes to an arrow. Hold down CTRL and drag the selection to the destination application. When the insertion point is in the proper location, release the mouse button.	
Move information from one application to another by using menu commands	Select the information in the source application to be moved. On the Standard toolbar, click the Cut button. Switch to the destination application and position the insertion point where you want to insert the moved information. On the Standard toolbar, click the Paste button.	
Move information from one application to another using drag-and-drop editing	Tile the windows for the source and destination applications so that both are visible on the screen. Select the information in the source application to be moved. Position the mouse pointer near the edge of the selection until the pointer changes to an arrow. Drag the selection to the destination application. When the insertion point is in the proper location, release the mouse button.	

For more information on	See in *Microsoft Office Getting Started*
Copying and moving information between applications	Chapter 4, "How Office Applications Work Together"
Sending a file to another user from within the application	Chapter 6, "Sharing Information with Others"

For online information about	From the Microsoft Office menu, choose <u>H</u>elp, click the Search button, and then
Copying information from one application to another by using menu commands	Type **copying and pasting**
Copying information from one application to another using drag-and-drop editing	Type **drag-and-drop editing**

Preview of the Next Lesson

In the next lesson, you'll learn how to insert, open, and edit information created by different applications. You'll also learn how to link information between two different applications so that the information is automatically updated when it changes in the source application.

Linking and Embedding Objects

You can link information between two documents in different applications so that the information is automatically updated when the original information changes. This can be useful when you have information in one document that you need in another document and both the information and the destination file change periodically, such as with a monthly status report.

You can also insert, open, and edit information that was created by a different application—using the resources of one application within another application. You're probably already familiar with inserting clip art graphics. You can use this same embedding process to insert files created in other types of applications.

For example, if you are creating a presentation in PowerPoint in which you need to include budget information, you might find it useful to use Microsoft Excel resources within the PowerPoint slides. You can use Microsoft Excel to handle the functions it does best, such as calculating and number formatting, while still working primarily in the PowerPoint document.

In this lesson, you'll learn how to link information to be automatically updated. You'll also learn how to insert, open, and edit information that was created by a different application. If you are working on a network and are running Microsoft Mail, you'll learn how to attach a file to a mail message.

You will learn how to:

- Link information in different applications.
- Edit and update linked information.
- Embed an existing file in another application.
- Create and insert new information by using another application.
- Edit and update inserted information.

Estimated lesson time: 40 minutes

Start the lesson

Start PowerPoint and open 03LESSN.PPT. Start Microsoft Excel and open 03LESSN.XLS.

1 Be sure that the Microsoft Office Manager is open.

The Microsoft Office Manager is open if the Office Manager toolbar appears on your desktop. If Microsoft Office Manager is not open, double-click the Microsoft Office icon in Program Manager.

Microsoft PowerPoint

2 On the Office Manager toolbar, click the Microsoft PowerPoint button. If the Tip Of The Day dialog box appears, choose the OK button.

3 When the application starts, select Open An Existing Presentation, and then choose the OK button.

4 From your PRACTICE directory, open 03LESSN.PPT.

This file consists of a portion of the new employee orientation presentation that will include current sales figures for the various Childs Play product lines. Be sure that both the PowerPoint window and the presentation window are maximized.

5 Save the presentation as **lessn03.ppt**. If you see the Summary Info dialog box, choose the OK button.

Microsoft Excel

6 On the Office Manager toolbar, click the Microsoft Excel button.

7 From your PRACTICE directory, open 03LESSN.XLS.

This workbook contains Childs Play sales figures that are updated monthly. Be sure that both the Microsoft Excel window and the workbook window are maximized.

8 Save the worksheet as **lessn03.xls**

Linking Objects Between Applications

You might be familiar with linking cells in Microsoft Excel. When the contents of the original cell are changed, the contents of the linked cell change automatically.

Likewise, you can select information in one file, and then *link* it to a file in another application. When you change the information in the original, or *source,* file, the contents of the linked *object* (or information) in the *destination* file change automatically. In this way, you have a live link between two files in two applications.

For example, you might have a Microsoft Excel workbook that contains ongoing budget information that is updated on a weekly basis. You can link a portion of this budget information to your regular monthly status report. By linking, you know that your status report will contain the most current information.

The process for linking objects between applications is similar to that for copying information between applications. You use the Copy command and the Paste Special command with the Clipboard to link objects.

The following illustration demonstrates how information is linked between files.

Source file

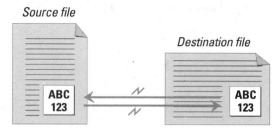

A linked object contains the same information as the source file.

Source file

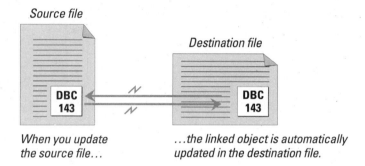

When you update   *...the linked object is automatically*
the source file...   *updated in the destination file.*

Linking is preferable to copying in the following instances:

- You need a live link to information stored in other files.
- You don't want to substantially increase the destination file size.
- All users have access to the source file.

When you link an object, the information is stored in the source file, and any editing takes place in the source file. When you double-click the linked object in the destination file, the source application and file open for you to edit.

Link an object

You have access to a sales workbook in Microsoft Excel that you want to use in your new employee orientation presentation. The figures in the sales workbook are updated on a monthly basis. You want the figures to be automatically updated in your presentation whenever this happens. Link the information from Microsoft Excel to your PowerPoint presentation.

1   In the Microsoft Excel workbook, be sure that the 1995 Sales-1 sheet is active.

2   Select all the information shown, from cell A1 through cell H7.

Copy

*Microsoft
PowerPoint*

3   On the Standard toolbar, click the Copy button.

4   On the Office Manager toolbar, click the Microsoft PowerPoint button to switch to the open PowerPoint presentation.

Be sure that Slide 1, with the heading "1995 Sales Performance," is displayed. This is where the information from Microsoft Excel will be inserted.

5   From the Edit menu, choose Paste Special.

The Paste Special dialog box appears.

6   In the Paste Special dialog box, select the Paste Link option button.

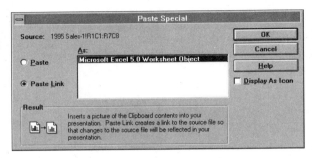

This option creates the link between the pasted information in the slide and the original information in Microsoft Excel, the source application.

7   Choose the OK button.

The Microsoft Excel information is inserted and linked to the slide. Now, whenever the information changes in the Microsoft Excel workbook, the information in the PowerPoint slide is automatically updated.

8   Use the sizing boxes around the object frame to adjust the size of the sheet object in the slide.

Your slide should look similar to the following illustration.

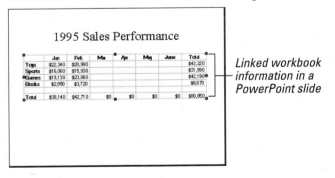

*Linked workbook
information in a
PowerPoint slide*

Save

9 On the Standard toolbar, click the Save button.

Update a linked object in an open file

Another month has gone by, and you have just received the sales figures for March. Enter the information into the Microsoft Excel workbook. Then, see how the changes in the source file in Microsoft Excel affect the linked information in the destination file in PowerPoint.

Microsoft Excel

1 On the Office Manager toolbar, click the Microsoft Excel button to switch back to the workbook.

2 In the March column, type the following figures in cells D2 through D5: **25,400**, **13,900**, **20,500**, and **4,020**

Tip Because these cells are formatted for currency, you don't need to type the dollar sign ($) or comma (,)—Microsoft Excel adds them as soon as you press ENTER.

---

3 On the Office Manager toolbar, click the Microsoft PowerPoint button to switch back to the presentation.

You'll see that the figures for March you just typed in the Excel workbook are also updated in your presentation, as shown in the following illustration.

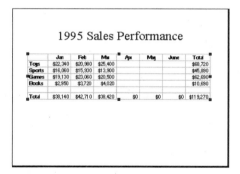

4 On the Standard toolbar, click the Save button.

5 From the File menu, choose Close.

The PowerPoint presentation closes.

Update a linked object in a closed file

Now you have the sales figures for April. Enter the information into the Microsoft Excel workbook. Then, see how the changes in the source file in Microsoft Excel affect the linked information in the destination file in PowerPoint—even when the file is closed.

Microsoft Excel

Save

Microsoft PowerPoint

1   On the Office Manager toolbar, click the Microsoft Excel button to switch to the workbook.

2   In the April column, type the following figures in cells E2 through E5: **26,200, 14,100, 19,400,** and **3,790**

3   On the Standard toolbar, click the Save button.

4   From the File menu, choose Close to close the workbook.

5   On the Office Manager toolbar, click the Microsoft PowerPoint button to switch back to the PowerPoint application.

6   From your PRACTICE directory, open LESSN03.PPT.

On Slide 1, you'll see that the figures for April that you typed in the Microsoft Excel workbook are updated in your presentation, even though the file was closed when you entered the data.

Edit a linked object from the destination file

You're working on the PowerPoint presentation containing the linked information, and you receive the new sales figures for May. Open the source application and file from within the linked object in PowerPoint, and then edit the workbook.

1   In the PowerPoint slide, double-click the linked object.

The file containing the linked information appears. You can now edit the linked information.

2   In the May column, type the following figures in cells F2 through F5: **26,400, 14,000, 19,500,** and **3,800**

3   On the Standard toolbar in Microsoft Excel, click the Save button.

4   From the File menu, choose Close.

5   On the Office Manager toolbar, click the Microsoft PowerPoint button.

The linked object is updated to reflect your changes for May.

6   On the Standard toolbar in PowerPoint, click the Save button.

Embedding Objects from Another Application

Embedding a file from another application is similar to inserting a piece of clip art. The clip art was created by a graphics application, but you need the art in a non-graphics application file. So you insert, or *embed*, a copy of the clip art in your application. The embedded clip art object becomes integrated with your file.

Likewise, you can insert information generated by another application into your current application, creating an *embedded object*. You can then double-click the embedded object to edit it. You can either embed information from an existing file, or create and embed a new object. Either way, you can use the full resources of another application within your file, as shown in the following illustration.

*Double-click the embedded object to open it in
its source application.*

Embedding is preferable to linking objects in the following instances:

- The information does not need to be updated frequently or automatically.
- You want to be able to edit the information without affecting other files.
- You do not need a live link to information stored in other files.
- File size is not a concern.
- A variety of users might need the file, but they might not have access to the source file.

When you embed an object, the information is stored and edited in the same file in which the object is embedded. This can significantly increase the size of the file. When you double-click the embedded object, it opens a small application window within the current application, and you can use the other application's menu and toolbars to edit, format, and make any other changes.

Note   Double-clicking an embedded object provides a different result than double-clicking a linked object. Double-clicking a linked object opens the source application and file for editing in a full screen. By contrast, when you edit an embedded object, the source file is unaffected. The changes take place only in the embedded object.

Embedding generally operates on an entire file. You embed the entire file, even though you might only view a portion of it. However, with some applications you can select a portion of a file, and then copy and paste it into the destination file. That portion is inserted, not as a static picture, but as an embedded object. You can double-click the object to open and edit it just like other embedded objects.

Embedding Objects from Existing Files

You can select information from another application's file, and then embed it as an object in your current application's file. If you double-click the embedded object to edit it, the original information from the source file remains unchanged. The embedded object is not linked to the source file. Instead, it is a copy of the source information that can be edited as if it were originally created in the destination application. In this way, you can use the full resources of another application within your file without affecting anything external to your file.

The process for embedding objects between applications is similar to that for inserting clip art from the ClipArt Gallery. You use the Object command from the Insert menu, specify the file, and then embed the file as an object.

Embed an object from an existing file

In another slide of the new employee orientation, embed a copy of an entire Microsoft Excel workbook.

Next Slide

1 In the PowerPoint presentation, go to Slide 2 by clicking the Next Slide button in the lower-right corner.

2 Click in the frame below the title "1995 Sales Performance."

This selects the text area of the slide, and it will be where the embedded workbook object is inserted.

3 From the Insert menu, choose Object.

The Insert Object dialog box appears.

4 Select the Create From File option.

The File box lists your current path, including the PRACTICE directory, as shown in the following illustration. If necessary, choose the Browse button to find the correct path.

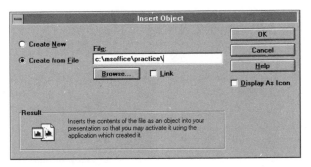

5 Click at the right end of the path, and type **lessn03.xls**

This specifies the location and the filename of the workbook you want to embed in your slide.

6   Choose the OK button.

PowerPoint embeds a copy of the Microsoft Excel workbook file in the selected slide. This might take a few seconds.

7   If necessary, drag the sizing boxes and the object frame to adjust the size and position of the embedded workbook. Your screen should look similar to the following illustration.

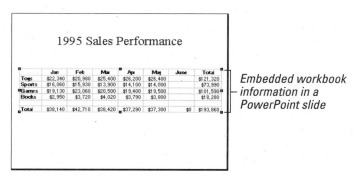

Embedded workbook information in a PowerPoint slide

Note   If the workbook contains multiple sheets, the sheet that was active when the workbook was last saved is shown in the embedded object. If necessary, you can change the active sheet by editing the embedded object.

Edit an object embedded from an existing file

You need to make some changes to the embedded Microsoft Excel workbook. Open and edit the embedded workbook.

1   Double-click the embedded workbook object.

Your PowerPoint menu and toolbars change to the Microsoft Excel menu and toolbars. You can now edit the embedded object using Microsoft Excel commands and tools.

2   Switch to the 1995 Sales-2 sheet. Your screen should look like the following illustration.

Microsoft Excel menu

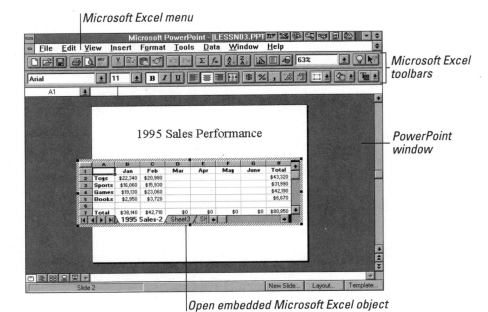

Microsoft Excel toolbars

PowerPoint window

Open embedded Microsoft Excel object

3   In the March column, type the following figures in cells D2 through D5: **25,400**, **13,900**, **20,500**, and **4,020**

4   Click outside the embedded workbook.

The embedded object is updated to reflect your changes for March. Your menu and toolbars change back to those of PowerPoint.

5   On the Standard toolbar, click the Save button.

Save

Edit an embedded object's source file

When you embedded the Microsoft Excel workbook in your presentation slide, you made an independent, unlinked copy of it. When the source workbook changes, the embedded object in the slide remains as it was. You've received sales figures for April. Enter them into the workbook. Then notice that those changes are not reflected in the embedded object.

1   On the Office Manager toolbar, click the Microsoft Excel button.

Microsoft Excel

2   From your PRACTICE directory, open LESSN03.XLS.

3   Be sure that the 1995 Sales-2 sheet is active.

You'll see that the changes you made to the sheet from within PowerPoint have not changed the Microsoft Excel source information.

4   In the April column, type the following figures in cells E2 through E5: **26,200**, **14,100**, **19,400**, and **3,790**

5   On the Standard toolbar in Microsoft Excel, click the Save button.

6   From the File menu, choose Close.

7   On the Office Manager toolbar, click the Microsoft PowerPoint button.

8   Be sure that Slide 2 is the active slide.

You'll see that the changes you made to the Microsoft Excel sheet have not changed the embedded object.

*Microsoft
PowerPoint*

Embedding a New Object

You can also use the resources from another application to create a new embedded object. For example, in a PowerPoint presentation you might want to include a table that contains figures that will need periodic updating and recalculation. Because Microsoft Excel handles this task best, you can embed the table as a Microsoft Excel workbook. You can then open the workbook from within the PowerPoint presentation anytime you needed to update it. The workbook exists only within the PowerPoint presentation, but it gives you all the capabilities of Microsoft Excel when you need them.

The process for embedding a new object is similar to that for embedding existing objects. You use the Object command from the Insert menu, indicate that you're creating new information, select the application, and then embed the object.

Create and embed a new object

You have sales performance information for January and February that you need to have only here in this presentation—it does not need to be in a separate workbook by itself. In another slide of the new employee presentation, embed a new workbook object and enter this information.

1   In the PowerPoint presentation, go to Slide 3 and click in the blank frame below the title "1995 Sales Performance."

This selects the text area of the slide, which is where the embedded workbook object will be inserted.

2   From the Insert menu, choose Object.

The Object dialog box appears. Be sure that the Create New option is selected.

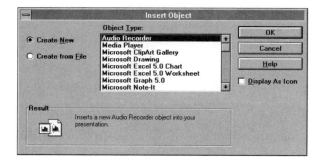

3 In the Object Type list, select Microsoft Excel 5.0 Worksheet.

4 Choose the OK button.

Microsoft Excel opens and displays a blank workbook. Your menu and toolbars change to the Microsoft Excel menu and toolbars.

5 Enter the following information into the sheet. You will add the information for March later.

	Jan	**Feb**	**Mar**
Toys	$22,340	$20,980	
Sports	$16,060	$15,930	
Games	$19,130	$23,060	
Books	$2,950	$3,720	

6 Use the sizing boxes around the object frame to adjust its size. This reflects how much of the worksheet is actually shown in the presentation slide. Adjust the object frame so that only those cells containing information are visible, as shown in the following illustration.

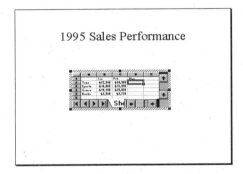

7 Click outside the workbook object.

PowerPoint embeds a copy of your new Microsoft Excel information in your presentation file, and your menu and toolbars change back to those of PowerPoint. Because you created the workbook from within your presentation file, this is the only place where this workbook is available. It is not a separate Microsoft Excel file external to PowerPoint.

8 Adjust the size and position of the embedded object frame to make it fit properly on the slide.

Your slide should look similar to the following illustration.

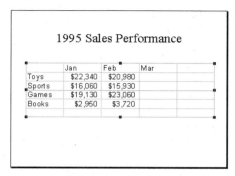

1995 Sales Performance

	Jan	Feb	Mar	
Toys	$22,340	$20,980		
Sports	$16,060	$15,930		
Games	$19,130	$23,060		
Books	$2,950	$3,720		

Save

9   On the Standard toolbar, click the Save button.

Edit a new embedded object

Make changes to the new embedded object to update the employee orientation slides with the latest available data.

1   In Slide 3, double-click the embedded object.

You can delete an object by selecting it and then pressing the DELETE key.

Your PowerPoint menu and toolbars change to the Microsoft Excel menu and toolbars. You can now edit the embedded object using Microsoft Excel commands and tools.

2   In the March column, type the following figures in cells D2 through D5: **$25,400**, **$13,900**, **$20,500**, and **$4,020**

3   Click outside the object.

The embedded object is updated to reflect your changes. Your menu and toolbars change back to those of PowerPoint.

4   On the Standard toolbar, click the Save button.

5   From the File menu, choose Close.

Attach a file to a mail message

You need to send this draft of the new employee orientation to another user on your network. Attach your presentation to a Microsoft Mail message and then send it to another user on your network.

Note   This exercise is optional, and works only if you have installed Microsoft Mail version 3.0 or later on your computer.

Microsoft Mail

1   On the Office Manager toolbar, click the Microsoft Mail button.

The Microsoft Mail window appears.

Note If you don't see this button on your toolbar, but you do have Microsoft Mail installed, add the button by choosing the Customize command from the Office Manager menu. On the Toolbar tab, select the Microsoft Mail check box, and choose OK.

2 Click the Compose button.

The Send Note dialog box appears.

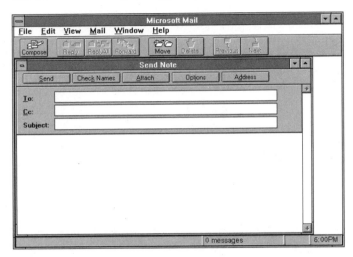

3 In the To box, type the mail user name of another user in your network. Also type your own user name.

If you do not know any other user names, using your own user name is sufficient.

4 In the Subject box, type **Microsoft Office Test**

5 In the Message Text, type **This is a test**, or any other message you prefer.

6 Click the Attach button.

The Attach dialog box appears.

7 From your PRACTICE directory, select LESSN03.PPT, choose the Attach button, and then choose the Close button.

The attached file appears in your message as a PowerPoint icon.

8 Choose the Send button.

The document and your message are sent to the users you specified, and they are in your mailbox as well. If the recipients have PowerPoint installed, they can then double-click the icon to view the presentation.

9 Hold down ALT and, on the Office Manager toolbar, click the Microsoft Mail button.

Microsoft Mail closes, and PowerPoint appears.

One Step Further

If you decide that you no longer need to have an object linked between applications, you can break the link. When you break a link, the information remains in your document as a static picture. Although the object will no longer be updated and cannot be edited, you can still move, resize, or delete the object.

Break the link to a linked object

You've decided that you no longer need a live link between the sales information in the Microsoft Excel workbook and your new orientation presentation. Break the link to convert the object into a static picture.

1   Be sure that PowerPoint is the active application.

2   From your PRACTICE directory, open LESSN03.PPT and go to Slide 1.

3   From the Edit menu, choose Links.

The Links dialog box appears.

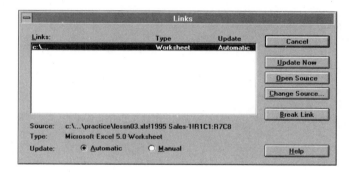

4   In the Links box, select the link you want to break.

5   Choose the Break Link button.

A message asks you to confirm that you want to convert the linked object to a picture.

6   Choose the OK button.

The link is removed from the list.

7   Choose the Close button.

The object looks the same as before, but it is now static information. If the information in Microsoft Excel changes, the object in PowerPoint will not be updated.

Update the unlinked information

You've just received new sales information for June. Update the Microsoft Excel workbook. Notice that the object in your PowerPoint presentation no longer accepts the updates, because the link is broken.

Microsoft Excel

1   On the Office Manager toolbar, click the Microsoft Excel button.

2   From the PRACTICE directory, open LESSN03.XLS and switch to the 1995 Sales-1 sheet.

3   In the June column, type the following figures in cells G2 through G5: **27,100, 14,200, 20,300,** and **4,000**

4   On the Standard toolbar, click the Save button.

Save

5   On the Office Manager toolbar, click the Microsoft PowerPoint button.

You'll see that the changes for June have not been updated in your slide, because the link no longer exists between the object and the Microsoft Excel file.

*Microsoft
PowerPoint*

6   On the Standard toolbar, click the Save button.

End the Lesson

1   Hold down ALT and, on the Office Manager toolbar, click the Microsoft PowerPoint button.

If you see the Save dialog box, choose Yes.

2   To continue to the next lesson, from the File menu in Microsoft Excel, choose Close. To quit for now, from the File menu in Microsoft Excel, choose Exit.

If you see the Save dialog box, choose Yes.

Lesson Summary

To	Do this
Link an object between two applications	In the source file, select the information to be linked and choose the Copy button. In the destination file, position the insertion point. From the Edit menu, choose Paste Special, select Paste Link, and then choose OK.
Edit and update a linked object from the source file	In the source file, edit the linked information. The object in the destination file is automatically updated.
Edit and update a linked object from the destination file	In the destination file, double-click the linked object. The source application and file open. Edit the object. The object in the destination file is automatically updated.

To	Do this
Embed an object from an existing file	Position the insertion point where you want the object to appear. From the Insert menu, choose Object. Select the Create From File option, and then type the path and filename for the file that contains the information to be embedded. Choose OK.
Edit and update an embedded object	Double-click the embedded object. The object's source application opens. Edit the object. Click outside the object when you're finished.
Create and embed a new object	Position the insertion point where you want the object to appear. From the Insert menu, choose Object. Select the Create New option, and then select the application from the Object Type list. Choose OK. In the launched application, create the object and adjust the object's size if necessary. Click outside the object when you're finished.
Attach a file to a mail message	In the Microsoft Mail window, click the Compose button. In the dialog box, address and compose your message. Click the Attach button. In the dialog box, select the file to attach, click the Attach button, and then choose Close. Choose Send to send your message.

For more information on	See in *Microsoft Office Getting Started*
Linking and embedding information between applications	Chapter 4, "How Office Applications Work Together"
Linking and embedding information into specific applications	Chapter 5, "Using Microsoft Office"
Attaching a file to a mail message	Chapter 6, "Sharing Information with Others"

For online information about	From the Microsoft Office menu, choose Help, click the Search button, and then
Linking an object between two applications	Type **linking**
Embedding an object from an existing file	Type **embedding, existing information**
Creating and embedding a new object	Type **embedding, new information**

Preview of the Next Lesson

In the next lesson, you'll learn how to open files created in other applications. You'll also learn how to save files to be used in another application.

Importing and Exporting Files

You can convert a file created in one application into a format that another application can interpret. This process of converting files between applications is called *importing* and *exporting*. The result is that once you import or export a file into another application, it looks as if it had originally been created in that application.

For example, if you have a PowerPoint presentation that you would like to use as the basis for a Word report, you can convert the presentation file so that it can be opened and used in Word. Then when you start Word and open that file, it appears as if it had originally been typed in Word.

In this lesson, you'll learn how to import and export files from one application into another. If you are working on a network and are running Microsoft Mail, you'll also learn how to route a file to several other users.

You will learn how to:

- Import a file from another application.
- Export a file to another application.

Estimated lesson time: 20 minutes

Start the lesson

Start Microsoft Excel and open 04LESSN.XLS. Start Word and open 04LESSN.DOC.

1 Be sure that the Microsoft Office Manager is open.

The Microsoft Office Manager is open if the Office Manager toolbar appears on your desktop. If Microsoft Office Manager is not open, double-click the Microsoft Office icon in the Windows Program Manager.

2 On the Office Manager toolbar, click the Microsoft Excel button.

Microsoft Excel

3 From your PRACTICE directory, open 04LESSN.XLS.

This workbook consists of a list of new employee information. Be sure that both the Microsoft Excel window and the workbook window are maximized.

4 Save the workbook as **lessn04.xls**

5 From the File menu in Microsoft Excel, choose Exit.

Microsoft Word

6 On the Office Manager toolbar, click the Microsoft Word button. If the Tip Of The Day dialog box appears, choose the OK button.

7   From your PRACTICE directory, open 04LESSN.DOC.

This document consists of a portion of the new employee orientation packet. Be sure that both the Word window and the document window are maximized.

8   Save the document as **lessn04.doc**

Importing a File from Another Application

Just as you can open a file that you previously saved under the current application, you can open a file that you have saved under a different application. This can be useful when you have information in one application that you would like to use as the basis for a new file in another application.

When you open a file originating in another application from the current application, a new file is created in the current application. This process is called *importing*. Importing converts a file from another application into a format that the currently active application can interpret. When you import a file, you open it in the current application, and the file looks and acts as if it had originally been created in this application.

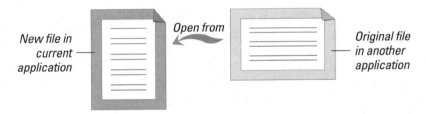

What is being converted between applications is the *file format*—the specific manner in which an application codes the information. The file format can be quite different between the various types and brands of applications. Microsoft Excel has a much different file format than PowerPoint, because they are different types of applications. But even among the same type of application—for example, Microsoft Excel and Lotus 1-2-3—the file formats are different.

Import a file to a different file format when your project meets all of the following criteria:

- You need all the information in a file created by another application.

- You want to bring the file from the other application into the current application.

- You do not need the resources of the source application to use the information.

- You might need to edit the information, and you can do so using the resources of the destination application.

When you import a file, you use the Open command, and then you select the file format in which the file was created. When you open the file, it is converted and opened in the file format of the active application.

The original file still exists in its original file format. You can choose to save the file under its original file format again, or you can save the file under the new file format. If you choose to do the latter, you'll have two versions of the file: the original file saved under the original file format, and the new file saved under the new file format.

Review the file to be imported

You have a Word document that contains a portion of the new employee orientation packet. You want to use this as the basis for the corresponding PowerPoint presentation for the orientation. Review the Word document outline to understand how it might be used to create the PowerPoint presentation.

1   From the View menu of Word, choose Outline to review the structure of the LESSN04.DOC document.

The document changes to Outline view, with the Outline toolbar displayed and the headings and subheadings marked as outline levels. This is the information that will be exported to PowerPoint.

2   From the View menu, choose Normal.

The document returns to Normal view.

You must close a file before you can import it into another application.

3   From the File menu, choose Close.

Import the file

Now that you have reviewed the document to be imported, switch to PowerPoint and import the Word outline into a new PowerPoint presentation.

Microsoft PowerPoint

1   On the Office Manager toolbar, click the Microsoft PowerPoint button. If the Tip Of The Day dialog box appears, choose the OK button.

2   In the PowerPoint dialog box, select Open An Existing Presentation, and then choose the OK button.

3   In the Open dialog box, select your PRACTICE directory.

4   In the List Files Of Type box, select Outlines.

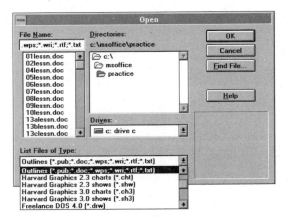

All files in your PRACTICE directory with the extension PUB, DOC, WPS, WRI, RTF, and TXT are listed. These are all files that are in some type of text file format that can be interpreted as an outline in PowerPoint.

5 In the File Name list, select LESSN04.DOC, and then choose the OK button.

The Word document is imported into the PowerPoint Outline view, looking and acting as if it had originally been created in PowerPoint. Your screen should look like the following illustration.

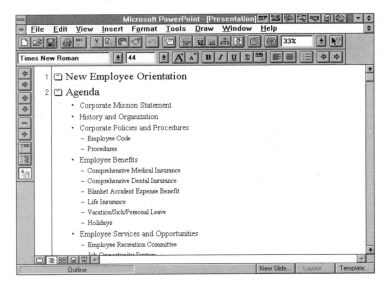

The source Word document still exists in its original form. However, now you also have a new version, converted to the PowerPoint file format.

Edit and save the imported file

Now that the Word outline has been imported to PowerPoint, modify the PowerPoint outline to better suit the presentation format.

1 Select the second bulleted item, "History and Organization."

Promote

2 On the Outlining toolbar, click the Promote button.

"History and Organization" moves from the second to the first outline level. All information at the first outline level will become a separate slide.

3 Select "Corporate Mission Statement."

Move Down

4 On the Outlining toolbar, click the Move Down button.

"Corporate Mission Statement" moves below "History and Organization."

5 Promote the next five major bullet items, from "Corporate Mission Statement" through "Company Map."

Each of these items moves from the second to the first outline level, to become individual slides in the presentation. You now have eight slides in the presentation outline.

6 From the View menu, choose Slides.

The presentation changes from Outline view to Slide view.

7 Page through the slides to see the results of the importing and editing process.

The imported information is edited to better suit the format of a slide presentation.

Save

8 On the Standard toolbar, click the Save button.

The Save As dialog box appears.

9 Save the presentation as **lessn04.ppt**, and then choose the OK button. If the Summary Info dialog box appears, choose the OK button.

Route the file to other users

You want to send the presentation to a few of your colleagues who you have asked to review and provide input on the orientation materials. Route the presentation file to other users. When you use the *routing* feature, Word adds instructions to your Mail message that tells recipients to send the message on when they are finished. Mail automatically sends the message to the next person on the list.

Note   This exercise is optional, and works only if you have installed Microsoft Mail version 3.0 or later on your computer.

1 From the File menu, choose Add Routing Slip.

The Routing Slip dialog box appears, with your name in the From box. The Subject box displays "Routing: New Employee Orientation." You can type a different subject if you want.

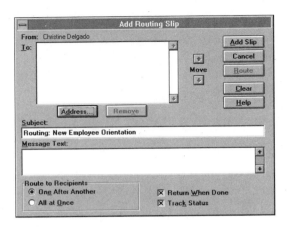

2   Choose the Address button, and select the names of at least two other users on your network. Also select your own user name.

3   Choose Add, and then choose the OK button.

4   In the Message Text box, type **This is a test. Please route to next user or back to me. Thanks.** Or type any other message you prefer.

5   In the Route To Recipients area, select the One After Another option.

This causes the file to be routed to the users in the order in which you entered their names in the To box.

6   Choose the Route button.

The presentation and your message are sent to each of the users you specified in the order that you typed their names. They can review the presentation in PowerPoint, provide you with feedback, and send the presentation on to the next user.

Exporting a File to Another Application

You can save a file that originated in the current application for use in another application. This can be useful when you have information in one application that you would like to use as the basis for a new file in another application. This process, called *exporting*, converts a file created in the current application into a format that another application can interpret. When you export a file, you are saving it in the file format of the destination application. You can then open the file in that application, and the file looks and acts as if it had originally been created there.

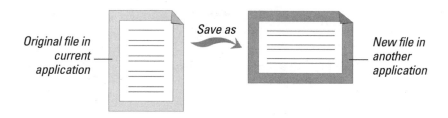

Original file in current application → *Save as* → New file in another application

Export a file to a different file format when your project meets all of the following criteria:

- You need all the information in a file created by another application.

- You want to send the file from the current application to the other application.

- You do not need the resources of the source application to use the information.

- You might need to edit the information, and can you do so using the resources of the destination application.

When you export a file, you typically use the Save As command, and then you select the file format to which you want to save the file. When you save the file, it is converted from the file format of the current (source) application into your selected file format.

Your original file still exists in its original file format. The difference is that now you have a copy of the file in a different file format. When you switch to the destination application, you can open that converted file as if it had been originally created there.

The main difference between importing and exporting is the direction from which you make the file conversion. When importing, you are opening a file created in another file format into your active application. When exporting, you are saving a file in your active application to another file format.

Export a file

You have a Microsoft Excel workbook that includes information on new employees. You want to use this information as a basis for a new document in Word. Export the workbook file to a format that Word can interpret.

Microsoft Excel

1 On the Office Manager toolbar, click the Microsoft Excel button.

2 From your PRACTICE directory, open LESSN04.XLS.

Be sure that Sheet1 is the active sheet.

3 From the File menu in Microsoft Excel, choose Save As.

To export a worksheet to a Word document with tabs between the fields, use the Text (tab delimited) file format. The file is exported and given the extension TXT. Then you can open the TXT file in Word.

4   In the Save File As Type box, select CSV (Comma delimited).

CSV stands for *comma-separated values*. This is a text file format that converts each Microsoft Excel row into a separate line in the Word file, and it separates the information in each cell with a comma. In the File Name box, the XLS extension changes to CSV.

5   Choose the OK button.

Although you cannot directly export a Microsoft Excel workbook to a Word document, you can take an intermediate route by exporting the workbook to this generic CSV text file format that Word can read. A message appears indicating that only the active sheet of the workbook will be exported.

6   Choose the OK button.

Microsoft Excel exports the sheet to the CSV file format. Your original Microsoft Excel workbook remains as it was.

7   From the File menu, choose Close.

A message asks if you want to save changes. Because you just saved this workbook in the CSV file format, and because you still have the original XLS version, it is not necessary to save again.

8   Choose the No button.

9   Hold down ALT and, on the Office Manager toolbar, click the Microsoft Excel button.

Microsoft Excel closes.

Microsoft Excel

Open the exported file

Open the file you just exported from Microsoft Excel to Word, so you can see the result of the export process.

1   On the Office Manager toolbar, click the Microsoft Word button.

Microsoft Word

2   On the Standard toolbar, click the Open button.

3   In the List Files Of Type box, select All Files (*.*).

All files in the PRACTICE directory are listed.

Open

4   In the File Name box, select LESSN04.CSV, and then choose the OK button. If the Convert File dialog box appears, choose the OK button.

The workbook that you had exported to the CSV file format opens on your screen. Instead of being contained in separate cells, each field of information is separated by a comma. The Microsoft Excel information looks and acts as if it had originally been created in Word. Your screen should look like the following illustration.

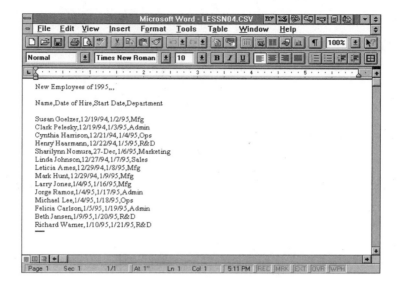

Edit and save an exported file in its new format

Take the conversion to its final step by saving it as a Word file.

1 Center the title and make it boldface type. Delete the three commas at the end of the title.

2 Delete the next line, which starts with "Name, Date of Hire."

3 From the File menu, choose Save As.

4 Save the document as **lessn04a.doc**

The Excel workbook still exists in its original file format. But now you also have a new version converted to a format that Word can interpret.

5 From the File menu, choose Exit.

A message asks if you want to save the formatting changes you just made. Choosing Yes will convert the file to Word format. Choosing No will maintain the file in a text-only (no formatting) CSV format.

6 Choose the Yes button.

7 In the Save Format dialog box, choose the Word button.

One Step Further

You can easily export a PowerPoint presentation to a Word report. On the Standard toolbar, the Report It button creates a Word file from your PowerPoint slides. Use this when you want to use your presentation slides as a basis for a more detailed report.

With the Report It button, your presentation is converted through *Rich Text Format,* or *RTF.* This is a sophisticated file format for converting text and formatting codes across different applications.

Export a PowerPoint presentation to a Word report

Export the PowerPoint presentation outline to Word, to create an outline and the basis for a new Word document.

1 On the Office Manager toolbar, click the Microsoft PowerPoint button.

The LESSN04.PPT presentation should still be open.

Microsoft PowerPoint

2 On the Standard toolbar, click the Report It button. If the Convert File dialog box appears, choose the OK button.

Report It

The presentation is converted and then opens in Word. If the Tip Of The Day dialog box appears, choose the OK button. Your screen should look like the following illustration.

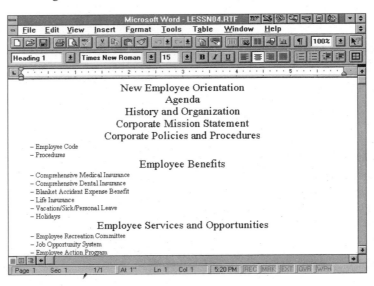

You can now edit the file and create a detailed report based on text from the presentation.

3 From the File menu, choose Save As.

4 Under Save File As Type, select Word Document.

5   Save the file as **lessn04b.doc** in your PRACTICE directory.

6   From the File menu, choose Exit.

End the Lesson

1   On the Office Manager toolbar, click the Microsoft PowerPoint button.

2   To continue to the next lesson, from the File menu in PowerPoint, choose Close. To quit for now, from the File menu in PowerPoint, choose Exit.

If you see the Save dialog box, choose Yes.

Lesson Summary

To	Do this
Import a file	From the Open dialog box of the current application, from the List Files of Type box select the file format of the file to be imported. Select the filename from the File Name box. Choose OK.
Route a file to other users	Open the file you want to route. From the File menu, choose Add Routing Slip. Type the user names and select your options, and then choose the Route button.
Export a file	Open the file you want to export. From the File menu, choose Save As. In the Save File As Type box, select the file format to which the file is to be exported. If necessary, type the filename. Choose OK.

For more information on	See in *Microsoft Office Getting Started*
Importing and exporting files	Chapter 5, "Using Microsoft Office"
Routing files through Microsoft Mail	Chapter 6, "Sharing Information with Others"

For online information about	Choose Search For Help On from the Help menu of
Importing an outline from Word to PowerPoint	PowerPoint, and then type **import outline**
Exporting an outline from Word to PowerPoint	Word, and then type **exporting documents**
Exporting a file from Microsoft Excel to Word	Microsoft Excel, and then type **exporting, by changing file format**

For online information about	Choose <u>S</u>earch For Help On from the <u>H</u>elp menu of
Importing a file from Microsoft Excel to Word	Word, and then type **importing**
Exporting a PowerPoint presentation to a Word report.	PowerPoint, and then type **report it**
Routing a file to other users from PowerPoint	PowerPoint, and then type **route**

Preview of the Next Lessons

In Part 2, you'll learn how to use the different integration techniques—copying and pasting, linking and embedding, and importing and exporting—to create compound Word documents. In the next lesson, you'll create a Word document using a workbook and a chart from Microsoft Excel.

Review & Practice

In the lessons in Part 1, you learned how to use common Microsoft Office resources, and to use the integration techniques to copy, move, link, embed, import, and export information between different applications. If you want to practice these skills and test your understanding before you proceed with the lessons in Part 2, you can work through the Review & Practice section following this lesson.

Part 1   Review & Practice

You can practice the skills you learned in Part 1 by working through the steps in this Review & Practice section. You will use the Office Manager toolbar, use common Microsoft Office resources, and copy, link, embed, and import information between different applications. If you are working on a network and are running Microsoft Mail, you will also send and route files to other users.

Scenario

The marketing department at Childs Play has developed the marketing strategy for a new line of educational toys. You've been asked to prepare the materials for the marketing plan proposal, including the strategy presentation and the accompanying report.

You will review and practice how to:

- Use common Microsoft Office resources in different applications.

- Copy information between applications.

- Link and embed information between applications.

- Import information between applications.

Estimated practice time: 20 minutes

Step 1: Copy Workbook Data into the Word Report

You have marketing method cost data from an Excel workbook that you would like to use in the Marketing Tools section of the marketing strategy report. You don't need the information to be automatically updated over time. In fact, you're certain you won't need to edit this information at all: You just need a picture of the information in the report. Because of this, copy the information from Microsoft Excel into your Word report. Then, send the proposal draft to a colleague to obtain feedback on your approach.

1 In Microsoft Excel, open the file P1REVIEW.XLS from your PRACTICE directory and save it as **reviewp1.xls**

2 In the Mktg Methods sheet, select and copy cells A5 through D15.

3 In Word, open the file P1REVIEW.DOC and save it as **reviewp1.doc**

4 On page 3, below the first paragraph under "Marketing Methods," paste the Microsoft Excel information.

5 If you are working on a network and are running Microsoft Mail, use the Send command on the File menu to send the file to another user.

6 Save and close the Word file.

7 Exit from Word.

For more information on	See
Copying information between applications	Lesson 2
Sending a file to another user from within an application	Lesson 2

Step 2: Import the Report into a Presentation

You've developed the outline and have started writing portions of the marketing strategy report. You want to use the major headings of the report as the basis for the presentation, to which you'll add additional information and graphics. As a result, you decide to import the Word report into your PowerPoint presentation.

1 Switch to PowerPoint.

2 From your PRACTICE directory, import REVIEWP1.DOC into PowerPoint. (Tip: Use the List Files Of Type box to select the Outlines file format.)

3 While still in Outline view, insert a new slide and move it into the Slide 1 position.

4 Promote the three items under the Budget slide—Marketing Costs, Past Sales, and Projected Sales—so that they each will have their own slide.

5 Switch to Slide view. In the new Slide 1 that you've created, change the layout to a title slide. (Tip: Use the Layout button in the lower right corner of the PowerPoint window.)

6 In the title frame, type **Childs Play**. In the subtitle frame, type **Marketing Strategy**

7 Save the presentation as **reviewp1.ppt**

For more information on	See
Importing a file from another application	Lesson 4
Exporting a file to another application	Lesson 4

Step 3: Link from a Workbook to a Slide

You have general marketing cost data from an Excel workbook that you would like to use in the marketing strategy presentation. You expect this information to change periodically as new data becomes available. Because you expect to be giving this presentation to several different groups over the next few weeks, you want the information in your presentation to be updated automatically, as soon as it changes. Link the information from Microsoft Excel to your PowerPoint presentation. When you're satisfied with your draft, attach it to a Mail message you're sending to your manager.

1 Switch to Microsoft Excel and, in the Mktg Costs sheet, select and copy cells A5 through C17.

2 Switch to PowerPoint and, on Slide 6, use the Paste Special command to link the Microsoft Excel information to the frame below the title.

3 Adjust the size and position of the worksheet object to make it fit the slide better, and then save the presentation.

4 Switch back to Microsoft Excel. (Tip: Double-click the linked object.)

5 Change cell B10 from 12,000 to **13,500**. In cell C8, change 60,000 to **57,000**, and then save the workbook and exit from Microsoft Excel.

6 Switch back to PowerPoint to see that the changes in the linked workbook information have been made in the presentation.

7 If you are working on a network and are running Microsoft Mail, switch to Microsoft Mail and use the Attach command to send the file to another user. When finished, exit from Microsoft Mail.

For more information on	See
Linking information between two different applications	Lesson 3
Attaching a file to a Microsoft Mail message	Lesson 3

Step 4: Embed a Workbook in the Presentation

You have projected sales data from an Excel workbook that you would like to use in the marketing strategy presentation. You don't want the information to be updated by the source, but you want to be able to edit the information in the presentation. You also need Microsoft Excel's formula capabilities in the presentation. Embed the Microsoft Excel workbook in your PowerPoint presentation, and then edit the workbook object. When you are finished, send the presentation draft to three individuals in accounting and sales to make sure your facts are accurate.

1 Switch to PowerPoint.

2 On Slide 8, use the Object command on the Insert menu to embed the REVIEWP1.XLS file in the frame below the slide title.

3 Open the embedded workbook object, and then adjust its size and position.

4 Switch to the Projected Sales sheet, and then change cell C7 from $389,000 to **$425,000**. Change cell E9 from $131,000 to **$150,000**.

5 Switch back to the PowerPoint menus and toolbars. (Tip: Click outside the embedded workbook object frame.)

6 Make any necessary adjustments to the size and position of the embedded workbook and then save the presentation.

7   If you are working on a network and are running Microsoft Mail, use the Add Routing Slip command from the File menu to send the presentation to three other users one after another.

For more information on	See
Embedding files in an application	Lesson 3
Routing a file to multiple users	Lesson 4

Step 5: Use WordArt in the Report and Slides

In the marketing strategy presentation, you want to include the Childs Play motto "It's All For Fun," stylized by using WordArt on the title slide.

1   Go to Slide 1 of the presentation, the title slide.

2   Use the Object command on the Insert menu to select WordArt 2.0.

3   Type **It's All For Fun** in the Enter Your Text Here dialog box.

4   Close the dialog box, and then click outside the object frame to redraw it.

5   From the Edit menu, choose WordArt Object, and then choose Open.

6   Choose a shape, fill, font, and any other effects you want the motto to display, and then choose the OK button.

7   Adjust the size and position of the motto to make it fit better on the slide, and then save the presentation.

For more information on	See
Using WordArt or other common Microsoft Office resources	Lesson 1
Using the Microsoft Office Manager toolbar and menu	Lesson 1

End the Lesson

1   From the File menu in PowerPoint, choose Exit.

    If you see the Save dialog box, choose Yes.

2   If you have any other applications running, use the Office Manager toolbar to exit from them.

    If you see the Save dialog box, click Yes.

2

Creating Documents in Word Using Integrated Information

Microsoft Word is a word processing application that you can use to write letters, reports, and other text-based documents. You can then edit and format the text with a variety of powerful and versatile tools.

In this part, you will learn how to use Word as the base application to bring numbers and calculations from Microsoft Excel into a Word document. You'll use a PowerPoint presentation outline as the basis for a new Word document. And you'll use data stored in a Microsoft Access table to create mail merged letters and summary reports.

Creating Documents with Workbook Data

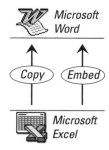

Microsoft
Word

Copy   Embed

Microsoft
Excel

You can insert Microsoft Excel sheets and charts wherever you need them in a Word report. For example, maybe you've been asked to create a marketing status report that includes sales performance tables and charts. Or, you might need to write a manufacturing report that, in addition to narrative text, includes a table of units produced and a pie chart of all products manufactured.

In this lesson, you'll enhance the Childs Play new employee orientation packet by copying and embedding detailed information from Microsoft Excel regarding 401(k) investment choices and strategies. To convey this information effectively, the document will include a narrative, numerical information, and graphic representations of numbers.

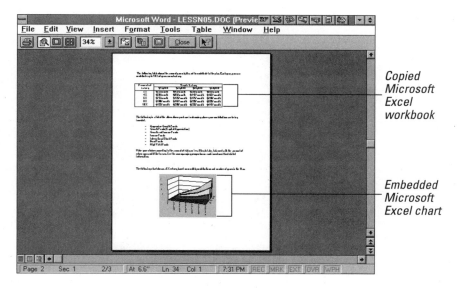

Copied
Microsoft
Excel
workbook

Embedded
Microsoft
Excel chart

You will learn how to:

- Copy a portion of a Microsoft Excel workbook into a Word document.
- Embed a Microsoft Excel chart in a Word document.

Estimated lesson time: 20 minutes

Start the lesson

Start Word and open 05LESSN.DOC. Start Microsoft Excel and open 05LESSN.XLS.

1 Be sure that the Microsoft Office Manager is open.

The Microsoft Office Manager is open if the Office Manager toolbar appears on your desktop. If Microsoft Office Manager is not open, double-click the Microsoft Office icon in the Windows Program Manager.

Microsoft Word

2 On the Office Manager toolbar, click the Microsoft Word button. If the Tip Of The Day dialog box appears, choose the OK button.

3 From your PRACTICE directory, open 05LESSN.DOC.

This document contains information to be included in the Childs Play new employee orientation packet. Be sure that both the Word window and the document window are maximized.

4 Save the document as **lessn05.doc**

Microsoft Excel

5 On the Office Manager toolbar, click the Microsoft Excel button.

6 From your PRACTICE directory, open 05LESSN.XLS.

This workbook contains detailed data and a chart on 401(k) contributions. Be sure that both the Microsoft Excel window and the workbook window are maximized.

7 Save the workbook as **lessn05.xls**

Copying a Workbook from Microsoft Excel

A simple way to include a Microsoft Excel workbook in your Word report is to copy and paste it. When you copy and paste a workbook into a Word document, it appears as a Word table. You can edit the contents of the table as if it originally had been created in Word.

Copying and pasting workbook information into a Word document is the best technique to use when your project meets all of the following criteria:

- You have tabular data that already exists in Microsoft Excel.

- You want to use this data as part of a Word document.

- You want the data to appear in a Word table, looking as if it originally had been created in Word.

- The information in the Word table will not need to be automatically updated by the source file in Microsoft Excel.

You copy a workbook into a document when you want the copied information in the *destination file* in Word to be independent of the *source file* in Microsoft Excel—if the information in Microsoft Excel changes, the copy in the Word report does not change.

Note   If you tile your Microsoft Excel and Word windows, you can use *drag-and-drop editing* to copy the information. When copying, remember to hold down CTRL while you drag. Otherwise the information is moved, rather than copied.

Copy a workbook from Microsoft Excel into Word

You are working on a Word document that explains 401(k) investment choices and strategies to new employees of Childs Play. You need to include information from a Microsoft Excel workbook in the document. Once the cells are inserted, you want to be able to edit the information like a Word table. Copy the cells and paste them into your Word document.

1   In the LESSN05.XLS workbook, be sure that the 401(k) Contributions sheet is active.

2   Select cells A5 through E11.

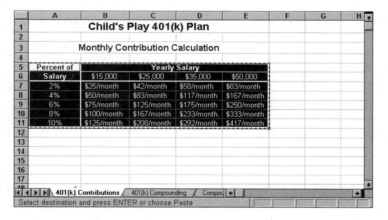

Percent of Salary	Yearly Salary			
	$15,000	$25,000	$35,000	$50,000
2%	$25/month	$42/month	$58/month	$83/month
4%	$50/month	$83/month	$117/month	$167/month
6%	$75/month	$125/month	$175/month	$250/month
8%	$100/month	$167/month	$233/month	$333/month
10%	$125/month	$208/month	$292/month	$417/month

Child's Play 401(k) Plan — Monthly Contribution Calculation

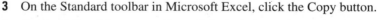

Select destination and press ENTER or choose Paste

Copy

3   On the Standard toolbar in Microsoft Excel, click the Copy button.

4   On the Office Manager toolbar, click the Microsoft Word button to switch to the open Word document.

5   On page 1, position the insertion point in the second blank line after the last paragraph, which starts with "The following table...."

This is where the copied information from Microsoft Excel will be pasted.

Paste

6   On the Standard toolbar in Word, click the Paste button.

The Microsoft Excel information appears in the document as a Word table, where it can be edited and formatted.

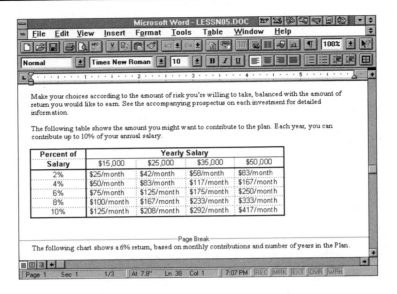

7   On the Standard toolbar in Word, click the Save button.

Embedding a Chart from Microsoft Excel

You can insert Microsoft Excel information into your Word document and keep all the power and functions of Microsoft Excel with the information. You might want to do this if you expect to add to or edit the information later, and if you will need resources unique to Microsoft Excel, such as formulas, analysis, and number formatting.

You do this by *embedding* the information as an *object*. When you double-click the object, you can use all the Microsoft Excel tools on the embedded information while you're still working in your Word document.

Embedding a Microsoft Excel workbook in a Word document is the best technique to use when your project meets all of the following criteria:

- You want the Microsoft Excel workbook to be an integral part of the Word document.

- You want to use the resources unique to Microsoft Excel, such as the calculating or charting capabilities.

- You want your Word document's resources to be self contained, particularly if you expect that your document might be used on another computer.

- File size of the Word document is not a concern.

- The information in the Word table will not need to be automatically updated by the source file in Microsoft Excel.

Embedding Microsoft Excel information in your Word document inserts the entire workbook file into the document.

When you double-click the embedded object in your Word document, your menu and toolbars change to those of the application that created the embedded object. For example, when you embed a Microsoft Excel object and then double-click the object, your menu and toolbars change to the Microsoft Excel menu and toolbars. When you click outside the object, the menu and toolbars change back to those of Word.

Embed a chart from Microsoft Excel in Word

You want to include a chart representing 401(k) investment strategies in your document. You also want the chart and its resources available within your document, because you'll need to update the numbers and edit the chart later. Embed the workbook containing the chart in your document.

1 In the LESSN05.DOC document, go to page 2.

2 Position the insertion point in the second blank line after the paragraph that starts with "The following chart...."

3 From the Insert menu, choose Object.

The Object dialog box appears.

4 Click the Create From File tab.

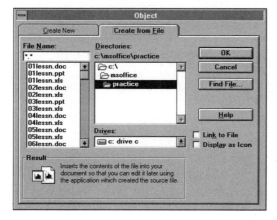

Because the workbook contains multiple sheets, the sheet that was active when the workbook was last saved is shown in the embedded object. You will change the active sheet in the following exercise.

5 From your PRACTICE directory, select LESSN05.XLS, and then choose the OK button.

Word embeds a copy of the Microsoft Excel workbook file at the insertion point. This might take a few seconds.

Edit the embedded area chart

Now that the workbook is embedded, open and edit the workbook to adjust its size, and then to switch to the sheet containing the chart you want to appear in your document.

1   Double-click the embedded workbook object.

   Your Word menu and toolbars change to Microsoft Excel menus and toolbars.

2   Use the sizing boxes on the four sides of the workbook object frame to adjust its size to show cells A1 through E11, as shown in the following illustration.

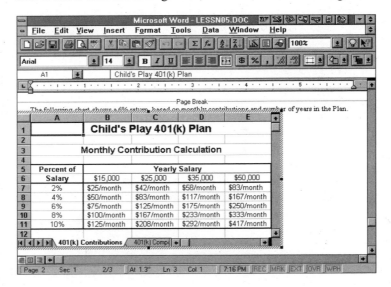

3   Switch to the workbook sheet called Compounding Chart.

   You can use the navigation buttons in the lower-left corner of the Microsoft Excel window to switch between sheets in the workbook.

4   Click outside the embedded workbook.

   The embedded object is updated to reflect the view of the area chart, and your menu and toolbars change back to those of Word.

5   If necessary, use the sizing boxes on the workbook object frame to adjust the size and proportions of the chart.

   Your screen should look similar to the following illustration.

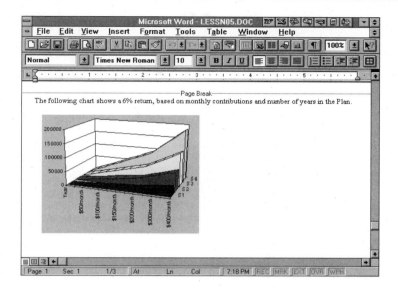

Save

6   On the Standard toolbar in Word, click the Save button.

One Step Further

You can create and embed a new Microsoft Excel worksheet within a Word document. This is useful when you need resources that Microsoft Excel provides; when the worksheet you create will be needed only within this Word document; and when you know exactly how large your worksheet needs to be.

When you use the Insert Microsoft Excel Worksheet button to embed your blank worksheet, your Word menu and toolbars change to those of Microsoft Excel. When you finish creating the worksheet, you click outside of the embedded object frame to return to Word.

Insert a new Microsoft Excel worksheet

You want to add numerical data regarding 401(k) compounding in a sheet format to your Word orientation packet. Embed a new Microsoft Excel worksheet in your Word document.

1   In the LESSN05.DOC document, go to page 3.

2   Position the insertion point in the blank line below the heading, "Tax Deferred Compounding."

Insert Microsoft
Excel Worksheet

3 On the Standard toolbar, click the Insert Microsoft Excel Worksheet button.

A box appears in which you specify the size of the worksheet.

4 Drag to specify five rows down by three columns across, and then release the mouse button.

A worksheet of the specified size appears at the insertion point, and the menu and toolbars change to those of Microsoft Excel.

Create the data in the new Microsoft Excel worksheet

Now that you have your new Microsoft Excel workbook embedded in your document, enter the information for it, and then edit it so that all the information is visible and easy to read.

1 Type the following information in the worksheet:

Year	5	10
$25/month	$1,753	$4,118
$50/month	$3,506	$8,235
$75/month	$5,259	$12,352
$100/month	$7,012	$16,470

Bold

2 Select cells A1 through C1, and then click the Bold button on the Formatting toolbar to change the text in those cells to boldface type.

3 With cells A1 through C1 still selected, click the Center button on the Formatting toolbar to center the text in the cells.

Center

4 Adjust the width of column A so that all the text is visible.

5 Click outside the worksheet.

The menu and toolbars change back to those of Word. Your report should look similar to the following illustration.

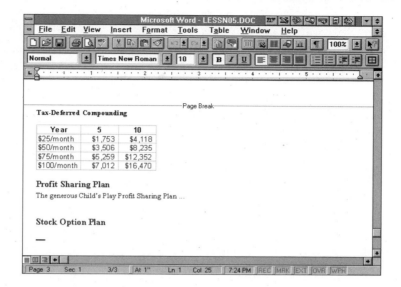

Save

6   On the Standard toolbar, click the Save button.

End the Lesson

1   To continue to the next lesson, from the File menu in Word, choose Close. To quit for now, from the File menu in Word, choose Exit.

If you see the Save dialog box, click Yes.

Microsoft Excel

2   Hold down ALT and then, on the Office Manager toolbar, click the Microsoft Excel button.

If you see the Save dialog box, click Yes.

Lesson Summary

To	Do this	Button
Copy a workbook from Microsoft Excel into Word	Select the workbook information, and on the Standard toolbar, click the Copy button. In the Word document, position the insertion point, and then, on the Standard toolbar, choose the Paste button.	

To	Do this
Embed an existing workbook or chart from Microsoft Excel in Word	Position the insertion point in the Word document. From the Insert menu, choose Object. Click the Create From File tab, and then select the file to embed.
Edit an embedded Microsoft Excel object in Word	Double-click the embedded object. The menu and toolbars change to Microsoft Excel. When you are finished editing, click outside the object. The menu and toolbars change back to those of Word.

For more information on	See in *Microsoft Office Getting Started*
Copying information and embedding files between applications	Chapter 4, "How Office Applications Work Together"
Inserting information from other applications into Word	Chapter 5, "Using Microsoft Office"

For online information about	Choose <u>S</u>earch For Help On from the <u>H</u>elp menu of
Copying information from Microsoft Excel into Word	Microsoft Excel, and then type **copying, to other applications**
Embedding information from other applications in Word	Microsoft Word, and then type **embedding**
Embedding Microsoft Excel information in another application	Microsoft Excel, and then type **embedding**

Preview of the Next Lesson

In the next lesson, you'll learn how to link a monthly report to data maintained and updated in Microsoft Excel on a regular basis. You'll see how the monthly report is automatically updated when the workbook data is updated.

Linking Workbook Information to Reports

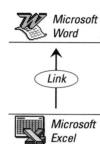

Microsoft Word

Link

Microsoft Excel

You can create a document in Word that includes automatically updated information from a Microsoft Excel workbook. For example, you might need to produce a monthly manufacturing report that summarizes figures that are maintained and calculated on a weekly basis in a Microsoft Excel workbook. Or, you might need to write a weekly sales summary report in Word that includes information from a workbook that tracks daily sales orders.

In this lesson, you'll create a report on the benefits chosen by the latest group of new Childs Play employees. The report is provided to upper management every month. It will be linked to an existing Microsoft Excel workbook file in which benefits information is maintained on an ongoing basis, as new employees make their choices. If you are working on a network and are running Microsoft Mail, you'll also learn how to route the report to three other users.

Source file in Microsoft Excel

New Employees of 1995

Name	Medical Premium Per Pay Period	Dental Premium Per Pay Period	Life Insurance Premium	401(k) Option	Initial Contribution (Rollover)	Contribution Per Pay Period
Swan Gaaker	$0.00	$0.00	$0.00	8%	$9,800.00	$125.00
Clark Polarky	$7.50	$6.00	$5.25	2%	$0.00	$12.50
Shanlynn Namura	$5.00	$4.00	$3.50	2%	$0.00	$24.00
Henry Heermann	$5.00	$4.00	$3.50	0%	$0.00	$0.00
Cynthia Harrian	$5.00	$4.00	$3.50	4%	$0.00	$38.00
Linda Johnran	$7.50	$6.00	$5.25	5%	$6,700.00	$78.00
Lotoa Amar	$7.50	$6.00	$5.25	2%	$0.00	$38.00
Mark Hunt	$10.00	$8.00	$7.00	1%	$0.00	$15.00
Jorgo Ramar	$0.00	$0.00	$0.00	2%	$4,100.00	$0.00
Larry Jamar	$2.50	$2.00	$1.75	8%	$0.00	$30.00
Michael Lee	$0.00	$0.00	$0.00	10%	$0.00	$190.00
Felisa Carlran	$2.50	$2.00	$1.75	7%	$0.00	$79.00
Beth Jonron	$12.50	$10.00	$8.75	4%	$2,300.00	$25.00
Richard Warner	$0.00	$0.00	$0.00	5%	$7,200.00	$37.00
TOTALS	$65.00	$52.00	$45.50		$30,100.00	$691.50

Medical Insurance - Dependents	Medical Premium Per Pay Period	Dental Insurance - Dependents	Dental Premium Per Pay Period	Life Insurance - Dependents	Life Insurance Premium	401(k) Option	Initial Contribution (Rollover)	Contribution Per Pay Period
26	$65.00	26	$52.00	26	$45.50		$30,100.00	$691.50

Please contact me if you have questions or concerns. Thank you.

Destination file in Word   *Linked information*

You will learn how to:

- Link information from a Microsoft Excel workbook to a Word report.
- Automatically update linked information from Microsoft Excel to Word.

Estimated lesson time: 20 minutes

Start the lesson

Start Word and open 06LESSN.DOC. Start Microsoft Excel and open 06LESSN.XLS.

1   Be sure that the Microsoft Office Manager is open.

The Microsoft Office Manager is open if the Office Manager toolbar appears on your desktop. If Microsoft Office Manager is not open, double-click the Microsoft Office icon in the Windows Program Manager.

Microsoft Word

2   On the Office Manager toolbar, click the Microsoft Word button. If the Tip Of The Day dialog box appears, choose the OK button.

3   From your PRACTICE directory, open 06LESSN.DOC.

This document is a new employee report to upper management. Be sure that both the Word window and the document window are maximized.

4   Save the document as **lessn06.doc**

5   On the Office Manager toolbar, click the Microsoft Excel button.

Microsoft Excel

6   From your PRACTICE directory, open 06LESSN.XLS.

This workbook contains a list of new employees and their benefits information. Be sure that both the Microsoft Excel window and the workbook window are maximized.

7   Save the workbook as **lessn06.xls**

Linking Workbook Information to a Word Report

Suppose you are writing a periodic report in Word that requires current information from a Microsoft Excel workbook that is updated regularly. You want your report to always reflect the latest changes from the workbook.

You create an automatically updating relationship between a Word report and a Microsoft Excel workbook by *linking* the two. When you link Microsoft Excel information to a Word document, any changes made to the *source* file in Microsoft Excel are automatically updated in the *destination* file in Word. This is especially useful when you are working with documents that constantly need up-to-date information from workbooks.

Linking Microsoft Excel information to a Word document is the best technique to use when your project meets all of the following criteria:

- Information exists in a Microsoft Excel workbook that you want to use in a Word document.

- The workbook information changes periodically.

- You update your Word document periodically as well, and you want each version to reflect the latest changes to the workbook information.

- The workbook file will always be available to you, or to anyone else who might be using the linked Word file.

Linking keeps your document file relatively small, because the actual source information is not stored with the document file. Only the link reference and the image of the information are stored there.

When you double-click the linked *object* in your document, Microsoft Excel opens and displays the source workbook. You can then make any changes there. As soon as you make the changes in the workbook, those changes are reflected in the linked object in your document.

Link Microsoft Excel information to a Word report

You are creating a Word report on new employee benefits that includes current information from a Microsoft Excel workbook. The information in the workbook is updated at least once a week, and you want to be sure that your report always reflects the latest changes. Link the information from the workbook to your document.

1 In Sheet1 of the Microsoft Excel workbook, select cells E3 through M3.

Copy

2 On the Standard toolbar in Microsoft Excel, click the Copy button.

3 On the Office Manager toolbar, click the Microsoft Word button to switch to the open Word report.

4 On page 1, position the insertion point in the second blank line after the second paragraph, which starts with "Totals for benefits...."

This is where the linked information from Microsoft Excel will be inserted.

5 From the Edit menu, choose Paste Special.

6 In the Paste Special dialog box, select the Paste Link option button.

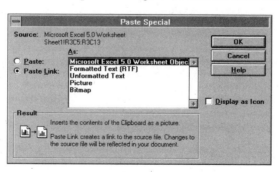

7 In the As list, select Microsoft Excel 5.0 Worksheet Object, and then choose the OK button.

The Microsoft Excel information is inserted and linked to the report.

If you were to choose Formatted Text (RTF) in the As list, the linked information would appear in your report as a formatted Word table and text. It would still be linked to the Microsoft Excel worksheet, but double-clicking the object would not open Microsoft Excel.

8   Switch to the Microsoft Excel workbook, and then select cells E21 through M21.

9   Repeat the process in steps 2 through 7 to link these just below the other linked row in your Word report.

Your screen should look similar to the following illustration.

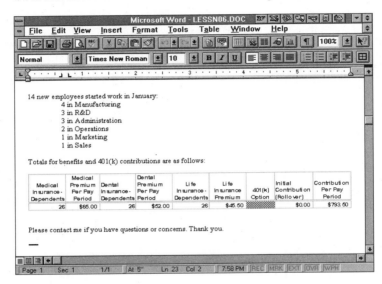

Now, whenever the source file in Microsoft Excel is edited, the corresponding information in your destination file in Word will automatically be updated.

Edit linked information

Another week has gone by, and there is new employee benefits information to be entered into the Microsoft Excel workbook. Edit the information in the Microsoft Excel workbook. Observe that the changes you make in the linked portion of the workbook are reflected immediately in your Word report.

Microsoft Excel

1   On the Office Manager toolbar, click the Microsoft Excel button to switch back to the workbook.

Tip   If your linked object is a Microsoft Excel Worksheet Object (rather than Formatted Text-RTF), you can also double-click the linked object to open Microsoft Excel and the source file.

---

2 Make the following changes in the indicated rows and columns.

Tip It's easy to make these changes when you split the window into two panes. Use the vertical split box and then scroll the right pane so you can view column A and column M at the same time.

		Column A	Column K	Column M
		Name	401(k) Option	Contribution Per Pay Period
Row 7		Sharilynn Nomura	2%	$24.00
Row 13		Jorge Ramos	3%	$30.00

You'll see that the figures you typed in column M change the formula result in cell M21, which is linked to your Word report.

Microsoft Word

3 On the Office Manager toolbar, click the Microsoft Word button to switch back to the report.

You'll notice that the changed formula result in the Microsoft Excel workbook is updated in your report.

Note If the destination Word document is open when you make the changes to the source workbook, the update takes place immediately. If the Word document is closed, the linked object will update as soon as you open the document.

Save

4 On the Standard toolbar in Word, click the Save button.

Route the report

Route the employee benefits report to your management through Microsoft Mail.

Note This exercise is optional, and works only if you have installed Microsoft Mail version 3.0 or later on your computer.

1 From the File menu in Word, choose Add Routing Slip.

The Routing Slip dialog box appears, with your name at the top. The Subject box displays "Routing:" followed by text from the first line of the document. You can type a different subject if you want.

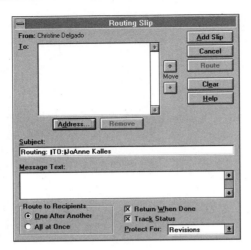

2   Choose the Address button, and select the names of at least two other users on your network. Then select your own user name.

3   Choose Add, and then choose the OK button.

4   In the Message Text box, type **This is a test. Please route to next user or back to me. Thanks.** Or type any other message you prefer.

5   In the Route To Recipients area, select the One After Another option.

This causes the report file to be routed to the users in the order in which you entered their names in the To box. Word automatically adds text to the message that instructs recipients to send it on to the next person. Because you typed your own user name last, the report file will be routed back to you after the other users have made their comments.

6   Choose the Route button.

The report and your message are sent to each of the users you specified in the order that you typed their names. They can review the report in Word, provide you with feedback, and send the report on to the next user.

One Step Further

As convenient as automatic updates are, sometimes you might prefer to have your linked objects updated only upon your request. You can do this by changing the automatic link to a manual link using the Links dialog box. In the dialog box, all the links in your document are referenced by their source filenames, the sheet name, and the row and column reference in R1C1 format.

Change an automatic link to a manual link

You've decided that you want more control over when your document is updated with the changes from the workbook. Change the automatic update link to a manual update link.

1   From the Edit menu in Word, choose Links.

The Links dialog box appears, listing your two links to the Microsoft Excel workbook.

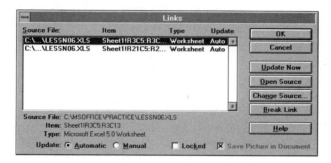

2   Select the second link, which indicates that its source is in row 21 (R21) of the LESSN06.XLS workbook.

To select more than one link at a time, hold down CTRL while selecting the link references.

3   Next to Update at the lower-left corner of the dialog box, select the Manual option, and then choose the OK button.

Now, when changes are made to Row 21 in the Microsoft Excel workbook, they will not be automatically updated in your report. The changes will be reflected only when you request the updates.

Request a manual link update

You're ready to receive any changes from the source file in Microsoft Excel. Request a manual link update.

Microsoft Excel

1   On the Office Manager toolbar, click the Microsoft Excel button to switch back to the workbook.

2   In column L, add the following initial contributions (rollovers) for the
individuals listed:

	Column A	Column L
	Name	Initial Contribution (Rollover)
Row 5	Susan Goelzer	**$9,800**
Row 10	Linda Johnson	**$6,700**
Row 13	Jorge Ramos	**$4,100**
Row 17	Beth Jansen	**$2,300**
Row 18	Richard Warner	**$7,200**

You'll see that the figures you typed in column L change the formula result in
cell L21, which is linked to your Word report.

Microsoft Word

3   On the Office Manager toolbar, click the Microsoft Word button to switch back
to the report.

You'll see that the changed formula result for Initial Contribution (Rollover) in
the workbook is not yet changed in your report.

4   From the Edit menu in Word, choose Links.

5   In the Links dialog box, select the second link to the Microsoft Excel workbook,
which is the one you changed to a manual update link.

6   Choose the Update Now button, and then choose the OK button.

The changed formula result from the workbook is now updated in your report.

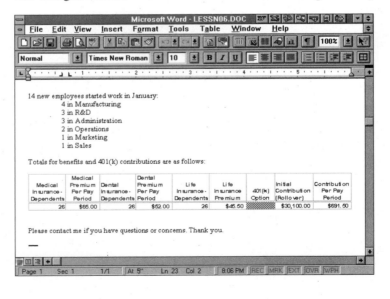

Save

7   On the Standard toolbar in Word, click the Save button.

Tip   Another way to update manual links is to select the linked information in the document and click the right mouse button. From the shortcut menu, choose Update Links.

End the Lesson

1   To continue to the next lesson, from the File menu in Word, choose Close. To quit for now, from the File menu in Word, choose Exit.

If you see the Save dialog box, click Yes.

Microsoft Excel

2   Hold down ALT, and then on the Office Manager toolbar, click the Microsoft Excel button.

If you see the Save dialog box, click Yes.

Lesson Summary

To	Do this
Link information from Microsoft Excel to Word	Select and copy the Microsoft Excel information, and then switch to Word. Position the insertion point where the linked information should be inserted. From the Edit menu, choose Paste Special. In the dialog box, select the Paste Link option button, and then choose the OK button.
Open the linked Microsoft Excel object from Word	Double-click the linked Microsoft Excel workbook object.
Route your file to other users	From the File menu, choose Add Routing Slip. Complete the dialog box and choose the Route button.

For more information on	See in *Microsoft Office Getting Started*
Linking information between applications	Chapter 4, "How Office Applications Work Together"
Inserting information from other applications into Word	Chapter 5, "Using Microsoft Office"
Routing files through Microsoft Mail	Chapter 6, "Sharing Information with Others"

For online information about	Choose <u>S</u>earch For Help On from the <u>H</u>elp menu of
Linking information from other applications to Word	Microsoft Word, and then type **linking**
Linking Microsoft Excel information to Word	Microsoft Excel, and then type **linking, source worksheets to dependent documents**
Manipulating linked information in Word	Microsoft Word, and then type **links**
Routing a file to other users	Microsoft Word, and then type **Microsoft Mail**

Preview of the Next Lesson

In the next lesson, you'll learn how to include an entire PowerPoint presentation within a Word document. You'll also learn how you can save a PowerPoint presentation as a Word document, so you can develop a document based on the information in the presentation.

Using PowerPoint Information in Word

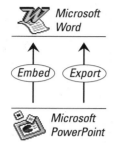

Microsoft
Word

Embed   Export

Microsoft
PowerPoint

You can insert an entire PowerPoint presentation into a Word document so that each slide can be viewed one at a time. For example, you might want to insert a seminar presentation into a memo so others can view the presentation while reading your memo on their computer. You can also convert a presentation into Word to create a document based on a presentation. For example, you might want to create a document to help your audience follow along and make notes on your presentation.

In this lesson, you will embed an entire PowerPoint presentation in a Word document, and you'll also export a PowerPoint presentation to Word.

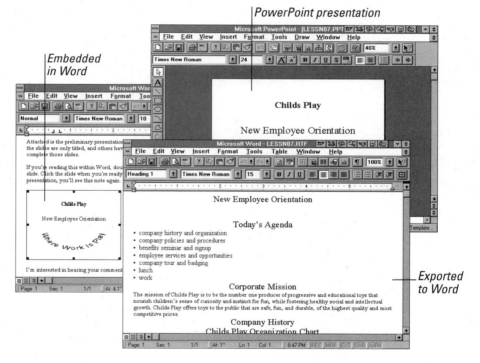

You will learn how to:

■ Embed a PowerPoint presentation in Word and then view it.

■ Export a presentation to a Word document, using the Report It button.

Estimated lesson time: 20 minutes

Start the lesson

Start PowerPoint and open 07LESSN.PPT. Start Word and open 07LESSN.DOC.

1   Be sure that the Microsoft Office Manager is open.

The Microsoft Office Manager is open if the Office Manager toolbar appears on your desktop. If Microsoft Office Manager is not open, double-click the Microsoft Office icon in the Windows Program Manager.

*Microsoft
PowerPoint*

2   On the Office Manager toolbar, click the Microsoft PowerPoint button. If the Tip Of The Day dialog box appears, choose the OK button.

3   From your PRACTICE directory, open 07LESSN.PPT.

This file is a portion of the new employee orientation presentation. Be sure that both the PowerPoint window and the presentation window are maximized.

4   Save the presentation as **lessn07.ppt**. If the Summary Info dialog box appears, choose the OK button.

Microsoft Word

5   On the Office Manager toolbar, click the Microsoft Word button.

6   From your PRACTICE directory, open 07LESSN.DOC.

This is a memo that will include the presentation for others to review. Be sure that both the Word window and the document window are maximized.

7   Save the document as **lessn07.doc**

Inserting and Viewing a Presentation in Word

Suppose you are developing a presentation in PowerPoint, and you want to include it in a Word document that you are sending to others in your workgroup for their review and feedback.

You can include a PowerPoint presentation in Word by *embedding* the presentation as an *object* in the Word document. Others can then review the document along with the presentation on their computers. The *PowerPoint Viewer* becomes a part of the embedded presentation, so even if others do not have PowerPoint installed on their computers, they'll still be able to view the complete presentation from within Word.

Note   The PowerPoint Viewer is a separate application included with PowerPoint. If the PowerPoint Viewer is not installed, use the Office Setup program to install it.

Embedding a PowerPoint presentation in a Word document is the best technique to use when your project meets any of the following criteria:

- You want to include a presentation within a Word document.
- You want to be able to view all the slides in the presentation.
- You're sending the document to others, and you want them to view the presentation.
- The person to whom you're sending the document does not have PowerPoint.

When you double-click the PowerPoint object in the document, the PowerPoint Viewer displays each slide in the presentation.

This can be useful when you want input or approval on a presentation draft. This can also be an alternative to giving a live presentation to your audience.

Note   You can also attach a PowerPoint presentation file to a Microsoft Mail message and then send it to other users on your network.

Embed a PowerPoint presentation file in Word

Embed the Childs Play new employee orientation presentation file from PowerPoint in your memo in Word so that it can be distributed for review.

1   In the Word memo, position the insertion point in the second blank line after the second paragraph, which starts with "If you're reading this."

2   From the Insert menu, choose Object.

3   In the Object dialog box, click the Create From File tab to make it active.

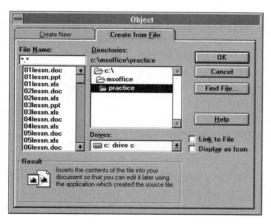

When you embed a presentation in a Word document, the entire file is included in the document. Because of this, the document file size can increase substantially.

4   From your PRACTICE directory, select LESSN07.PPT, and then choose the OK button.

Word embeds a copy of the PowerPoint presentation at the insertion point. This might take a few seconds. The first slide appears in the object frame, which might fill your screen.

5   If necessary, scroll upward or downward through the document to see the edge of the presentation.

6   Click the object to make the object frame appear.

7   Drag the sizing boxes in the object frame to make the object smaller to fit and look better on your page. Your screen should look similar to the following illustration.

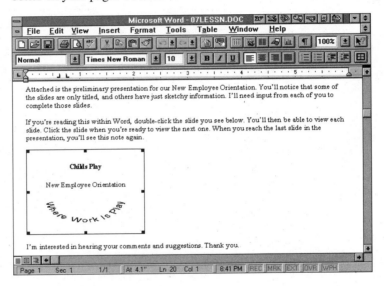

Save

8   On the Standard toolbar, click the Save button.

View the PowerPoint presentation within Word

Suppose that now you are one of the recipients of the memo. You've received the file either through electronic mail or on a diskette, and you want to review the presentation.

1   Double-click the embedded presentation object in the memo.

The screen clears for a moment, and then the PowerPoint Viewer displays a full-screen view of the first slide of the presentation.

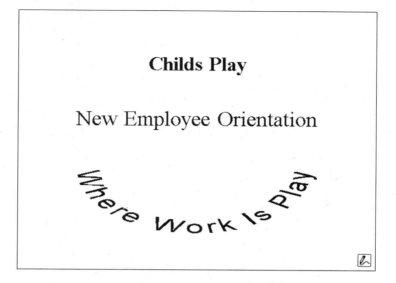

2   Click the slide.

The second slide in the presentation appears.

3   Click all succeeding slides to review the rest of the presentation.

When you click the last slide, the PowerPoint Viewer closes, and the Word memo appears again. You can view PowerPoint slides in a Word document like this, even if you do not have PowerPoint installed on your computer.

4   From the File menu in Word, choose Close.

If you see the Save dialog box, click Yes.

Exporting a Presentation to a Word Report

You might want to create a new Word document based on an existing PowerPoint presentation. This can be useful if you want your audience to have an accompanying document that they can use to make notes on the presentation, keep for future reference, or study for more in-depth information.

You can create a document that's based directly on your presentation by *exporting* the presentation file to Word. With exporting, you can convert a PowerPoint presentation into *Rich Text Format (RTF)*, which is a document *file format* that Word can read. Once you've exported the information from PowerPoint, you can open the new Word document, and the information looks as though it originally had been created in Word.

Exporting a PowerPoint presentation to a Word document is the best technique to use when your project meets all of the following criteria:

■   You want to convert an entire presentation file to create a new Word document,

■   You want to create a report or handout based on the information in an existing presentation.

■   You want much of the PowerPoint formatting to be retained in the new Word document.

Note   Whenever you export to send information from PowerPoint to Word, you're operating on whole files. You export the entire current file to create an entirely new Word file.

Importing works the same way. Whenever you import to bring information from PowerPoint into Word, you're bringing the entire file into the current application to create a new file.

The easiest way to export information from PowerPoint to Word is to use the Report It button on the Standard toolbar in PowerPoint. You click the Report It button to export the current presentation to a Word file by the same name.

Export a PowerPoint presentation to Word with Report It

You want the new employees to have an orientation packet that corresponds with your orientation presentation. Export the PowerPoint presentation to a new Word document.

Microsoft PowerPoint

1   On the Office Manager toolbar, click the Microsoft PowerPoint button.

The open LESSN07.PPT presentation in PowerPoint appears.

Report It

If the Tip Of The Day dialog box appears, choose the OK button.

2   On the Standard toolbar in PowerPoint, click the Report It button.

3   If the Convert File dialog box appears, be sure that Rich Text Format (RTF) is selected, and then choose the OK button.

RTF is a sophisticated text format that converts text as well as formatting from one application to another. Your presentation file is converted into RTF, which Word can read. Then, the RTF file appears in Word with the filename LESSN07.RTF. Your screen should look like the following illustration.

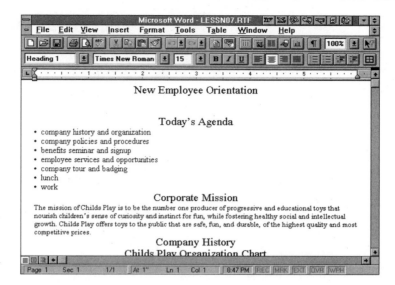

The new document can now be edited to create a detailed report based on text from the presentation.

4   From the File menu, choose Save As.

5   Double-click the PRACTICE directory.

6   Under Save File As Type, select Word Document.

7   Save the file as **lessn07a.doc**

This stores the file permanently as a Word document, and you can now edit and format the document to create an appropriate handout for the presentation.

8   From the File menu, choose Close.

One Step Further

An alternate method for exporting information from PowerPoint to Word is through the Save As command on the File menu. You choose the Outline (RTF) file format from the Save File As Type box to convert the presentation for use by Word.

Export a PowerPoint presentation to Word

Experiment with the another method for exporting a PowerPoint presentation to a Word document, using the Save As command.

1   From the File menu in PowerPoint, choose Save As.

The Save As dialog box appears.

2   In the Save File As Type box, select Outline (RTF).

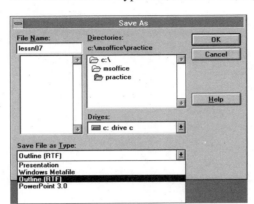

3   In the File Name box, type **lessn07b**, and then choose the OK button.

PowerPoint creates a file named LESSN07B.RTF, indicating that the presentation has been exported to Rich Text Format (RTF), a format that Word can interpret.

Open the exported presentation file in Word

Open, view, and save the exported RTF presentation file as a Word document file.

Microsoft Word

Open

1   On the Office Manager toolbar, click the Microsoft Word button.

2   On the Standard toolbar, click the Open button.

3   Be sure that the PRACTICE directory is selected.

4   In the List Files Of Type box, select Rich Text Format (*.rtf).

All RTF files in the PRACTICE directory are listed in the File Name box. When you exported the presentation file as an RTF file, it was saved with the RTF extension.

5   Select LESSN07B.RTF, and choose the OK button.

6   If the Convert File dialog box appears, be sure that Rich Text Format (RTF) is selected, and then choose the OK button.

The presentation that you had exported from PowerPoint to RTF appears on your screen. The new document is now ready for editing to create a detailed report based on text from the presentation.

7   From the File menu, choose Save As.

8   In the Save File As Type box, select Word Document.

9   Save the file as **lessn07b.doc**

End the Lesson

1   To continue to the next lesson, from the File menu in Word, choose Close. To quit for now, from the File menu in Word, choose Exit.

If you see the Save dialog box, click Yes.

Microsoft
PowerPoint

2   Hold down ALT and then, on the Office Manager toolbar, click the Microsoft PowerPoint button.

If you see the Save dialog box, click Yes.

Lesson Summary

To	Do this	Button
Embed a PowerPoint presentation file in Word	Position the insertion point in the Word document. From the Insert menu, choose Object. Click the Create From File tab, and then select the presentation file to be embedded. Click OK.	
View a PowerPoint presentation in Word	Double-click the presentation object in the Word document. Click a slide to view the next slide. When you click the last slide, the PowerPoint viewer closes.	
Export a presentation file from PowerPoint to Word using the Report It button	With the PowerPoint presentation open, on the Standard toolbar click the Report It button. If the Convert File dialog box appears, be sure Rich Text Format (RTF) is selected. From the File menu in Word, choose Save As. Under Save File As Type, select Word Document. Enter a new name for the file.	

For more information on	See in *Microsoft Office Getting Started*
Importing and exporting information between applications	Chapter 5, "Using Microsoft Office"
Converting documents from other applications	Chapter 6, "Sharing Information with Others"

For online information on	Choose <u>S</u>earch For Help On from the <u>H</u>elp menu of
Inserting information from other applications into Word	Microsoft Word, and then type **embedding**
Sending PowerPoint information to Word	Microsoft PowerPoint, and then type **Report It**
Using the PowerPoint Viewer	Microsoft PowerPoint, and then type **PowerPoint Viewer**
Converting PowerPoint information to RTF	Microsoft PowerPoint, and then type **export**

Preview of the Next Lesson

In the next lesson, you'll learn how to personalize form letters by merging names, addresses, and other information in a Microsoft Access database with a form letter created in Word.

Personalizing a Letter Using a Database

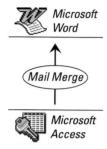

Microsoft
Word

Mail Merge

Microsoft
Access

Suppose you're writing a form letter to be mailed to a list of potential clients, and you'd like to personalize it with specific client information you have stored in a database. In the letter, you want to include the person's name and address, and you want to refer to the product in which they've expressed interest. With Microsoft Office, you can automate this process with a *mail merge*.

In this lesson, you'll create a set of personalized form letters in Word to be sent to new employees of Childs Play. These letters will contain information merged from a Microsoft Access table.

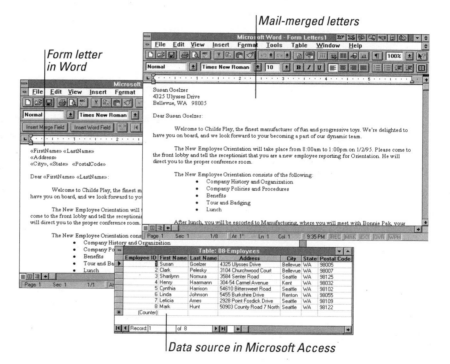

Mail-merged letters

Form letter
in Word

Data source in Microsoft Access

You will learn how to:

■ Set up a form letter to accept information from a Microsoft Access database.

■ Merge data into a Word form letter from either Word or Microsoft Access.

Estimated lesson time: 30 minutes

Start the lesson

Start Microsoft Access and open SBSDATA.MDB. Start Word and open 08LESSN.DOC.

1   Be sure that the Microsoft Office Manager is open.

The Microsoft Office Manager is open if the Office Manager toolbar appears on your desktop. If Microsoft Office Manager is not open, double-click the Microsoft Office icon in the Windows Program Manager.

Microsoft Access

2   On the Office Manager toolbar, click the Microsoft Access button. If the Welcome message appears, double-click the Control-menu box to close it.

3   From your PRACTICE directory, open SBSDATA.MDB.

4   Double-click the 08-Employees table to open it.

This table contains specific information about the new Childs Play employees.

Microsoft Word

5   On the Office Manager toolbar, click the Microsoft Word button. If the Tip Of The Day dialog box appears, choose the OK button.

6   From your PRACTICE directory, open 08LESSN.DOC.

This is the form letter into which you want to merge the specific information from the database table. Be sure that both the Word window and the document window are maximized.

7   Save the document as **lessn08.doc**

Setting Up Merge Fields

Suppose you have a generic form letter in Word that you would like to personalize for each recipient. Instead of filling in the specific information for each recipient manually, you can create personal letters automatically by using information already stored in a Microsoft Access database table.

You can merge database information into a form letter written in Word to make it look as if you wrote each letter individually. Using a process called *mail merge*, you can merge specific information about an individual on your mailing list into a form letter. In this way, you can quickly create personalized letters to all your addressees. Your letter is written with Word, while the specific information, such as the individuals' names, addresses, and other detailed information, is stored in a Microsoft Access database. With the Word letter as your *main document*, you can use the Microsoft Access database as your *data source* for the merge.

Using a Microsoft Access database table as the data source for a mail merge with a Word document is the best technique to use when your project meets any of the following criteria:

■   You want to personalize a form letter with a mail merge.

■   You already have a Microsoft Access database table that includes the information you need for the mail merge.

■ You don't have a data source set up yet, and you want to use the mail merge data source as the starting point for a larger database with a wider range of uses.

Note   Other possible data sources include a Microsoft Excel workbook and a Word table.

When preparing a form letter for a mail merge, you insert *merge fields* into your letter. These merge fields indicate where the specific database information is to be placed in your letter.

When merging into a Word document from a Microsoft Access database, the merge fields correspond with the field names of the database table.

Identify a Microsoft Access table as the merge data source

In Word, you have the main text for the standard letter to new Childs Play employees. You want to create a set of personal letters for the new employees. Identify the Microsoft Access database table as the data source for the mail merge. This is the table that contains the names, addresses, and other specific information you want to use to personalize the letters.

1   From the Tools menu in Word, choose Mail Merge.

The Mail Merge Helper dialog box appears.

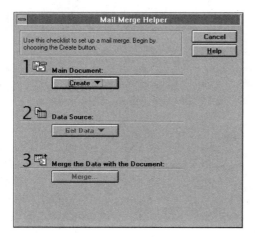

2   Choose the Create button, and then choose Form Letters.

This identifies the format and source of the main document for the merge.

3   Choose the Active Window button.

This indicates that your current file will be your main document for the mail merge.

4   In the Mail Merge Helper dialog box, choose the Get Data button, and then choose Open Data Source.

The Open Data Source dialog box appears.

If you do not have Microsoft Access, or if you have mail merge data in a Microsoft Excel workbook or in another Word file, you would identify the source here in the Open Data Source dialog box.

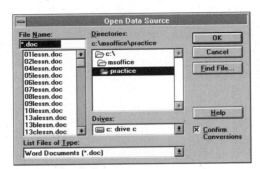

5   In the Open Data Source dialog box, be sure that your PRACTICE directory is selected.

6   Type **sbsdata.mdb** in the File Name box, and then choose the OK button. If the Confirm Data Source dialog box appears, choose the OK button.

7   In the Microsoft Access dialog box, click the Tables tab to make it active, select the 08-Employees table, and then choose the OK button.

The 08-Employees table is now identified as the data source for the mail merge. A message appears that states that there are no merge fields in the main document.

8   Choose the Edit Main Document button.

This sets up the document so you can insert the merge fields into appropriate places in the form letter.

The Mail Merge toolbar appears in your Word window.

The Mail Merge toolbar appears with any document that includes merge fields.

Insert merge fields into a Word form letter

Now insert merge fields for the names and addresses of the new employees. Then, insert merge fields in the body of the letter that add to or replace generic information with personalized information regarding the employee's start date, department, and supervisor. Be sure to press ENTER or SPACEBAR and to type appropriate punctuation, as necessary.

Insert Merge Field

1 Position the insertion point at the top of the Word letter, and then on the Mail Merge toolbar, click the Insert Merge Field button.

All data source fields from your selected database table appear.

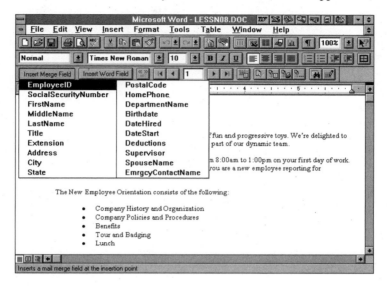

2 From the Insert Merge Field list, choose FirstName.

The <<FirstName>> field appears in your letter at the insertion point.

3 Press the SPACEBAR, and then on the Mail Merge toolbar, click the Insert Merge Field button again.

4 Choose LastName, and then press ENTER to add a new line for the address information.

5 Follow the same process to insert the Address field on the next line, and then City, State, and PostalCode on the third line.

Be sure to press ENTER and the SPACEBAR wherever you need a new line or a space, and type a comma between the City and State fields.

6 In the greeting line, select the words "New Employee" (but don't select the colon), and then from the Insert Merge Field list, choose FirstName, press the SPACEBAR, and then choose LastName.

By doing this, you're replacing the generic, impersonal information in the letter with specific, personalized information. The chosen fields appear in your letter.

7 In the second paragraph, select the words "your first day of work" (but don't select the period), and then, from the Insert Merge Field list, choose DateStart.

So far, your letter should look similar to the following illustration.

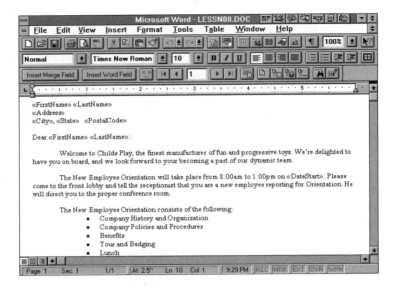

8   In the paragraph after the bulleted list, select the words "your department" (but don't select the comma), and then, from the Insert Merge Field list, choose DepartmentName.

When the mail merge is complete, the individual employee's specific department name will be inserted at this field.

9   In the same paragraph, position the insertion point just before the words "your supervisor." From the Insert Merge Field list, choose Supervisor, and then type a comma and press the SPACEBAR.

Now the merge fields are all inserted into the proper places in the letter. At this point, you're ready to start the mail merge.

Merging Microsoft Access Data into a Word Letter

Your form letter is written and includes all the necessary merge fields. Now you're ready to merge Microsoft Access database information with the form letter. The result will be a new document containing all the mail-merged letters, ready for you to print and send. A separate letter is created for each record in the selected database table.

You can initiate the mail merge from Word by using the Mail Merge command from the Tools menu. Or, you can initiate the mail merge from Microsoft Access by using the Merge It button on the Standard toolbar. The result is identical, regardless of the application from which you initiate the mail merge. Choose whichever method is most convenient for you. If you're currently working in Microsoft Access, it's probably more convenient to initiate the mail merge there. Likewise, if you're working in Word, it's quicker to start the mail merge there.

Start the merge from Word

You're currently working in Word, so initiate the mail merge from there.

1 From the Tools menu in Word, choose Mail Merge.

2 In the Mail Merge Helper dialog box, choose the Merge button.

The Merge dialog box appears, letting you set mail merge options.

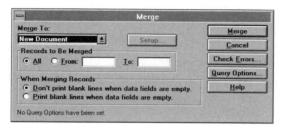

3 In the Merge dialog box, choose the Merge button.

The information from the selected Microsoft Access database merges into the form letter at the appropriate fields. A new document is created that contains a separate letter for each record in the database table, as shown in the following illustration.

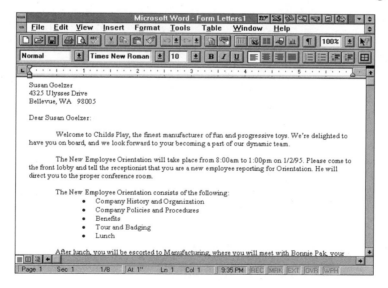

4 Scroll through the merged document and notice that each letter is separated by a section break.

Your original form letter is still intact, so you can use it again later.

Save

5 On the Standard toolbar, click the Save button.

6 Save the merged document as **lessn08a.doc**

7 From the File menu, choose Close.

Start the merge from Microsoft Access

Experiment with starting the mail merge from Microsoft Access, and notice how the process and resulting letters are identical to that of the previous exercise. It's more convenient to initiate the merge from Microsoft Access, if you're already using it.

Microsoft Access

1 On the Office Manager toolbar, click the Microsoft Access button.

Microsoft Access appears, displaying the open SBSDATA.MDB database and the 08-Employees table.

2 Click the database window to make it active. Or, from the Window menu, choose Database: SBSDATA.

Merge It

3 On the Standard toolbar in Microsoft Access, click the Merge It button.

The Microsoft Word Mail Merge Wizard appears.

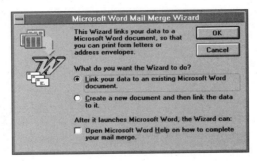

4 Be sure that the first option—to link your data to an existing Word document—is selected, and then choose the OK button.

5 From the Select Microsoft Word Document dialog box, select LESSN08.DOC from your PRACTICE directory, and then choose the OK button.

Word and your selected document appear. Be sure that both the Word window and the document window are maximized.

Mail Merge

6 On the Mail Merge toolbar in Word, click the Mail Merge button.

7 In the Merge dialog box, choose the Merge button.

The information from your selected Microsoft Access table merges into the selected form letter at the appropriate merge fields. A new Word document is created that contains a separate letter for each record in the database table.

8 Save the merged document as **lessn8b.doc**

9 From the File menu, choose Close.

One Step Further

You can use the same mail merge process from Microsoft Access into Word to create mailing labels. You choose the appropriate mailing label size and format, and then you set up the label's merge fields, including the addressees' names and addresses. You end up with a sheet of mailing labels ready to be printed and affixed to your mailing.

Identify the mailing label document and data source

Now that your mail merged letters are created, you want to create mailing labels for the envelopes. Follow the mail merge process, but this time, choose mailing labels as the document type.

1 From the Tools menu in Word, choose Mail Merge.

2 In the Mail Merge Helper dialog box, choose the Create button, and then choose Mailing Labels.

3 In the next dialog box, choose the New Main Document button.

This will set up your main mailing label document in a new document, rather than using the document currently open on your screen.

4 In the Mail Merge Helper dialog box, choose the Get Data button, and then choose Open Data Source.

5 In the Open Data Source dialog box, be sure that your PRACTICE directory is selected.

6 In the File Name box, type **sbsdata.mdb**, and then choose the OK button. If the Confirm Data Source dialog box appears, choose the OK button.

This indicates that the SBSDATA.MDB database contains the table that you want to use as your data source.

7 In the Microsoft Access dialog box, click the Tables tab to make it active, select the 08-Employees table, and then choose the OK button.

This indicates that the 08-Employees table is the data source for the mailing labels.

8 In the Microsoft Word dialog box, choose the Set Up Main Document button.

The Label Options dialog box appears, in which you can select printer and label information.

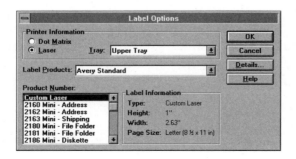

9 Choose the OK button.

The Create Labels dialog box appears.

Insert merge fields into the mailing label

Now that the label document and the data source are set up, insert the merge fields from the data source into the mailing label.

1 In the Create Labels dialog box, choose the Insert Merge Field button.

All the data source fields from your selected database table appear.

2 Choose FirstName.

The <<FirstName>> field appears on the first line of your sample mailing label.

3 Press the SPACEBAR, choose the Insert Merge Field button, and then choose LastName.

4 Press ENTER.

5 Repeat this process to insert the Address field on the second line, and the City, State, and PostalCode fields on the third line.

Be sure to press ENTER and the SPACEBAR where appropriate, and type a comma between the City and State fields. Your sample label should look like the following illustration.

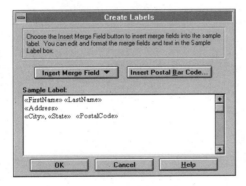

6 Choose the OK button.

The Mail Merge Helper dialog box appears.

Merge the database information into the mailing label

Now merge the information from the Microsoft Access data source with the mailing labels in Word.

1   In the Mail Merge Helper dialog box, choose the Merge button.

2   In the Merge dialog box, choose the Merge button.

Microsoft Word creates the main document for the mailing labels. It then merges the selected Microsoft Access data source information with it, to create a new merged mailing label document, ready for printing and use. The merged mailing label document includes a separate label for each record in the database table, as shown in the following illustration.

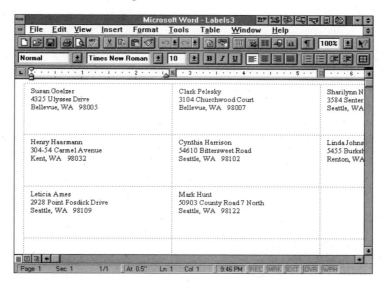

3   Save the merged mailing label document as **lessn08c.doc**

4   From the File menu, choose Close.

The mailing label main document appears, with all the merge fields inserted.

5   Save the main label document as **lessn08d.doc**

6   From the File menu, choose Close.

End the Lesson

1   To continue to the next lesson, close the 08-Employees table in Microsoft Access. To quit for now, from the File menu in Microsoft Access, choose Exit.

If you see the Save dialog box, click Yes.

2   To continue to the next lesson, from the File menu in Word, choose Close. To quit for now, from the File menu in Word, choose Exit.

If you see the Save dialog box, click Yes.

Lesson Summary

To	Do this	Button
Set up the main document for a mail merge	From the Tools menu in Word, choose Mail Merge. Choose the Create button, and then choose the type of document you want to create.	
Identify the Microsoft Access database and table to be used as the merge data source	From the Tools menu in Word, choose Mail Merge. Choose the Get Data button, and then choose the Open Data Source button. Select the Microsoft Access database field and then select the table.	
Insert a mail merge field from Microsoft Access into your Word document	Position the insertion point where the field should be inserted. On the Mail Merge toolbar, click the Insert Merge Field button. Choose the field to be inserted.	Insert Merge Field
Initiate the mail merge from a Word document	On the Mail Merge toolbar, click the Mail Merge Helper button. In the dialog box, choose the Merge button. Save the merged document with a new name.	
Initiate the mail merge from Microsoft Access	With the Access database active, on the Standard toolbar, click the Merge It button. Select the first option button and choose OK. In the dialog box, select the Word document, and choose OK. On the Mail Merge toolbar in Word, click the Mail Merge button, and then choose the Merge button in the dialog box. Save the merged document with a new name.	

For more information on	See in *Microsoft Office Getting Started*
Creating a mail merge in Word using Microsoft Access information	Chapter 5, "Using Microsoft Office"
Sharing database information across a network	Chapter 6, "Sharing Information with Others"

For online information about	From the Help menu of
Opening a data source from another application	Microsoft Word, choose Search For Help On, and then type **Microsoft Access**
Creating a mail merged form letter	Microsoft Word, choose Search For Help On, and then type **form letter**
Creating a mail merged mailing list	Microsoft Word, choose Search For Help On, and then type **mailing list**
Initiating mail merge from Microsoft Access	Microsoft Access, choose Search, and then type **mail merge**

Preview of the Next Lesson

In the next lesson, you'll learn how to create a Word report using database information. You'll insert a database table into Word to create a Word table, and you'll export database report information to a format that Word can interpret.

Writing a Report Using a Database

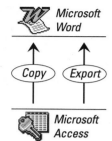

Microsoft Word

↑ Copy ↑ Export

Microsoft Access

You can bring database information, such as sales figures, customer information, or manufacturing details, from Microsoft Access into a Word document to create reports. For example, you want to create a sales report in Word that includes sales figures and customer information from a database. Or, you might need to write a manufacturing report indicating the number of units produced, quality specifications, and amount of scrap.

In this lesson, you'll learn how to use Microsoft Access database information in a Word document. You'll create an employment report for Childs Play management by inserting a database table into a Word document. You'll also convert a Microsoft Access database report into a format that Word can read and use in this document.

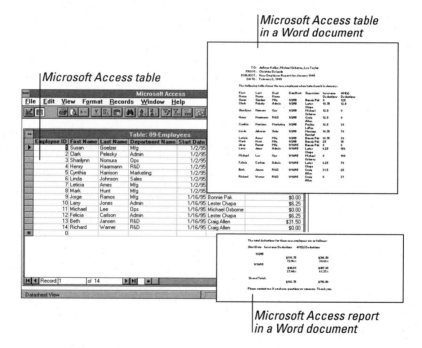

Microsoft Access table

Microsoft Access table in a Word document

Microsoft Access report in a Word document

You will learn how to:

- Insert a database table into Word as a Word table.
- Convert a database report into a format that Word can interpret.

Estimated lesson time: 25 minutes

Start the lesson

From Microsoft Access, open the 09-Employees table. From Word, open the 09LESSN.DOC file.

1   Be sure that the Microsoft Office Manager is open.

The Microsoft Office Manager is open if the Office Manager toolbar appears on your desktop. If Microsoft Office Manager is not open, double-click the Microsoft Office icon in the Windows Program Manager.

Microsoft Access

2   On the Office Manager toolbar, click the Microsoft Access button. If the Welcome message appears, double-click the Control-menu box to close it.

3   From your PRACTICE directory, open SBSDATA.MDB.

4   Double-click the 09-Employees table to open it.

This table stores the benefits choices made by new Childs Play employees.

Microsoft Word

5   On the Office Manager toolbar, click the Microsoft Word button. If the Tip Of The Day dialog box appears, choose the OK button.

6   From your PRACTICE directory, open 09LESSN.DOC.

This document is a report to upper management regarding new employee statistics. Be sure that both the Word window and the document window are maximized.

7   Save the document as **lessn09.doc**

Inserting a Database Table into a Word Document

Suppose you want to insert a Microsoft Access database table into a Word document. There are two methods for doing this. If you want to insert the entire table, you use the Database command on the Insert menu in Word. If you want to insert just a portion of the table, you use the Copy command in Microsoft Access, and then the Paste command in Word.

With either method, you're inserting a copy of the Microsoft Access table into your document, and it looks and acts as if you had originally created the table in Word.

Insert an entire database table into Word

Insert the benefits table in Microsoft Access into your Word report to upper management.

1   In the Word report, position the insertion point in the second blank line after the first paragraph, which starts with "The following table."

2   From the Insert menu, choose Database.

The Database dialog box appears.

With the Query Options button, you can select which fields you want to insert. You can also apply comparison and sorting operations.

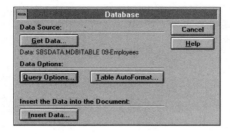

3 Choose the Get Data button.

The Open Data Source dialog box appears.

Be sure that your PRACTICE directory is selected.

4 In the File Name box, type **sbsdata.mdb**, and then choose the OK button. If the Confirm Data Source dialog box appears, choose the OK button.

5 In the Microsoft Access dialog box, click the Tables tab to make it active, select the 09-Employees table, and then choose the OK button.

The Database dialog box appears again.

You can instantly apply a table format by choosing the Table AutoFormat button in the Database dialog box.

6 Choose the Insert Data button.

7 In the Insert Data dialog box, choose the OK button.

All records in the selected database table are inserted into your Word report as a Word table, and Microsoft Access appears.

8 On the Office Manager toolbar, click the Microsoft Word button.

Your report should look similar to the following illustration.

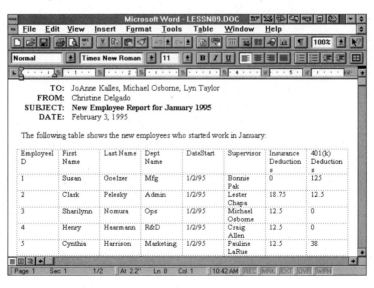

Edit the table

Now that your Microsoft Access table is inserted into your Word report, edit and format the table to make it more suitable for your management report. Delete the Employee ID column, because it's not necessary in this context. Then adjust the column sizes so that all the text fits properly.

1   Click anywhere in the Employee ID column.

2   From the Table menu in Word, choose Select Column. Or, select the column with the mouse by clicking just above the column header cell.

The Employee ID column is selected.

Cut

3   From the Table menu, choose Delete Columns. Or, click the Cut button on the Standard toolbar.

The Employee ID column is deleted.

4   Adjust the table's column sizes so that the text fits properly. Do this by dragging the right edge of each column to the new location.

5   Select the first row that includes the field names.

Bold

6   On the Formatting toolbar, click the Bold button.

Your formatted table should look similar to the following illustration.

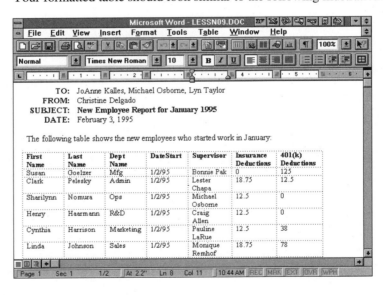

Save

7   On the Standard toolbar, click the Save button.

Copy a portion of a database table into Word

You discover that you don't need the entire table in your report, but only a few selected fields. Experiment with copying three columns from a database table and pasting them into your Word report.

Microsoft Access

Copy

Microsoft Word

Paste

1 On the Office Manager toolbar, click the Microsoft Access button.

2 In the 09-Employees table, drag across the field names in the column titles to select the First Name, Last Name, and Department Name columns.

3 On the Standard toolbar, click the Copy button.

4 On the Office Manager toolbar, click the Microsoft Word button.

5 Position the insertion point at the top of the second page of the report, immediately after the page break.

6 On the Standard toolbar, click the Paste button.

The selected columns are inserted into your Word report at the insertion point, as shown in the following illustration.

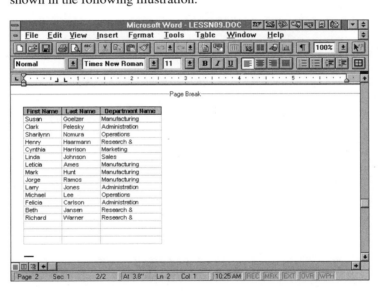

You can now edit the table using any of the commands on the Table menu.

7 On the Standard toolbar, click the Save button.

Converting a Database Report into a Word Format

You have a database report generated in Microsoft Access that you'd like to include in a Word document. A *database report* usually summarizes extensive database information that originates in a database *table* or *query*. This kind of information can be quite useful in a Word document that deals with the topic.

To use a database report in Word, you must convert the information into *Rich Text Format (RTF)*, which is a document *file format* that Word can interpret and use.

When you output a database form to RTF format, Microsoft Access converts the underlying table or query on which the form is based.

You convert a Microsoft Access object, such as a report or table, with the Output To command on the File menu in Microsoft Access. You choose the RTF format, and Microsoft Access converts the information into a separate RTF file. You can then build a Word document around the converted information, or you can copy and paste it into another existing document. This is an automated process that is similar to *exporting* Microsoft Access information to Word.

Convert a database report into RTF

In another section of your document, you want to include a database report that summarizes the benefits choices made by the new employees. From Microsoft Access, convert the 09-Employees report to RTF and output it to Word.

Microsoft Access

1   On the Office Manager toolbar, click the Microsoft Access button.

Microsoft Access appears, displaying the open SBSDATA.MDB database and the 09-Employees table.

Database Window

2   On the Standard toolbar, click the Database Window button. Or, switch to the Database window by clicking the window.

3   In the Database window, click the Report tab.

4   Select 09-Employee Benefits Summary, and then click the Preview button.

The preview of the Employee Benefits Summary report appears.

5   From the File menu, choose Output To.

The Output To dialog box appears.

You can also just select the report name from the Database window, and then choose Output To from the File menu.

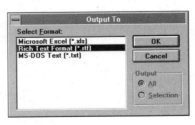

6   Select Rich Text Format (*.rtf), and then choose the OK button.

Another Output To dialog box appears, indicating that the new converted file will be named 09-EMPLO.RTF.

7 In the File Name box, type **lessn09a.doc**

Be sure to type the .DOC extension.

8 Select the AutoStart check box, and then choose the OK button.

Microsoft Access converts the selected database report to an RTF file.

9 If the Convert File dialog box appears, be sure that Rich Text Format (RTF) is selected, and then choose the OK button.

The RTF report appears in a new Word document.

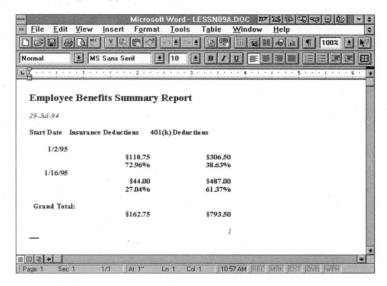

You can now build a Word document around the converted database report, or you can copy and paste it into an existing Word document.

Insert exported information into an existing Word document

Copy and paste the converted database report into your Word document.

1 From the Edit menu, choose Select All.

Copy

2 On the Standard toolbar, click the Copy button.

3 From the File menu, choose Close.

LESSN09.DOC appears.

4 Position the insertion point on page 1 in the blank line after the second paragraph, which starts with "The total deductions."

Paste

5 On the Standard toolbar, click the Paste button.

The Microsoft Access summary report is inserted into your Word document.

You can now make any editing changes and adjustments you want.

6 Delete the lines containing the summary report's title, date, and page number.

Your report should look similar to the following illustration.

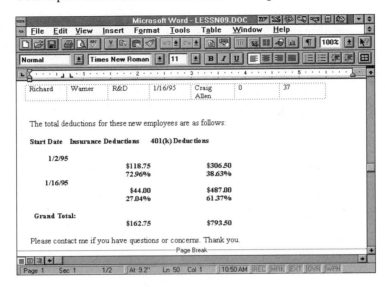

Save

7 On the Standard toolbar in Word, click the Save button.

One Step Further

Earlier in this lesson, you learned two methods of inserting a database table into a Word document. Another way to use a Microsoft Access table in Word is to convert it to RTF. You follow the same process as when you convert a database report to RTF. A database table converted to RTF and brought into Word retains its formatting and therefore looks more polished than a Microsoft Access report brought into Word.

Export a database table to Word

Microsoft Access

1 On the Office Manager toolbar, click the Microsoft Access button.

2 On the Standard toolbar, click the Database Window button. Or, switch to the Database window by clicking on it.

Database Window

3 Click the Table tab, select 09-Employees, and then choose Open.

4 From the File menu, choose Output To.

The Output To dialog box appears.

5 In the Output area, select the All option button.

6 Select Rich Text Format (*.RTF), and then choose the OK button.

Another Output To dialog box appears.

7 In the File Name box, type **lessn09b.doc**

Be sure to type the .DOC extension.

8 Select the AutoStart check box, and then choose the OK button.

Microsoft Access converts the selected table to an RTF file.

If the Tip Of The Day dialog box appears, choose the OK button.

9 If the Convert File dialog box appears, be sure that Rich Text Format (RTF) is selected, and then choose the OK button.

The RTF file appears in Word, displaying the table. You can now build a Word document around the exported database table, or you can copy and paste it into an existing Word document.

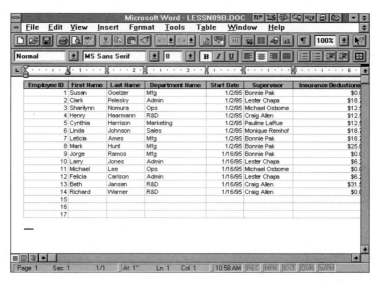

10 From the File menu, choose Close.

Note   A simple way to use all or part of a Microsoft Access table in Word is to simply copy and paste it. When you use the Copy and Paste commands with Microsoft Access table information, the RTF conversion takes place automatically. Instead of creating a separate file, you can paste the copied table information directly into an existing Word report. With copying and pasting, you can also select certain rows or columns of the table.

End the Lesson

1   To continue to the next lesson, from the <u>F</u>ile menu in Word, choose <u>C</u>lose. To quit for now, from the <u>F</u>ile menu in Word, choose E<u>x</u>it.

If you see the Save dialog box, click Yes.

Microsoft Access

2   Hold down ALT and then, on the Office Manager toolbar, click the Microsoft Access button.

If you see the Save dialog box, click Yes.

Lesson Summary

To	Do this
Insert a Microsoft Access table into Word	Position the insertion point in Word where you want the table to appear. From the Insert menu in Word, choose Database. Choose the Get Data button. Select the database file. In the Microsoft Access dialog box, select the table name. Choose the Insert Data button, and then choose the OK button.
Copy and paste selected rows or columns of a Microsoft Access table into Word.	In the Microsoft Access table, select the columns or rows to copy. On the Standard toolbar, click the Copy button. In the Word document, position the insertion point and then, on the Standard toolbar, click the Paste button.
Export Microsoft Access database information to RTF	In the Microsoft Access Database window, select the object (table, report, query, and so on), and then select the item that you want to export. From the File menu, choose Output To. Select Rich Text Format (*.RTF), and then choose the OK button.

For more information on	See in *Microsoft Office Getting Started*
Copying and pasting information between applications	Chapter 4, "How Office Applications Work Together"
Inserting database information into Word	Chapter 5, "Using Microsoft Office"
Sharing database information across a network	Chapter 6, "Sharing Information with Others"

For online information on	From the <u>H</u>elp menu of
Inserting a database as an object in Word	Microsoft Word, choose <u>S</u>earch For Help On, and then type **Database command**
	Microsoft Word, choose <u>S</u>earch For Help On, and then type **RTF**
Converting database information into RTF	Microsoft Access, choose <u>S</u>earch, and then type **output to**
Copying database information to Word	Microsoft Access, choose <u>S</u>earch, and then type **copying objects**

Preview of the Next Lessons

In Part 3, you'll learn how to create compound Microsoft Excel workbooks using the different integration techniques—copying and pasting, linking and embedding, and importing and exporting. In the next lesson, you'll learn how to create a Microsoft Excel workbook including text from Word.

Review & Practice

In the lessons in Part 2, you learned how to use information from different applications to create and enhance Word documents. If you want to practice these skills and test your understanding before you proceed with the lessons in Part 3, you can work through the Review & Practice section following this lesson.

Part 2   Review & Practice

You can practice the skills you learned in Part 2 by working through the steps in this Review & Practice section. You will create Word documents using information originating in Microsoft Excel, PowerPoint, and Microsoft Access.

Scenario

You've been asked to prepare three documents incorporating marketing and sales information from a variety of sources in Microsoft Excel, Microsoft Access, and PowerPoint. You'll prepare a marketing strategy proposal for a new line of educational toys, which you'll then send out for review. The proposal will be based on an existing presentation. You'll also write a monthly marketing status report by obtaining existing information from a Microsoft Excel workbook and a Microsoft Access database. Finally, you'll personalize a form letter to customer sales representatives by doing a mail merge with Microsoft Access information.

You will review and practice how to:

- Include a PowerPoint presentation within a Word document by embedding it, and then route it to other users in your workgroup.
- Save a PowerPoint presentation as a Word document.
- Copy a Microsoft Excel workbook and embed a Microsoft Excel chart into a Word document.
- Include an automatically updated workbook in a Word document.
- Insert a Microsoft Access table and summary report in a Word document.
- Create personalized form letters in Word using data from Microsoft Access.

Estimated practice time: 35 minutes

Step 1: Insert a Presentation into a Document

You want feedback from other marketing team members regarding the PowerPoint presentation on the marketing strategy proposal. Embed the presentation in a memo so that other marketing team members can view it whether they have PowerPoint on their computers or not. Then route the memo through Microsoft Mail.

1   In PowerPoint, open the file P2REVIEW.PPT from your PRACTICE directory and save it as **reviewp2.ppt**

2   In Word, open the file P2AREV.DOC, and save it as **revp2a.doc**

3   After the second paragraph, which starts with "If you're reading this within Word...," embed the PowerPoint file REVIEWP2.PPT in the memo. (Tip: Use the Insert menu in Word.)

4   Reduce the size of the embedded presentation object to approximately three inches square, and then center the object.

5   View the PowerPoint file from within the memo.

6   If you are working on a network and are running Microsoft Mail, route the file to at least two other users in your group. (Tip: Use the Add Routing Slip command.)

7   Save and close the Word file.

For more information on	See
Embedding a file from one application within another application	Lesson 3
Embedding a PowerPoint presentation in a Word document	Lesson 7
Routing a file to other users in a workgroup	Lesson 6

Step 2: Save a Presentation as a Word Document

You've decided that the PowerPoint presentation contains much of the basic information you need for your marketing strategy proposal. Convert the presentation file to a format that Word can read.

1   In PowerPoint, export the file REVIEWP2.PPT to Word. (Tip: Use the Report It button.)

2   In Word, insert page breaks above each of the major headings: "Goal," "Positioning," "Marketing Methods," and "Budget."

3   Save the file as a Word document called **rev2b.doc**, and then close it.

4   Exit from PowerPoint.

For more information on	See
Exporting a file from one application to be used in another application	Lesson 4
Exporting a PowerPoint presentation file to Word	Lesson 7

Step 3: Include a Workbook in a Word Document

In your marketing strategy proposal, you need to include a Microsoft Excel sheet on projected marketing costs, as well as a chart on projected sales revenues. Another team member has given you the Microsoft Excel workbook with the projected costs, and she has assured you that these figures are accurate and fixed, and you don't expect to make any content changes. Because of this, just copy and paste the workbook into your proposal.

In the same workbook is a chart of projected sales revenues. You expect some changes to the figures, but these changes will only affect this proposal. Because of these factors, embed a copy of the chart in the proposal.

1 In Microsoft Excel, open the file P2REVIEW.XLS and save it as **reviewp2.xls**

2 In the Mktg Costs sheet, copy cells A5 through C17.

3 In Word, open the file P2CREV.DOC and save it as **revp2c.doc**

4 On page 4, in the blank line after the "Marketing Costs" heading, paste the copied information.

5 On the same page, in the blank line after the "Projected Sales" heading, embed the workbook REVIEWP2.XLS in the proposal. (Tip: Use the Insert menu in Word.)

6 Open the object and switch to the Sales Chart sheet in the workbook. If necessary, resize the workbook.

7 Return to Word, and then save and close the Word file.

For more information on	See
Copying and pasting information from one application to another application	Lesson 2
Copying and pasting information from Microsoft Excel into Word	Lesson 5
Embedding information from one application in the file of another application	Lesson 3
Embedding a Microsoft Excel chart within a Word document	Lesson 5

Step 4: Link a Workbook to a Word Document

Upper management needs a monthly marketing status report, including sales and customer information. You already keep sales information in a separate Microsoft Excel workbook, and you update it on a weekly basis. Because you want to automate the production of the monthly status report as much as possible, create a link between the Microsoft Excel workbook on sales and your monthly status report.

1 In the Microsoft Excel REVIEWP2.XLS file, switch to the Weekly Sales sheet.

2 Copy cells A4 through O11.

3 In Word, open the file P2DREV.DOC and save it as **revp2d.doc**

4 In the blank line after the first paragraph, which starts with "The following figures...," link the copied information as a worksheet object (rather than an RTF object). (Tip: Use the Paste Special command.)

5   Switch to the Microsoft Excel source workbook, and then in the Weekly Sales sheet, type **39,200**, **32,000**, **22,000**, and **11,000** in the column for week 5.

6   Save the file and exit Microsoft Excel.

7   Switch to and save the Word file.

For more information on	See
Linking information, for automatic updates, from one application to be used in another application	Lesson 3
Linking Microsoft Excel workbook information to a Word document	Lesson 6

Step 5:   Use Database Information in a Document

As part of the same marketing status report, you want to include information on the company's customer sales representatives. Detailed customer representative records are maintained in a Microsoft Access database. Insert a customer representative table, and then convert a Microsoft Access sales performance report into the Word status report.

1   In the Word REVP2D.DOC document, after the second paragraph which starts with "This table shows...," insert the Microsoft Access P2-Reps General table from the database file SBSDATA.MDB. (Tip: Use the Insert menu in Word.)

2   In Word, delete the P2-RepsID column (the first column), change the table font size to 8 points, and adjust the column widths so that the text fits properly. Make any other adjustments to the table format that you want.

3   From the same database file, convert the database report P2-Reps Total into RTF, and then insert it into page 2 of the Word report in the blank line after the paragraph which starts with "The following information". (Tip: Output the database report to RTF, and then copy and paste it.)

4   Delete any extra spacing between lines, and make any adjustments to the report format in Word that you want.

5   Save and close the Word file.

For more information on	See
Inserting Microsoft Access table information into Word	Lesson 9
Converting a Microsoft Access database report into a Word file format	Lesson 9

Step 6: Create Letters Using Database Information

You maintain records in a Microsoft Access database on Childs Play customer representatives. These records include names, addresses, and sales performance information. You want to send personalized form letters to each representative. Use the specific representative information in the Microsoft Access database to personalize a form letter in Word, by performing a mail merge between the two applications.

1   In Word, open the file P2EREV.DOC and save it as **revp2e.doc**

2   Start the mail merge process, and identify the Microsoft Access P2-Reps Detailed table within the SBSDATA.MDB database as the mail merge data source for your form letter. (Tip: Use the Mail Merge command from the Tools menu in Word.)

3   Insert merge fields to add the address and salutation at the beginning of the letter, and personalize the regional manager's name in the third paragraph. (Tip: Insert the merge fields <<FIRSTNAME>>, <<LASTNAME>>, <<ADDRESS>>, <<CITY>>, <<STATE>>, <<POSTALCODE>>, and <<REGIONALMGR>>.)

4   Merge the form letters with the data fields to create a new document containing all the merged letters.

5   Save the merged letters file as **revp2f.doc**, and then close it.

6   Save the main document file.

For more information on	See
Setting up a mail merge between a Microsoft Access database and a Word form letter	Lesson 8
Merging information between Microsoft Access and Word	Lesson 8

End the Lesson

▶   Hold down ALT and, on the Office Manager toolbar, click the button for each open application.

If you see the Save dialog box, click Yes.

3

Creating Workbooks in Microsoft Excel Using Integrated Information

Microsoft Excel is a spreadsheet application that you can use to store, manipulate, and analyze numerical information. With Microsoft Excel, you enter numbers and text into a column and row format, much like in a ledger. You can run the numbers through formulas to perform calculations, and you can transform the numbers into a variety of charts.

In this part, you will use Microsoft Excel as the base application with which you will use the sophisticated text formatting capabilities in Word. You will insert a PowerPoint presentation into a workbook, which can be invaluable if you're sending your workbook files to others. If you have Microsoft Access, you will also bring numerical information from a database into Microsoft Excel to analyze the information.

Creating Workbooks with Word Text

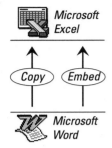

Microsoft Excel

Copy   Embed

Microsoft Word

If you have a table in Word on which you'd like to perform calculations or create a chart, you can bring it into Microsoft Excel. You can then use the features unique to Microsoft Excel. For example, you might have a table of test scores in Word that you want to use in a Microsoft Excel workbook. You can calculate averages and means with Microsoft Excel formulas, and then you can create a bar chart from this table. You can also use Word's special text formatting capabilities in Microsoft Excel to format text with bulleted or numbered lists, or other formatting.

In this lesson, you create a workbook containing 401(k) information for new employees of Childs Play that includes text created in a Word document.

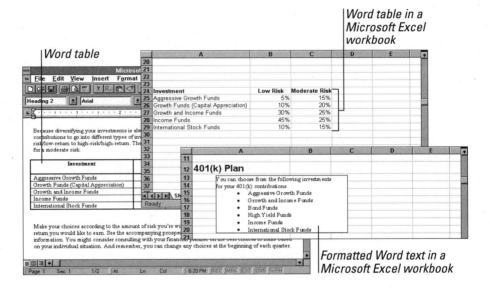

Word table in a Microsoft Excel workbook

Word table

Formatted Word text in a Microsoft Excel workbook

You will learn how to:

- Copy a Word table and paste it into a Microsoft Excel workbook.
- Link a Word table to a Microsoft Excel workbook for automatic updates.
- Create and embed a new Word document in a Microsoft Excel workbook.
- Insert a formatted Word document into a Microsoft Excel workbook.

Estimated lesson time: 35 minutes

Start the lesson

Start Word and open 10LESSN.DOC. Start Microsoft Excel and open 10LESSN.XLS.

1   Be sure that the Microsoft Office Manager is open.

The Microsoft Office Manager is open if the Office Manager toolbar appears on your desktop. If Microsoft Office Manager is not open, double-click the Microsoft Office icon in the Windows Program Manager.

Microsoft Excel

2   On the Office Manager toolbar, click the Microsoft Excel button.

3   From your PRACTICE directory, open 10LESSN.XLS.

This workbook will detail figures regarding employee retirement benefits, including the 401(k) plan. Be sure that both the Microsoft Excel window and the workbook window are maximized.

4   Save the workbook as **lessn10.xls**

Microsoft Word

5   On the Office Manager toolbar, click the Microsoft Word button. If the Tip Of The Day dialog box appears, choose the OK button.

6   From your PRACTICE directory, open 10LESSN.DOC.

This document includes information regarding Childs Play employee retirement benefits, including the company 401(k) plan. Be sure that both the Word window and the document window are maximized.

7   Save the document as **lessn10.doc**

Copying a Word Table into a Workbook

You want to create a workbook in Microsoft Excel that explains 401(k) information and investment strategies. This workbook will be used by new employees to help them make decisions about their retirement plan. You have a 401(k) table that you had originally created in Word, but you now want to use it in this workbook.

You can simply copy the Word table and paste it into your workbook. It will appear in your workbook as if you had originally created it with Microsoft Excel. The information in each cell in the table will be placed in a separate cell in the workbook.

Copying and pasting information from Word into Microsoft Excel is the best technique to use when your project meets all of the following criteria:

■   You want the information to look as if it originated in Microsoft Excel.

- You do not need any special text formatting provided by Word.

- You do not need the copied information in Microsoft Excel to be automatically updated when the original information in Word changes.

Copy a table from Word into a Microsoft Excel workbook

1   In Word, position the insertion point anywhere in the Investments table (the second table in the document), which is located toward the bottom of the page.

2   From the Table menu, choose Select Table.

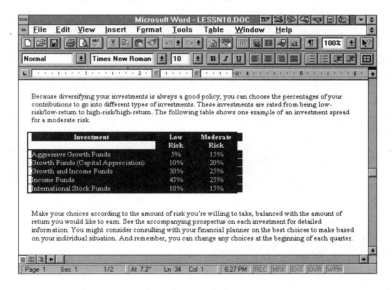

Copy

Paste

3   On the Standard toolbar in Word, click the Copy button.

4   On the Office Manager toolbar, click the Microsoft Excel button.

5   Be sure that Sheet1 is the active sheet, and then select cell A24.

6   On the Standard toolbar in Microsoft Excel, click the Paste button.

The Word table is inserted into the Microsoft Excel workbook as data in a range of cells.

```
┌──────────────────────────────────────────────────────────────────────┐
│              Microsoft Excel - LESSN10.XLS                             │
│ □  File  Edit  View  Insert  Format  Tools  Data  Window  Help         │
│ ┌──────────────────────────────────────────────────────────────┐      │
│ │ [toolbar icons]                              100%              │      │
│ ├──────────────────────────────────────────────────────────────┤      │
│ │ Arial         ▼ 10 ▼  B I U  ≡ ≡ ≡ ▦  $ % ,  .00 .00          │      │
│ ├──────────────────────────────────────────────────────────────┤      │
│ │   A37    ▼                                                     │      │
│ ├────┬─────────────────────┬────────┬──────────┬──────┬──────┐  │      │
│ │    │        A            │   B    │    C     │  D   │  E   │  │      │
│ ├────┼─────────────────────┼────────┼──────────┼──────┼──────┤  │      │
│ │ 20 │                     │        │          │      │      │  │      │
│ │ 21 │                     │        │          │      │      │  │      │
│ │ 22 │                     │        │          │      │      │  │      │
│ │ 23 │                     │        │          │      │      │  │      │
│ │ 24 │Investment           │Low Risk│Moderate Risk│   │      │  │      │
│ │ 25 │Aggressive Growth Funds│  5%  │   15%    │      │      │  │      │
│ │ 26 │Growth Funds (Capital Appreciation)│10%│20%│   │      │  │      │
│ │ 27 │Growth and Income Funds│ 30%  │   25%    │      │      │  │      │
│ │ 28 │Income Funds         │  45%   │   25%    │      │      │  │      │
│ │ 29 │International Stock Funds│ 10% │   15%    │      │      │  │      │
│ │ 30 │                     │        │          │      │      │  │      │
│ │ 31 │                     │        │          │      │      │  │      │
│ │ 32 │                     │        │          │      │      │  │      │
│ │ 33 │                     │        │          │      │      │  │      │
│ │ 34 │                     │        │          │      │      │  │      │
│ │ 35 │                     │        │          │      │      │  │      │
│ │ 36 │                     │        │          │      │      │  │      │
│ │ 37 │                     │        │          │      │      │  │      │
│ ├────┴─────────────────────┴────────┴──────────┴──────┴──────┘  │      │
│ │ Sheet1 / Sheet2 / Sheet3 / Sheet4 / Sheet5 / Sheet6            │      │
│ │ Ready                                                          │      │
└──────────────────────────────────────────────────────────────────────┘
```

Save

7   On the Standard toolbar in Microsoft Excel, click the Save button.

You can now manipulate, format, and calculate the cell contents as if you had originally typed them into the cells.

Edit the information in Microsoft Excel

Now that the Word table is copied into your workbook, you want to make some additions. Edit the information as you would any other workbook information.

1   In Sheet1, add a column to the right of the table and enter figures for a high-risk/high-return investment strategy, as follows:

High Risk

30%

35%

10%

10%

15%

You have now edited and added information to the table you copied from Word into your workbook. The information appears as if you had typed it in Microsoft Excel. This table is independent of the table in the Word source file. Changes you make in either file do not affect data in the other one.

2   On the Standard toolbar in Microsoft Excel, click the Save button.

Linking Word Information to a Workbook

You might have information in a Word document that is periodically updated, and you want those changes to be reflected in the same information in a Microsoft Excel workbook. You can make sure this happens automatically by *linking* the information to your workbook.

Linking information from Word to Microsoft Excel is the best technique to use when your project meets all of the following criteria:

- You have changing information in Word that you want to use in Microsoft Excel.
- You want to be sure that the information in Microsoft Excel is updated whenever the source file in Word changes.
- The destination file in Microsoft Excel will always have access to the source file in Word so that the link can be maintained.

When you create a link, the information in the workbook is automatically updated as soon as the information changes in the Word source file. You can also double-click the object in the workbook to open the Word source file and then edit the source file. Changes in the source file are then automatically reflected in the destination file in Microsoft Excel.

Link a table from Word to a Microsoft Excel workbook

You have more 401(k) information in another table in your Word document. This information is continually changing, and you want those changes to be reflected in your Microsoft Excel workbook as soon as they take place. You'll be using the workbook every few weeks at each new employee orientation, and you want to present the most current information. Link the table from the Word document to your workbook.

Microsoft Word

Copy

Microsoft Excel

1   On the Office Manager toolbar, click the Microsoft Word button.

2   In the Word document, select the Salary table, which is the first table on the page.

3   On the Standard toolbar in Word, click the Copy button.

4   On the Office Manager toolbar, click the Microsoft Excel button.

5   Select cell A32 to make it active.

6   From the Edit menu in Microsoft Excel, choose Paste Special.

The Paste Special dialog box appears.

7   Select the Paste Link option button.

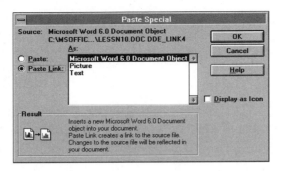

You can use this same process to link formatted text from Word to your Microsoft Excel workbook.

8 Be sure that Microsoft Word 6.0 Document Object is selected, and then choose the OK button.

The Word table is inserted into the Microsoft Excel workbook as a linked object, as shown in the following illustration.

Linked Word object

	A	B	C	D	E
24	Investment	Low Risk	Moderate Risk	High Risk	
25	Aggressive Growth Funds	5%	15%	30%	
26	Growth Funds (Capital Appreciation)	10%	20%	35%	
27	Growth and Income Funds	30%	25%	10%	
28	Income Funds	45%	25%	10%	
29	International Stock Funds	10%	15%	15%	
30					
31					
32	Percent of		Yearly Salary		
33	Salary	$15,000	$25,000	$35,000	$50,000
34	2%	$25/month	$42/month	$58/month	
35	4%	$50/month	$83/month	$117/month	
36	6%	$75/month	$125/month	$175/month	
37	8%	$100/month	$167/month	$233/month	
38	10%				
39					
40					
41					

Sheet1 / Sheet2 / Sheet3 / Sheet4 / Sheet5 / Sheet6

Ready

Any changes made to the source file in Word will be automatically updated in the destination file here in Microsoft Excel.

9 On the Standard toolbar in Microsoft Excel, click the Save button.

Save

Edit the table in Word

You've decided that you need to add a column showing examples for a $50,000 salary. Edit the table in Word, and then switch to the Microsoft Excel workbook. You'll notice that the change is reflected in the linked table.

1 On the Office Manager toolbar, click the Microsoft Word button.

Microsoft Word

2   In the table, add the following figures in the $50,000 column.

	$50,000
2%	**$83/month**
4%	**$167/month**
6%	**$250/month**
8%	**$333/month**

3   On the Standard toolbar in Word, click the Save button.

4   On the Office Manager toolbar, click the Microsoft Excel button.

Microsoft Excel

5   Notice that the changes you made to the linked table in Word are reflected in the linked object in Microsoft Excel.

6   On the Standard toolbar in Microsoft Excel, click the Save button.

Edit the information in Microsoft Excel

You're editing the workbook, and you decide that you would like another row in the table. Because the table is a linked object, you cannot make the change directly in Microsoft Excel. Rather, the change must be made in Word. You can switch quickly from the destination application to the source application and file by double-clicking the linked object. You can then edit the file and then return to Microsoft Excel.

1   In the Microsoft Excel workbook, be sure that Sheet1 is active.

2   Double-click the linked object.

Microsoft Word appears, along with the source file LESSN10.DOC.

3   In the Salary table, add the following figures for the 10% row.

	$15,000	$25,000	$35,000	$50,000
10%	**$125/month**	**$208/month**	**$292/month**	**$417/month**

4   On the Office Manager toolbar, click the Microsoft Excel button.

You'll see that the changes you made in the source file in Word are also changed automatically in your linked object in the workbook.

5   On the Standard toolbar in Microsoft Excel, click the Save button.

Embedding Word Text in a Workbook

You have a workbook in which you want to use text formatting capabilities that Word can provide, such as bulleted and numbered lists.

You can insert, or *embed*, a Word document in your Microsoft Excel workbook. This makes all the resources available in Word to become available in Microsoft Excel. When you double-click the Word object embedded in your workbook, your menu and toolbars change to those of Word. When you click outside the embedded object, the menu and toolbars change back to those of Microsoft Excel.

Embedding can cause your document size to increase significantly, because you are inserting the entire document file within your workbook file.

Embedding also ensures that all the pieces you need for a workbook file are in one place. This can be particularly useful if the workbook file might be used or viewed on other computers where the source file in Word might not be readily available.

You have three choices when embedding a Word document in a workbook:

- You can create and embed an entirely new Word document in your workbook.
- You can embed a selected area of an existing Word document.
- You can embed an existing Word document as an independent copy of the source file.

Create and embed a new Word document in a workbook

In your Microsoft Excel workbook explaining 401(k) information, you want to include detailed and attractively formatted text to clearly explain the sheets and charts. Specifically, you want to format indented and numbered lists. Since Microsoft Excel is not designed to do this kind of text formatting, create and embed a new Word object in your workbook.

1   In Microsoft Excel, select cell B14 to make it active.

This location will become the upper-left corner of the embedded object.

2   From the Insert menu in Microsoft Excel, choose Object.

The Object dialog box appears. Be sure that the Create New tab is active.

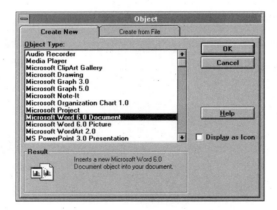

3   Select Microsoft Word 6.0 Document, and then choose the OK button.

A Word window appears within your workbook, and your Microsoft Excel menu and toolbars change to those of Word.

4   Drag the sizing box on the bottom edge of the Word window down to row 20 to make the object window larger.

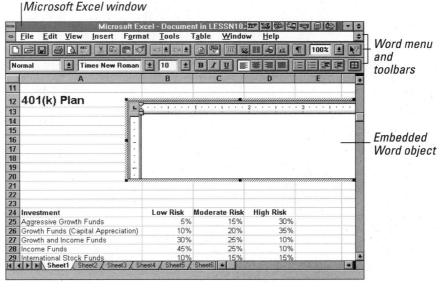

Microsoft Excel window

Word menu and toolbars

Embedded Word object

5   Enter the following text:

> **You can choose from the following investments for your 401(k) contributions:**
> **Aggressive Growth Funds**
> **Growth and Income Funds**
> **Bond Funds**
> **High Yield Funds**

Bullets

6   Select the four list items and, on the Formatting toolbar, click the Bullets button.

Bullets are added in front of the four list items.

7   With the four bulleted list items still selected, on the Formatting toolbar, click the Increase Indent button.

Increase Indent

The list items are indented.

8   Click outside the Word window on the Microsoft Excel worksheet.

Your menu and toolbars change back to those of Microsoft Excel. Your screen should look similar to the following illustration.

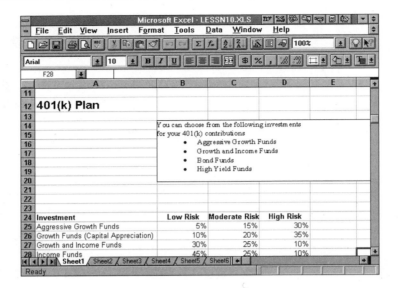

Save

9   On the Standard toolbar in Microsoft Excel, click the Save button.

Embed part of an existing Word document in a workbook

You have a Word document that includes text summarizing the retirement planning options. You want to include that text in your Microsoft Excel workbook on the same topic. Select and embed that portion of the Word document in your Microsoft Excel workbook.

Microsoft Word

1   On the Office Manager toolbar, click the Microsoft Word button.

2   At the top of the page, select the "Retirement Planning" heading, the first paragraph, and the numbered list.

Copy

3   On the Standard toolbar in Word, click the Copy button.

4   On the Office Manager toolbar, click the Microsoft Excel button.

Microsoft Excel

5   Select cell A3 to make it active.

This location will become the upper-left corner of the embedded Word object.

6   From the Edit menu in Microsoft Excel, choose Paste Special.

The Paste Special dialog box appears.

7 Be sure that the Paste option is selected, and then select Microsoft Word 6.0 Document Object.

8 Choose the OK button.

The selected Word object is embedded in your workbook, starting at the current cell.

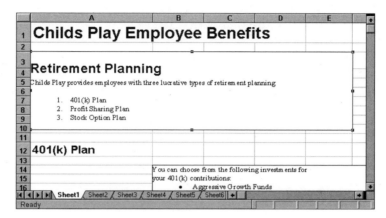

9 If you need to adjust the size of the Word object, double-click the object to open it, and then drag the sizing boxes on the edges of the Word object frame until it is the size you want. When you are finished editing, click outside the object frame.

Note There are actually two ways to adjust the size of an embedded object frame. If you double-click, as in step 9, you can crop or expand the object frame without affecting the size of the information inside the object. If you simply select the object by clicking once, adjusting the object frame size changes the size of the characters or graphics proportionally.

Edit a Word object embedded in a workbook

You want to edit the embedded Word text object on 401(k) investment types. Add two more investment types and format them in the same way as the other entries in the list.

1 Double-click the embedded Word object containing the list of 401(k) investment types (at cell B14).

The Word editing window appears within the workbook, and the Microsoft Excel menu and toolbars change to those of Word.

Microsoft Excel window

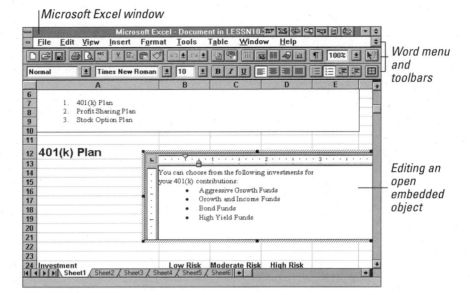

Word menu and toolbars

Editing an open embedded object

2 Add the following two investment types to the bulleted list:

Income Funds

International Stock Funds

Be sure that these items are bulleted and indented like the others.

3 Click outside the Word object frame.

The Word menu and toolbars change back to those of Microsoft Excel.

Save

4 On the Standard toolbar in Microsoft Excel, click the Save button.

One Step Further

Suppose your workbook will be read by others on their computers. You can display the embedded Word object as a Word icon. Although the workbook file size is the same, this can save space on your page. When others are reviewing the workbook and see the icon, they can double-click the icon and view the contents of the embedded object, as long as they have Word installed on their computers.

Display an embedded object as an icon

1 In Microsoft Excel, select cell B42 to make it active.

2 From the Insert menu in Microsoft Excel, choose Object.

The Object dialog box appears.

3   Click the Create From File tab to make it active.

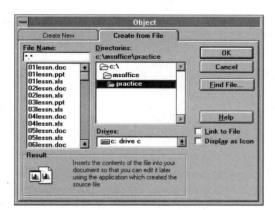

4   Be sure that your PRACTICE directory is selected, and then select LESSN10.DOC.

You can also link an entire file to its existing source file by selecting the Link To File check box in the Object dialog box. This is useful if you want to insert the entire file into the workbook and still have an automatically updating link to the source file.

5   Select the Display As Icon check box (below the Help button), and then choose the OK button.

The Microsoft Word icon and the filename appear in your workbook starting at the active cell.

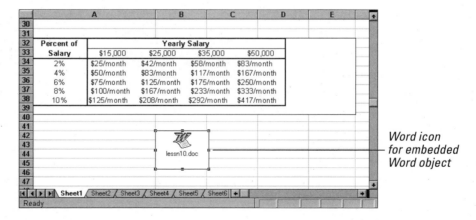

Word icon for embedded Word object

6   Double-click the Microsoft Word icon to view the embedded object.

The embedded Word object opens in its own window.

7   From the File menu, choose Close And Return To LESSN10.XLS.

8   On the Standard toolbar in Microsoft Excel, click the Save button.

End the Lesson

1   To continue to the next lesson, from the File menu in Microsoft Excel, choose Close. To quit for now, from the File menu in Microsoft Excel, choose Exit.

If you see the Save dialog box, click Yes.

Microsoft Word

2   Hold down ALT and, on the Office Manager toolbar, click the Microsoft Word button.

If you see the Save dialog box, click Yes.

Lesson Summary

To	Do this
Copy Word information into a Microsoft Excel workbook	Select the information in Word, and click the Copy button. Switch to Microsoft Excel, select the cell where you want the information to begin, and then click the Paste button.
Edit information pasted from Word into Microsoft Excel	Use the same editing techniques as if the information had been originally entered with Microsoft Excel.
Link Word information to a Microsoft Excel workbook for automatic updates	Select the information in Word, and click the Copy button. Switch to Microsoft Excel and select the cell where you want the information to begin. From the Edit menu, choose Paste Special. Select the Paste Link option button and Microsoft Word 6.0 Document Object, and then choose the OK button.
Edit information linked from Word to Microsoft Excel	Double-click the linked object. The source file appears in Word for you to edit.
Embed a new Word document in a Microsoft Excel workbook	Select the cell where you want the embedded information to begin. From the Insert menu, choose Object. Select Microsoft Word 6.0 Document, and then choose the OK button. A blank Word object window appears in your workbook, where you can create the document using Word tools and resources. When finished, click outside the Word object frame.
Embed part of an existing Word document in a Microsoft Excel workbook	In the Word document, select the text you want to embed, and click the Copy button. In Microsoft Excel, select the cell where you want the embedded information to begin. From the Edit menu, choose Paste Special. Select the Paste option button and Microsoft Word 6.0 Document Object, and then choose the OK button.

To	Do this
Edit an embedded Word object in Microsoft Excel	Double-click the embedded object. When finished editing, click outside the Word object frame.

For more information on	See in *Microsoft Office Getting Started*
Copying, linking, and embedding information between applications	Chapter 4, "How Office Applications Work Together"
Inserting information from other applications into Microsoft Excel	Chapter 5, "Using Microsoft Office"

For online information about	Choose <u>S</u>earch For Help On from the <u>H</u>elp menu of
Copying information from Word into Microsoft Excel	Microsoft Excel, and then type **copying, from other applications**
Linking information from Word to Microsoft Excel	Microsoft Excel, and then type **linking, source worksheets to dependent documents**
Linking information from Word to Microsoft Excel	Microsoft Word, and then type **linking**
Embedding information from Word in Microsoft Excel	Microsoft Excel, and then type **embedded objects, creating**
Editing Word objects embedded in Microsoft Excel	Microsoft Excel, and then type **embedded objects, editing**

Preview of the Next Lesson

In the next lesson, you'll learn how to insert selected slides or an entire presentation from PowerPoint into a Microsoft Excel workbook. You'll also view slides that are inserted into a workbook.

Inserting a Presentation into a Workbook

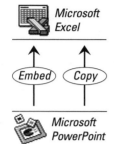

Microsoft Excel

Embed   Copy

Microsoft PowerPoint

You can include a PowerPoint presentation in your Microsoft Excel workbook. This can be particularly useful if the workbook will be reviewed by others on their computers. For example, you might want to insert a manufacturing presentation within a workbook with other production information that you're sending to the shop supervisors. They will be able to review the presentation whether or not they have PowerPoint installed on their computers.

In this lesson, you'll insert the PowerPoint presentation for the Childs Play new employee orientation within a Microsoft Excel workbook, which includes information on the new employees and data that supplements the presentation material. If you are working on a network and are running Microsoft Mail, you can also send the workbook file to another user on your network.

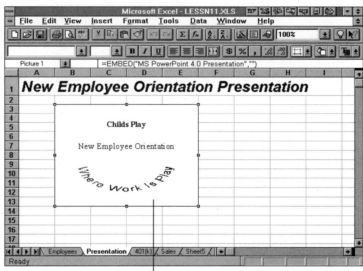

PowerPoint presentation in a Microsoft Excel workbook

You will learn how to:

- Insert an entire PowerPoint presentation file within a Microsoft Excel workbook.
- Insert selected PowerPoint presentation slides within a Microsoft Excel workbook.
- View a PowerPoint presentation embedded within a Microsoft Excel workbook.

Estimated lesson time: 20 minutes

Start the lesson

Start PowerPoint and open 11LESSN.PPT. Start Microsoft Excel and open 11LESSN.XLS.

1 Be sure that the Microsoft Office Manager is open.

The Microsoft Office Manager is open if the Office Manager toolbar appears on your desktop. If Microsoft Office Manager is not open, double-click the Microsoft Office icon in the Windows Program Manager.

Microsoft PowerPoint

2 On the Office Manager toolbar, click the Microsoft PowerPoint button. If the Tip Of The Day dialog box appears, choose the OK button.

3 From your PRACTICE directory, open 11LESSN.PPT.

This file contains a portion of the Childs Play new employee orientation. Be sure that both the PowerPoint window and the presentation window are maximized.

4 Save the presentation as **lessn11.ppt**. If the Summary Info dialog box appears, choose the OK button.

Microsoft Excel

5 On the Office Manager toolbar, click the Microsoft Excel button.

6 From your PRACTICE directory, open 11LESSN.XLS.

This workbook includes several sheets to be used as part of the new employee orientation. Be sure that both the Microsoft Excel window and the workbook window are maximized.

7 Save the document as **lessn11.xls**

Inserting a Presentation into a Workbook

Suppose you need to include a presentation created in PowerPoint within a Microsoft Excel workbook on the same topic. You can *embed* the PowerPoint presentation as an *object* in your Microsoft Excel workbook. Others can then view the workbook along with the presentation on their computers. The *PowerPoint Viewer* becomes a part of the embedded presentation, so even if others do not have PowerPoint installed on their computers, they'll still be able to view the complete presentation from Microsoft Excel.

Note The PowerPoint Viewer is a separate application included with PowerPoint. If the PowerPoint Viewer is not installed, use the Office Setup program to install it.

Embedding a presentation in your Microsoft Excel workbook is the best technique to use when your project meets all of the following criteria:

■ You want the presentation to be an integral part of the workbook.

■ You want all related information from different sources to be together in a single file.

■ You want anyone reviewing the workbook file on their computers to be able to view all the slides in the PowerPoint presentation.

When embedding a PowerPoint presentation in Microsoft Excel, you insert the presentation file as an object within the workbook. When you double-click the object, the PowerPoint Viewer displays each slide in the presentation. You switch to the next slide by clicking the current slide. When you click the last slide in the presentation, the PowerPoint Viewer closes, and the workbook appears again.

Note You can embed a presentation in Microsoft Mail as well. You can attach a PowerPoint presentation file to a Microsoft Mail message and send it to other users on your network. With the PowerPoint Viewer embedded with the presentation file, they can view the presentation even if they do not have PowerPoint installed on their computers.

Embed a PowerPoint presentation file in a workbook

You need to include the new employee orientation presentation in your Microsoft Excel workbook. This workbook includes all pertinent information on the new employees as well as the orientation itself. Embed the presentation in the workbook.

1 In the Microsoft Excel workbook, click the Presentation tab to make that sheet active.

2 Select cell B3 to make it active.

3 From the Insert menu, choose Object.

4 In the Object dialog box, click the Create From File tab.

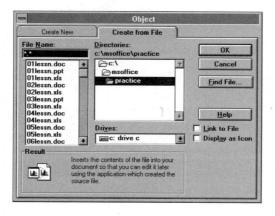

Because the entire presentation file is included within the workbook file when you embed, the workbook file size can increase substantially.

5 From your PRACTICE directory, select LESSN11.PPT, and then choose the OK button.

Microsoft Excel embeds a copy of the PowerPoint presentation, beginning at the active cell. This might take a few seconds.

6 Drag the sizing boxes on the embedded object frame until the object covers cells B3 through E13.

Your screen should look similar to the following illustration.

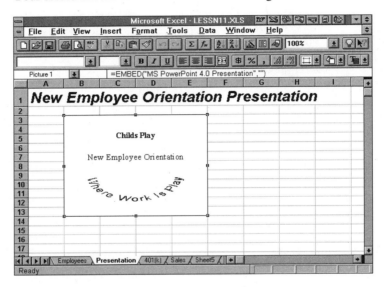

7 On the Standard toolbar, click the Save button.

Save

View a PowerPoint presentation in a workbook

Now view the presentation you just embedded in the workbook.

1 In the Microsoft Excel workbook, double-click the embedded presentation object.

The screen clears for a moment, and then the PowerPoint Viewer displays a full-screen view of the first slide of the embedded PowerPoint presentation.

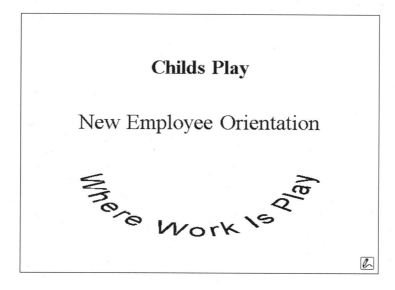

2   Click anywhere in the slide.

The second slide in the presentation appears.

3   Click all succeeding slides.

When you click the last slide, the PowerPoint Viewer closes, and the Microsoft Excel workbook appears.

Embedding PowerPoint Slides in a Workbook

You might not want to embed an entire presentation in your workbook. Maybe you only need a few slides. You can select individual slides from a PowerPoint presentation, and then embed them within your workbook. You use Slide Sorter view in PowerPoint to select the slides you want.

The process is similar to copying and pasting. But in this case, when you choose the Paste command, the selected slides along with the PowerPoint Viewer are embedded as an object in your workbook.

Embed individual slides in a workbook

There is another PowerPoint presentation that includes information you would like to use in your workbook. However, it is a lengthy presentation file, and you only need three of the individual slides.

*Microsoft
PowerPoint*

Slide Sorter View

1   On the Office Manager toolbar, click the Microsoft PowerPoint button.

2   Click the Slide Sorter View button at the bottom left of the window. Or from the View menu in PowerPoint, choose Slide Sorter.

The screen changes to Slide Sorter view.

3   If slide 1 is selected, click it to deselect it. Hold down SHIFT while clicking slides 2, 5, and 6 to select all three of these slides.

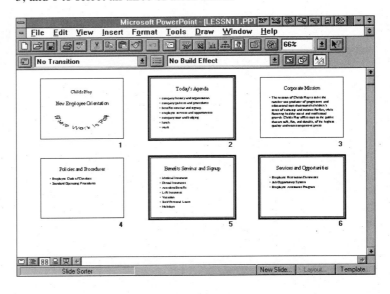

Copy

Microsoft Excel

Paste

4   On the Standard toolbar, click the Copy button.

5   On the Office Manager toolbar, click the Microsoft Excel button.

Be sure that the Presentation sheet is active.

6   Click cell D16 to make it the active cell.

7   On the Standard toolbar in Microsoft Excel, click the Paste button.

Microsoft Excel embeds the PowerPoint slides you selected as a single presentation object placed at the active cell. This might take a few seconds. You will see the first selected slide displayed in the object frame.

8   Drag the sizing boxes on the embedded slide object frame until the object covers cells D16 through G26.

Your screen should look like the following illustration.

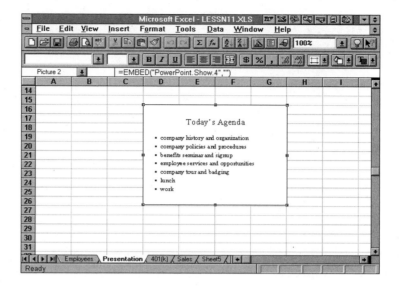

Save

9   On the Standard toolbar, click the Save button.

View the embedded slides

When you double-click to view this embedded object, you'll see only the selected slides, rather than all slides in the presentation file.

1   Double-click the embedded slide object, which starts at cell D16.

The screen clears for a moment, and then a full-screen view of the first embedded slide appears.

2   Click the next two slides.

When you click the third slide, the PowerPoint Viewer closes, and the Microsoft Excel workbook appears. Only the three slides you selected and copied from Slide Sorter view in PowerPoint are embedded in your workbook.

Note   You can also copy any text or graphics from a PowerPoint slide and paste it into a Microsoft Excel workbook. To do this, you select the text or graphic in PowerPoint, and click the Copy button on the Standard toolbar. In Microsoft Excel, you select the location for the information, and then you click the Paste button on the Standard toolbar. If you paste text, it is inserted as standard text that you can edit. If you paste a graphic, however, it is inserted as a static picture that you cannot change.

One Step Further

If you are working on a network and are running Microsoft Mail version 3.0 or later, you can send your workbook file to another user on your network.

Mail the workbook to another user

Use the Send command from the File menu to send the workbook to another user.

1 From the File menu, choose Send.

A dialog box appears that allows you to send a message with the file attached.

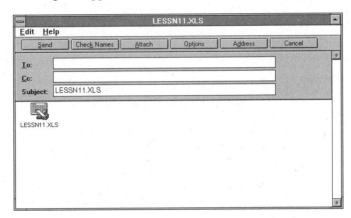

2 In the To box, type the mail user name of another user in your network. Also type your own user name so that you will receive a copy of the report. If you want to select user names, choose the Address button.

3 In the Subject box, select any existing text, and then type **Microsoft Office Test**

4 In the Message Text box after the LESSN11.XLS icon, type **This is a test**, or any other message you prefer.

5 Click the Send button.

The document and your message is sent to the user you specified, and it will be in your mailbox as well.

End the Lesson

1 To continue to the next lesson, from the File menu in Microsoft Excel, choose Close. To quit for now, from the File menu in Microsoft Excel, choose Exit.

If you see the Save dialog box, click Yes.

*Microsoft
PowerPoint*

2 Hold down ALT and, on the Office Manager toolbar, click the Microsoft PowerPoint button.

If you see the Save dialog box, click Yes.

Lesson Summary

To	Do this
Embed an entire PowerPoint presentation file in a Microsoft Excel workbook	Click the cell where you want the embedded presentation to be placed. From the Insert menu, choose Object. Click the Create From File tab, and then select the presentation file you want to embed. Choose the OK button.
View a PowerPoint presentation file embedded in a Microsoft Excel workbook	Double-click the embedded object. When you're ready to view the next slide, click the current slide.
Embed selected slides from a PowerPoint presentation file in a Microsoft Excel workbook	From the View menu in PowerPoint, choose Slide Sorter. Hold down SHIFT and select the slides you want to insert into your workbook. Choose Copy. In Microsoft Excel, click the cell where you want the selected slides to be placed. Choose Paste.

For more information on	See in *Microsoft Office Getting Started*
Embedding and copying information between applications	Chapter 4, "How Office Applications Work Together"
Inserting information from PowerPoint into Microsoft Excel	Chapter 5, "Using Microsoft Office"
Using Microsoft Mail to send Microsoft Excel workbooks to other users	Chapter 6, "Sharing Information with Others"

For online information about	Choose Search For Help On from the Help menu of
Embedding a PowerPoint presentation file in Microsoft Excel	Microsoft Excel, and then type **embedding**
Copying and pasting PowerPoint information	Microsoft PowerPoint, and then type **copy**
Working in Slide Sorter view in PowerPoint	Microsoft PowerPoint, and then type **Slide Sorter view**
Viewing a PowerPoint presentation file embedded in Microsoft Excel	Microsoft PowerPoint, and then type **PowerPoint Viewer**

For online information about	Choose <u>S</u>earch For Help On from the <u>H</u>elp menu of
Using Microsoft Mail to send a Microsoft Excel workbook to another user	Microsoft Excel, and then type **Send**

Preview of the Next Lesson

In the next lesson, you'll convert information stored in a Microsoft Access database into the Microsoft Excel format. You'll copy and paste information from a Microsoft Access database into a Microsoft Excel workbook. In addition, you'll learn special options for analyzing the database information using Microsoft Excel tools.

Analyzing Database Data in a Workbook

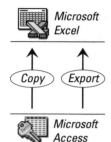

Microsoft Excel

Copy   Export

Microsoft Access

You can bring database information into a workbook to perform calculations on the numbers in the database, or to arrange the information into different categories to examine their relationships. For example, you might have a sales database that has a record on each item sold, including the cost and the sales representative. If you want to create a summary of the total amount sold per sales representative, you can transfer the database information into a workbook, and then group, summarize, and analyze the data there.

In this lesson, you'll convert information from the Childs Play employee database in Microsoft Access into a workbook in Microsoft Excel. Then, in Microsoft Excel, you'll create a table that analyzes employee benefits by department.

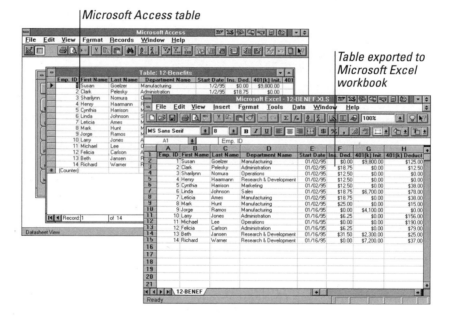

Microsoft Access table

Table exported to Microsoft Excel workbook

You will learn how to:

- Export information from a Microsoft Access database to Microsoft Excel format.
- Create a pivot table to summarize and analyze the data in different combinations.
- Copy information from Microsoft Access and paste it into a workbook.

Estimated lesson time: 25 minutes

Start the lesson

Start Microsoft Excel. Start Microsoft Access and open SBSDATA.MDB.

1 Be sure that the Microsoft Office Manager is open.

   The Microsoft Office Manager is open if the Office Manager toolbar appears on your desktop. If Microsoft Office Manager is not open, double-click the Microsoft Office icon in the Windows Program Manager.

2 On the Office Manager toolbar, click the Microsoft Excel button.

Microsoft Excel

   Be sure that the Microsoft Excel window is maximized.

3 On the Office Manager toolbar, click the Microsoft Access button. If the Welcome message appears, double-click the Control-menu box to close it.

Microsoft Access

4 From your PRACTICE directory, open SBSDATA.MDB.

   This is the Childs Play employee database, which includes tables on new employee information, including benefits choices.

Exporting a Database Table to a Workbook

You might want to create a workbook in Microsoft Excel that summarizes and analyzes information stored in a Microsoft Access database table.

You can convert the Microsoft Access table into the Microsoft Excel file format by *exporting* the table to create a workbook. You can then open the workbook in Microsoft Excel, and the table appears as if you had originally created it there. Each field of the database is placed in a separate cell in the new workbook.

Exporting database information from Microsoft Access to Microsoft Excel is the best technique to use when your project meets all of the following criteria:

- You have database information that you want to analyze in a Microsoft Excel workbook.

- You want to use some or all the information in a database table, query, or report in a Microsoft Excel workbook.

- You want to create an entirely new workbook file from the database information.

When you export, you are converting all the information in the selected database object, such as the individual table, to the selected *file format*. Exporting creates an entirely new file.

There are two commands in Microsoft Access that convert database information to the Microsoft Excel file format: Output To and Export—both on the File menu. With the Output To command, the text is copied as a Microsoft Excel file, and is formatted as it was in Microsoft Access. You can also export a selected portion of a table, query, or other database object with the Output To command. With the Export command, the text appears in Microsoft Excel in the default format of the workbook. You also have the choice of converting to earlier versions of Microsoft Excel, as well as to other database formats.

Microsoft Access has a toolbar button, Analyze It With MS Excel, that automatically executes the Output To command and opens the new file in Microsoft Excel.

Output a Microsoft Access table to Microsoft Excel

You want to create a workbook in Microsoft Excel that summarizes the benefits information of Childs Play employees. Much of the information you need is already stored in a Microsoft Access database table. Output the table to Microsoft Excel.

1 In Microsoft Access, select the 12-Benefits table. You do not need to open the table.

Analyze It With MS Excel

2 On the Standard toolbar in Microsoft Access, click the Analyze It With MS Excel button.

The selected table is converted into a workbook called 12-BENEF.XLS, and it appears in Microsoft Excel, retaining its format from Microsoft Access, as shown in the following illustration.

You can also choose the Output To command from the File menu, and then select Microsoft Excel. This is available from the Database window as well as the Table window.

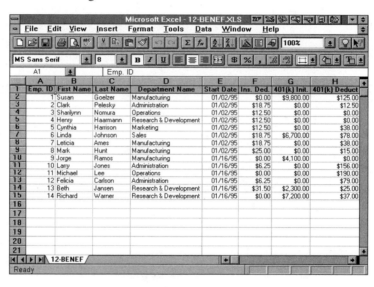

You can now work with this information as if you had originally created it in Microsoft Excel.

3 From the File menu, choose Save As.

4 In the Save As dialog box, type **lessn12a.xls** in the File Name box, and then choose OK.

Note When you use the Analyze It With MS Excel button, the resulting column headings in Microsoft Excel are taken from the field caption names you see in the Microsoft Access Datasheet view.

Export a Microsoft Access table to Microsoft Excel

Another method for converting a database table into a workbook is to use the Export command in Microsoft Access. Notice the differences between the two methods.

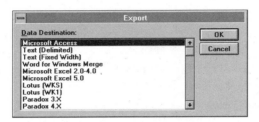

Microsoft Access

1   On the Office Manager toolbar, click the Microsoft Access button.

2   Be sure that the 12-Benefits table is still selected.

3   From the File menu in the Microsoft Access Database window, choose Export.

The Export dialog box appears.

You can select the Export command while either the Database window or the Datasheet window is active.

4   Select Microsoft Excel 5.0 as the data destination, and then choose the OK button.

The Select Microsoft Access Object dialog box appears. Be sure that the Tables option at the bottom of the dialog box is selected.

5   From the Objects list, select 12-Benefits, and then choose the OK button.

The Export To File dialog box appears, assigning the name 12-BENEF.XLS to the exported workbook file.

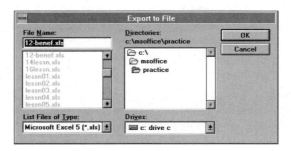

6 Change the filename to **lessn12b.xls** under your PRACTICE directory, and then choose the OK button.

The selected table is exported to a Microsoft Excel workbook.

Microsoft Excel

7 On the Office Manager toolbar, click the Microsoft Excel button.

8 On the Standard toolbar in Microsoft Excel, click the Open button.

Open

9 In your PRACTICE directory, select the new workbook file LESSN12B.XLS, and then choose the OK button.

The exported database table appears in the Microsoft Excel workbook in the default Microsoft Excel format, as shown in the following illustration.

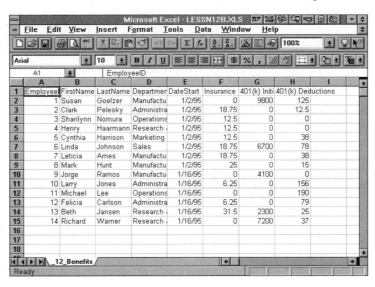

You can now work with this information as if you had originally created it in Microsoft Excel.

> **Note**   When you use the Export command in Microsoft Access to export a table, the resulting column headings in Microsoft Excel are taken from the field names as identified in the table's Design view.

Creating a Workbook Pivot Table from a Database

You might have different types of information in a Microsoft Access table that you would like to focus on and analyze in various ways. You can export the database table from Microsoft Access to a Microsoft Excel workbook, and then analyze the data using *pivot tables*.

A pivot table displays two-dimensional summaries of selected data from a database in different combinations. Microsoft Excel's PivotTable Wizard helps you create these summaries.

You can create a pivot table from any tabular sheet or database that includes row or column headings containing data in the cells.

Create a pivot table from exported Microsoft Access data

Now that you have exported your Microsoft Access database table to Microsoft Excel, you are ready to group, summarize, and analyze the information.

1   From the Window menu in Microsoft Excel, choose LESSN12A.XLS.

2   Select any cell within the data table, and then from the Data menu, choose PivotTable.

Step 1 of the PivotTable Wizard appears. Be sure that the Microsoft Excel List Or Database option button is selected.

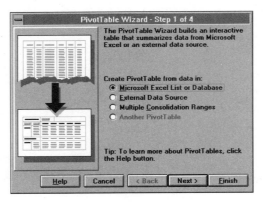

3   Choose the Next button.

Step 2 of the PivotTable Wizard appears. The Range field should be completed with $A$1:$H$15. If it is not, enter that range. A moving border appears around this range on the sheet.

4 Choose the Next button.

Step 3 of the PivotTable Wizard appears.

5 Drag the Department field into the Row area.

6 Drag the Ins. Ded, 401(k) Init., and 401(k) Ded. fields into the Data area, as shown in the following illustration.

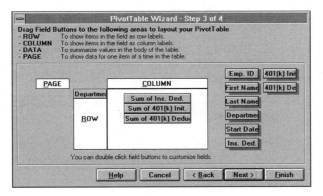

7 Choose the Next button.

Step 4 of the PivotTable Wizard appears.

8 Choose the Finish button.

The pivot table you specified appears, along with the Query and Pivot toolbar. The new pivot table displays a summary of deductions per department, and should look similar to the following illustration.

You can drag the Query And Pivot toolbar to dock on any of the four edges of the window. Or, you can close the toolbar by double-clicking its Control-menu box.

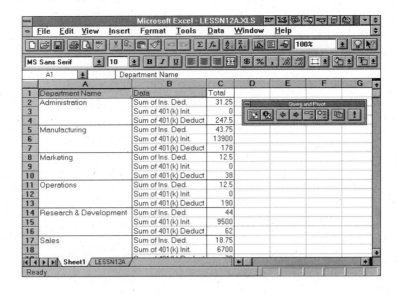

The pivot table is stored in the first sheet of your workbook, named Sheet1. Your original information is stored in the second sheet of the workbook, named LESSN12A.

Save

9 On the Standard toolbar, click the Save button. If you see a message asking if you want to update the file to the current version of Microsoft Excel, choose the Yes button.

You can now format, manipulate, or print the information in the pivot table. If you want to change the layout of the pivot table, choose PivotTable or PivotTable Field from the Data menu.

Copying Database Information into a Workbook

If you have selected information in a database table that you would like to use in your Microsoft Excel workbook, you can simply select and copy the information in the database, and then paste it into a sheet in Microsoft Excel. Each copied field from the database is inserted into a separate cell beginning at the selected cell in your workbook.

Copying and pasting database information from Microsoft Access into Microsoft Excel is the best technique to use when your project meets all of the following criteria:

- You have information from a database table or query that you want to use in a Microsoft Excel workbook.

- You want to use just a portion of the table or query in a Microsoft Excel workbook.

- You want to place the database information into an existing Microsoft Excel workbook.

Copy information from a database table into a workbook

You have most of the information you need in your benefits workbook. But there is another Microsoft Access table that has some information you want to use. Use the Copy and Paste commands to transfer information between the table and the workbook.

Microsoft Access

Copy

Microsoft Excel

Paste

1 On the Office Manager toolbar, click the Microsoft Access button.

2 Double-click the 12-Employees table to open it.

3 Select records 1 through 8 by dragging down the row headers.

These are the records of all employees who started work on 1/2/95.

4 On the Standard toolbar in Microsoft Access, click the Copy button.

5 On the Office Manager toolbar, click the Microsoft Excel button.

6 In Sheet1, click cell A25 to select it.

7 On the Standard toolbar in Microsoft Excel, click the Paste button.

The records from Microsoft Access are inserted into your workbook in the default Microsoft Excel format, starting at the active cell.

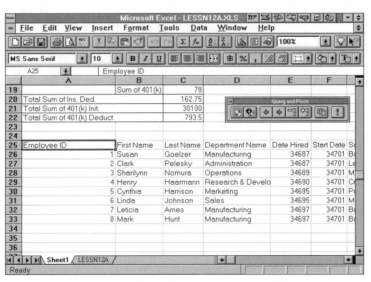

8 On the Standard toolbar, click the Save button.

One Step Further

Suppose you need to use a selected portion of a Microsoft Access database object in your Microsoft Excel workbook. You can export a selected portion of a database table, query, or report to your workbook, using the Output To command from the File menu.

Output a portion of a table to Microsoft Excel

Export a selected portion of the employee database table to your Microsoft Excel workbook. Because you want to retain the Microsoft Access table formatting, use the Output To command from the File menu.

Microsoft Access

1 On the Office Manager toolbar, click the Microsoft Access button.

Be sure that the 12-Employees table is open.

2 Select records 9 through 14 by dragging down the row headers.

These are the records of all employees who started work on 1/16/95.

3 From the File menu, choose Output To.

The Output To dialog box appears. Be sure that the Microsoft Excel (*.xls) format is selected. Also be sure that the Selection option button under Output is selected.

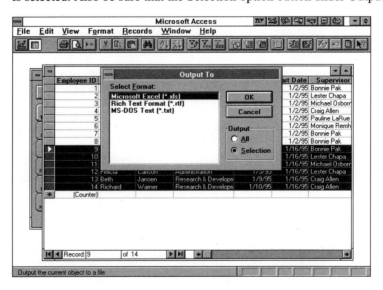

4 Choose the OK button.

A second Output To dialog box appears, assigning the name 12-EMPLO.XLS to the new workbook file.

5 Change the filename to **lessn12c.xls**, and then choose the OK button.

The selected records are converted into a Microsoft Excel workbook.

Microsoft Excel

6 On the Office Manager toolbar, click the Microsoft Excel button.

7 On the Standard toolbar in Microsoft Excel, click the Open button.

Open

8 In your PRACTICE directory, select the new workbook file LESSN12C.XLS, and then choose the OK button.

The selected records of the database table appear in the Microsoft Excel workbook, retaining its format from Microsoft Access, as shown in the following illustration.

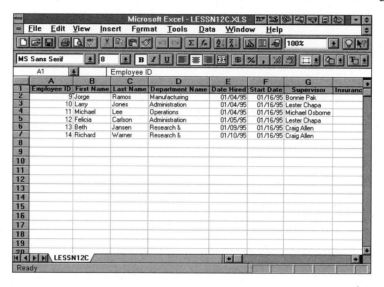

You could now work with this information as if you had originally created it in Microsoft Excel. You could also copy the data to another workbook, if needed.

Save

9 On the Standard toolbar, click the Save button. If you see a message asking if you want to update the file to the current version of Microsoft Excel, choose the Yes button.

End the Lesson

1 To continue to the next lesson, from the File menu in Microsoft Excel, choose Close three times, to close the three open files. To quit for now, from the File menu in Microsoft Excel, choose Exit.

If you see the Save dialog box, click Yes.

2 Hold down ALT and, on the Office Manager toolbar, click the Microsoft Access button.

If you see the Save dialog box, click Yes.

Lesson Summary

To	Do this	Button
Output a Microsoft Access database object to Microsoft Excel	In the Database window in Microsoft Access, select the object you want to output to Microsoft Excel. On the Standard toolbar, click the Analyze It With MS Excel button.	
Export a Microsoft Access database object to Microsoft Excel	From the Database window File menu, choose Export. Select Microsoft Export 5.0, and then choose the OK button. Select the object you want to export, and then choose OK.	
Create a pivot table from exported Microsoft Access data	Export or copy the database information from Microsoft Access into Microsoft Excel. From the Data menu in Microsoft Excel, choose PivotTable and follow the directions in the PivotTable Wizard.	
Copy information from Microsoft Access into Microsoft Excel	Select the Microsoft Access database information you want, and then click the Copy button. In Microsoft Excel, select the cell where you want the pasted information to be placed, and then click the Paste button.	

For more information on	See in *Microsoft Office Getting Started*
Copying and pasting information between applications	Chapter 4, "How Office Applications Work Together"
Inserting information from other applications into Microsoft Excel	Chapter 5, "Using Microsoft Office"
Exporting documents with different file formats to Microsoft Excel format	Chapter 6, "Sharing Information with Others"

For online information about	From the <u>H</u>elp menu of
Copying information from Microsoft Access into Microsoft Excel	Microsoft Access, choose <u>S</u>earch, and then type **copying records** *or* Microsoft Excel, choose <u>S</u>earch For Help On, and then type **pasting from other applications**
Exporting a database object from Microsoft Access to Microsoft Excel	Microsoft Access, choose <u>S</u>earch, and then type **exporting data: basics**
Using the Output To command to convert a database object to Microsoft Excel	Microsoft Access, choose <u>S</u>earch, and then type **Output To**
Creating a pivot table	Microsoft Excel, choose <u>S</u>earch For Help On, and then type **pivot tables**
Modifying a pivot table	Microsoft Excel, choose <u>S</u>earch For Help On, and then type **pivot tables, editing**

Preview of the Next Lessons

In Part 4, you'll learn how to create compound PowerPoint presentations using the different integration techniques—copying and pasting, linking and embedding, and importing and exporting. In the next lesson, you'll learn how to create a PowerPoint presentation including text from Word.

Review & Practice

In the lessons in Part 3, you learned how to use information from different applications to create and enhance Microsoft Excel workbooks. If you want to practice these skills and test your understanding before you proceed with the lessons in Part 4, you can work through the Review & Practice section following this lesson.

Part 3   Review & Practice

In Part 3, you learned how to create and enhance Microsoft Excel workbooks by bringing information from other applications. You can practice these skills by working through the steps in this Review & Practice section. You will create a workbook by copying, linking, embedding, and exporting information from Word, PowerPoint, and Microsoft Access.

Scenario

Two new sales executives have joined the company, and they need a concise encapsulation of the Childs Play marketing and sales picture. To provide this, you want to create a single workbook that includes a variety of marketing and sales information originating from sources in Word, PowerPoint, and Microsoft Access. The workbook will include narrative text on marketing goals, tables on marketing costs, a customer representative database, and a presentation outlining the new marketing strategy. When completed, you will send the workbook to the executives through Microsoft Mail.

You will review and practice how to:

- Export information from a Microsoft Access database to Microsoft Excel format.
- Create a pivot table to summarize and analyze the data in different combinations.
- Insert a formatted Word document into a Microsoft Excel workbook.
- Create and embed a new Word document within a Microsoft Excel workbook.
- Link a Word table to a Microsoft Excel workbook for automatic updates.
- Insert an entire PowerPoint presentation file within a Microsoft Excel workbook.

Estimated practice time: 25 minutes

Step 1: Export a Database Table to a Workbook

You want to create a new workbook with information from the customer representative database that includes their areas and recent sales activity. Output the database table to the Microsoft Excel file format.

1   In Microsoft Access, open the file SBSDATA.MDB from your PRACTICE directory.

2   Select the database table named P3-Customer Reps.

3   Output the table to Microsoft Excel. (Tip: Use the Analyze It With MS Excel toolbar button.)

4 In Microsoft Excel, save the new workbook file with the exported database table as **reviewp3.xls** in your PRACTICE directory.

5 Exit the Microsoft Access application.

For more information on	See
Exporting a file from one application to another	Lesson 4
Exporting and copying information from Microsoft Access to Microsoft Excel	Lesson 12

Step 2: Create a Pivot Table from a Database

You want to rearrange some of the information exported from the Microsoft Access database so that one can quickly see each region's sales performance. Create a simple pivot table based on the exported database table.

1 In Microsoft Excel, start the PivotTable Wizard. (Tip: Use the PivotTable command from the Data menu.)

2 Design the pivot table so that you will see total sales revenues by region. (Tip: Drag the Region field to the Row area, and drag the Revenues field to the Data area.)

3 Finish the PivotTable Wizard, and then review the resulting pivot table.

4 Save the workbook file.

For more information on	See
Creating a pivot table from exported database information.	Lesson 12

Step 3: Embed Existing Word Text in a Workbook

There is information in an existing Word document that you want to use in your workbook. The information is nicely formatted, and you want to retain its formatting when you bring it into Microsoft Excel. Embed the Word information in your workbook.

1 In Microsoft Excel, choose Worksheet from the Insert menu to insert a new sheet in the workbook.

2 Switch to Word, open the file P3REVIEW.DOC, and save it as **reviewp3.doc**

3 On page 1 of the document, select and copy the "Goal" heading, the next two paragraphs, and the numbered list.

4 In Microsoft Excel, embed the copied information at the top of the new Sheet2, starting at cell A3. (Tip: Use the Paste Special command.)

5 Save the workbook.

For more information on	See
Embedding information from one application in another	Lesson 3
Embedding part of an existing Word document in a Microsoft Excel workbook	Lesson 10

Step 4: Embed New Word Text in a Workbook

You want to create handsomely formatted narrative text in your workbook that is beyond the text formatting resources provided by Microsoft Excel, but is provided by Word. Embed new Word text and format it as a Word object in your workbook.

1   Embed a new Word object in Sheet2 of your workbook, starting at cell B20. (Tip: Use the Object command from the Insert menu.)

2   Size the embedded Word window as necessary.

3   Type the following text:

The following are the primary marketing methods we will be employing in next year's strategy:

magazine display ads
television commercials
catalogs
promotions

4   Add bullets in front of the four list items.

5   Indent the bullet list. (Tip: Use the Increase Indent toolbar button.)

6   Click outside the Word object.

7   Edit the Word object to add the following two marketing methods to the bulleted list:

trade shows
newspaper display ads

8   Click outside the Word object.

9   Save the workbook.

For more information on	See
Embedding information from one application in another	Lesson 3
Embedding a new Word object in a Microsoft Excel workbook	Lesson 10

Step 5: Link Word Information to a Workbook

There is a Word table on marketing costs that is periodically updated. You want to use that table in your workbook, and you want the information in the workbook to be automatically updated whenever the original table in Word changes. Copy and link the table from Word to Microsoft Excel. Then change the information in the source document.

1   Switch to Word, and copy the entire Marketing Costs table on Page 4 at the end of the document.

2   Switch to Microsoft Excel, and then link the table starting at cell B30. (Tip: Use the Paste Special command.)

3   In the Word source document, change the actual expenditure for catalogs from 24,000 to **26,000**. Then change the planned expenditure for promotions from 12,000 to **15,000**.

4   In Microsoft Excel, see that the changes you made in the source document are automatically reflected in the linked table in your workbook.

5   Save the workbook.

6   Exit the Word application, and save your changes.

For more information on	**See**
Linking information from one application to another	Lesson 3
Linking information from Word to Microsoft Excel	Lesson 10

Step 6: Embed a Presentation in a Workbook

You have a presentation created in PowerPoint that you've been using to present the 1995 marketing strategy. You want to include this in the workbook. Embed the PowerPoint presentation in the workbook. Then use Microsoft Mail to send the workbook file to the executives for review on their computers.

1   In PowerPoint, open the file P3REVIEW.PPT and save it as **reviewp3.ppt**

2   Exit PowerPoint.

3   In Microsoft Excel, click Sheet1 to make it the active sheet.

4   Embed the REVIEWP3.PPT presentation file starting at cell D2. (Tip: Use the Object command on the Insert menu.)

5   Size the embedded presentation object so that it covers cells D2 through G12.

6   View the embedded presentation object.

7   If you are working on a network and are running Microsoft Mail, use the Send command on the File menu to send the file to at least one other user on your network.

8   Save the workbook.

For more information on	See
Embedding information from one application in another	Lesson 3
Embedding a PowerPoint presentation in a Microsoft Excel workbook	Lesson 11

End the Lesson

▶   Close the Microsoft Excel application.

If you see the Save dialog box, click Yes.

4 Creating Presentations in PowerPoint Using Integrated Information

With PowerPoint you can combine text, graphics, and other resources to create attractive presentation slides for meetings, training sessions, speeches, and other group talks. You can add formatting templates to your presentation to make each slide look professionally designed. You can also add special effects for the transitions between slides. Presentations can be made into overhead transparency foils, they can be made into photographic slides, or they can be viewed on a computer.

In this part, you'll learn how to use PowerPoint as the base application in conjunction with Word and Microsoft Excel. You will create a new presentation based on a Word document, add new slides from a Word document to an existing presentation, and insert and update specialized information in your presentations.

Creating a Presentation with Word Text

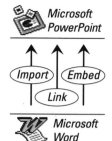

Microsoft PowerPoint

Import   Embed
Link

Microsoft Word

You can convert or insert Word information into a PowerPoint presentation outline to create a new presentation or to add slides to an existing presentation. For example, you might have a Word report about your company's new customer service policies and procedures, and you want to give a presentation on this topic to the service representatives. Or, perhaps you want to transform the company's annual report into a presentation to be given at the annual shareholders meeting.

In this lesson, you'll create and enhance the Childs Play new employee orientation presentation in PowerPoint based on text created in Word. You'll open a Word outline in PowerPoint, add new slides from another Word document outline, link Word information to a slide, and create and insert a new Word table.

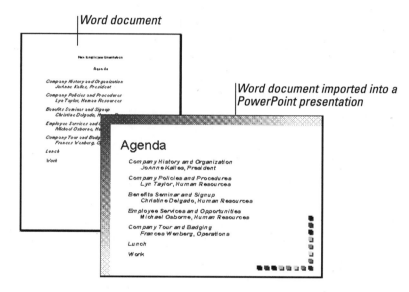

Word document

Word document imported into a PowerPoint presentation

You will learn how to:

- Convert a Word outline to PowerPoint format.
- Insert Word information as new slides into an existing PowerPoint presentation.
- Link Word information to a PowerPoint slide for automatic updates.
- Embed a Word table in a PowerPoint slide.

Estimated lesson time: 35 minutes

Start the lesson

Start Word and open 13ALESSN.DOC, 13BLESSN.DOC, and 13CLESSN.DOC. Start PowerPoint.

Microsoft Word

1   On the Office Manager toolbar, click the Microsoft Word button. If the Tip Of The Day dialog box appears, choose the OK button.

2   From your PRACTICE directory, open 13ALESSN.DOC. Be sure that both the Word window and the document window are maximized.

This is part of the Childs Play employee orientation packet created in Word, which includes an outline you'll import into a PowerPoint outline. You'll then use that outline as the basis for a new PowerPoint presentation.

3   Save the document as **lessn13a.doc**, and then close it.

4   From your PRACTICE directory, open 13BLESSN.DOC.

This is a Word document that contains an outline you'll import as a new slide within an existing PowerPoint presentation.

5   Save the document as **lessn13b.doc**, and then close it.

6   From your PRACTICE directory, open 13CLESSN.DOC.

This is a periodically changing Word document that you'll include in a PowerPoint slide.

7   Save the document as **lessn13c.doc**

*Microsoft
PowerPoint*

8   On the Office Manager toolbar, click the Microsoft PowerPoint button. If the Tip Of The Day dialog box appears, choose the OK button.

9   In the PowerPoint dialog box, choose the Cancel button.

Be sure that the PowerPoint window is maximized.

Importing a Word Outline into a Presentation

Using an existing Word outline as the basis for a PowerPoint presentation can save you time and effort when you already have a Word document, or at least an outline structure that corresponds to a presentation you're giving.

You convert the Word document into the PowerPoint *file format* by *importing* the document's outline to create a new presentation file. The imported Word file appears as if you had originally created it in PowerPoint.

Importing an outline from Word to PowerPoint is the best technique to use for creating a new presentation when your project meets all of the following criteria:

■   You are currently working in PowerPoint.

■   You have a Word outline that corresponds to the presentation you're giving.

■   You want the Word outline to be the basis for an entirely new presentation file.

To see the document's outline structure, from the View menu in Word, choose Outline. You can change the order and the level of items in the document by using the outline tools in Outline view.

When you import information from Word into PowerPoint, each Heading 1 outline level becomes a separate slide. Heading 2 and Heading 3 levels are included as subordinate, bulleted information in the slide. Your document includes Heading styles if you're importing a document based on a Word outline, or if you have applied Heading styles in the Word document.

You import a Word outline into PowerPoint by opening the Word document within PowerPoint and specifying the Outline file type.

Import a Word document into a PowerPoint presentation

In Word, you have created the outline structure and have begun to write the text for the new employee orientation packet. You will use this Word document to create the orientation presentation in PowerPoint that will correspond to the packet.

Open

1   On the Standard toolbar in PowerPoint, click the Open button.

Importing is like opening the document outline as a new presentation file. Importing creates an entirely new file.

2   In the Open dialog box, select Outlines from the List Files Of Type list.

A document must be closed in its original application before it can be imported.

3   In the File Name list of your PRACTICE directory, select LESSN13A.DOC, and then choose the OK button.

The Word document is imported and converted into PowerPoint format. This might take a few seconds. The new presentation appears in Outline view, as shown in the following illustration.

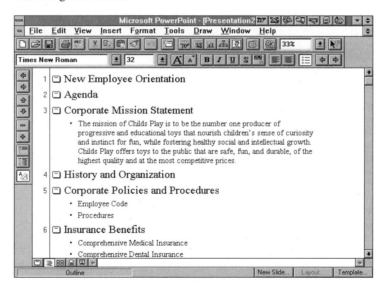

Slide View

4   Click the Slide View button in the lower-left corner of the PowerPoint window.

The imported outline appears as slides in Slide view.

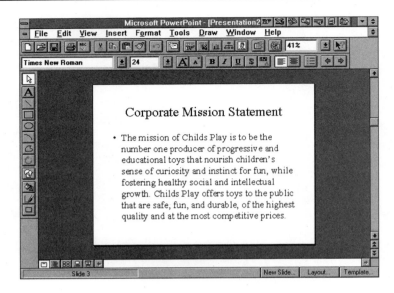

5   Use the PowerPoint navigation buttons in the lower-right corner of the window to page through the different slides.

6   On the Standard toolbar, click the Save button.

Save

7   In the Save As dialog box, type **lessn13.ppt**, and then choose the OK button. If the Summary Info dialog box appears, choose the OK button.

Note   You can make the same type of conversion if you're currently working in Word. Instead of importing, you can *export* from Word to PowerPoint. To do this, open the document in Word. From the File menu, choose Save As. In the Save File As Type list, select Rich Text Format (RTF), and then choose the OK button. Word copies and converts the document to RTF, which is a format that PowerPoint can interpret. The document is saved with the RTF extension. Close the document, go to PowerPoint, and open the converted RTF file.

Edit the imported presentation

Now that your Word document is in the form of a PowerPoint presentation, use PowerPoint's formatting tools to improve the appearance of two slides.

1   Use the PowerPoint navigation buttons to switch to Slide 3.

2   Select the text of the mission statement, from "The" through "prices."

Italic

3   On the Formatting toolbar, click the Italic button to change the font to italic.

4   Switch to Slide 8, and select the bulleted holiday names, from "New Year's Day" through "New Year's Eve."

5   On the Formatting toolbar, use the Font Size box to change the font size to 24 points.

The text of the slides are now edited and formatted to better suit the slide presentation layout.

Apply a template to an imported Word outline

Apply a model PowerPoint format to your new presentation to make it look more polished and professional.

1   In the LESSN13.PPT presentation, be sure that Slide 8, "Holidays," is displayed on your screen.

2   From the Format menu, choose Presentation Template.

The Presentation Template dialog box appears.

3   Open the MSOFFICE\POWERPNT\TEMPLATE\CLROVRHD directory and then, in the File Name list, select COLORBXC.PPT.

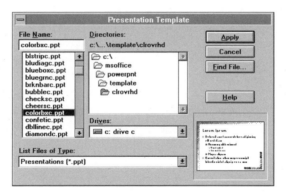

Using this same technique, you can apply a template to an exported Word outline as well.

4   Choose the Apply button.

PowerPoint formats all the slides in your presentation according to the selected template. Your screen should look similar to the following illustration.

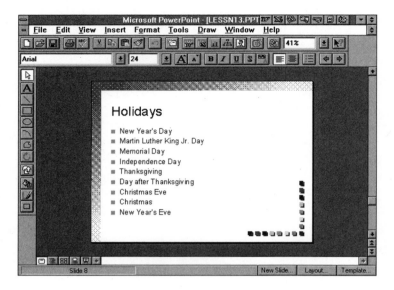

Save

5 On the Standard toolbar, click the Save button.

Inserting New Slides from Word Information

You can transform a Word outline into one or more slides in an existing PowerPoint presentation. This is useful when you have the outline of a Word document that contains information you want to use in a presentation you've already created.

You can convert and insert a new slide from a Word document. Each Word paragraph marked with a Heading 1 style becomes a separate slide inserted into your presentation. Heading 2 and Heading 3 levels are included as subordinate, bulleted information in the slide.

Inserting an outline from Word into an existing PowerPoint presentation is the best technique to use when your project meets all of the following criteria:

- You have an existing PowerPoint presentation.

- You have a Word outline that you want to use in its entirety in the presentation.

- You want to add the Word outline to the existing presentation file, rather than create a new presentation file.

You insert, or import, a Word outline into an existing PowerPoint presentation by using the Slides From Outline command.

Insert a Word outline as a slide in an existing presentation

Add retirement benefits information to the PowerPoint presentation that you have already created by importing the outline of a second Word document on the topic.

1   Be sure that Slide 8 of LESSN13.PPT is displayed.

This is the slide after which the new slide will be inserted.

2   From the Insert menu, choose Slides From Outline.

The Insert Outline dialog box appears.

3   From your PRACTICE directory, select LESSN13B.DOC, and then choose the OK button.

The outline of the Word document is converted from the Word format to the PowerPoint format. This Word document contains a single Heading 1, so it is inserted as one new slide after Slide 8.

4   Use the PowerPoint navigation buttons to view the changes in your presentation.

You'll see that a slide on Retirement Planning is inserted as the new Slide 9, as shown in the following illustration.

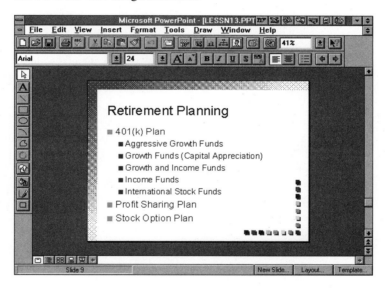

The former Slide 9 is now Slide 10.

5   On the Standard toolbar, click the Save button.

Linking Word Information to a PowerPoint Slide

You can copy information from Word into PowerPoint so that when the information changes in Word, the same information in the PowerPoint slide will be automatically updated. This is especially useful if there is source text in Word that you want to use in PowerPoint, and you want the information to always be up to date.

To avoid having to manually update the PowerPoint presentation when the Word text changes, you can *link* selected information from the Word document for use and automatic update in the PowerPoint presentation.

Linking information from Word to PowerPoint is the best technique to use when your project meets all of the following criteria:

- You have information in Word that is updated periodically.

- You want to use this same information in a PowerPoint presentation.

- You want the PowerPoint version to be automatically updated whenever the Word version is edited.

You link the information in Word, the *source application*, to PowerPoint, the *destination application*, by using the Paste Special command in PowerPoint.

Link Word text to a slide for automatic updates

The agenda and speakers for the Childs Play new employee orientation change somewhat each month. You keep this information updated in the LESSN13C.DOC Word document. You also use similar information in your orientation presentation. Link the Word agenda text to the PowerPoint agenda slide.

Microsoft Word

1   On the Office Manager toolbar, click the Microsoft Word button.

The LESSN13C.DOC document file appears.

2   Select the agenda text from "Company History and Organization" through "Work."

Copy

3   On the Standard toolbar, click the Copy button.

4   On the Office Manager toolbar, click the Microsoft PowerPoint button.

Microsoft PowerPoint

5   Switch to Slide 2, click the text that reads "Click to add text," and then press the SPACEBAR to clear the text.

6   On the Formatting toolbar, click the Bullet On/Off button to turn the bulleted list formatting off.

Bullet On/Off

7   From the Edit menu, choose Paste Special.

8   Select the Paste Link option button.

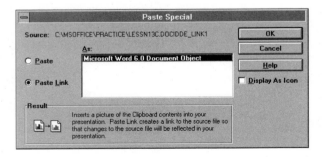

9   Be sure that Microsoft Word 6.0 Document Object is selected, and then choose the OK button.

The selected and copied Word text is pasted and linked to Slide 2.

10   Drag the object frame so that it is positioned under the title, as shown in the following illustration.

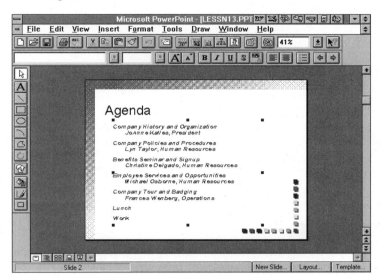

Note that the text retains the formatting from the Word source document. Now, whenever the information changes in Word, it will also be updated in PowerPoint.

Note   If your information does not need to be updated, you can use a similar process to simply copy and paste information from Word to PowerPoint. Instead of choosing Paste Special, choose Paste. The copied information from Word is placed at the insertion point, but it is not linked to the source document. You should copy and paste text and graphics separately, because PowerPoint uses different processes to paste text and graphics.

Update linked Word text

Because some of the staff names in the orientation agenda have been changed, edit the source file in Word, and observe that the linked information is automatically updated in the destination file in PowerPoint.

1   While still in Slide 2, double-click the linked Word document object.

The source file in Word appears.

2   Change "Lyn Taylor" to **Christine Delgado**. Change "Frances Wenberg" to **Mel Ocazu**

Save

*Microsoft
PowerPoint*

3   On the Standard toolbar in Word, click the Save button.

4   On the Office Manager toolbar, click the Microsoft PowerPoint button.

In Slide 2, notice that the changes you made in the Word source document are reflected automatically in your PowerPoint slide.

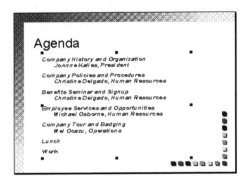

5   On the Standard toolbar in PowerPoint, click the Save button.

Embedding a Word Table in a PowerPoint Slide

You can create a Word table within a PowerPoint slide. This is useful if you have information to present that is best laid out in rows and columns, and if you want to use Word's table editing and formatting capabilities.

To do this, you can create and *embed* a new Word table within an existing PowerPoint slide.

Embedding a new Word table in a PowerPoint slide is the best technique to use when your project meets all of the following criteria:

- You want to create new information in PowerPoint that should be presented in columns and rows.

- You want to use the columns and rows of the Word table feature to enter and lay out information in the table.

- You think you might need to update the table later on.

- You do not need the table to exist in a separate independent file.

It makes no difference whether you create the table first in Word and then embed it in PowerPoint, or create it as a new table existing only within PowerPoint. The table editing and formatting capabilities act the same in either instance. The main distinction is the existence of a separate Word file independent of PowerPoint.

You can embed a new Word table in PowerPoint by changing the slide layout to the Table layout.

Embed and create a new Word table in a PowerPoint slide

You are creating slides in your PowerPoint presentation that cover Childs Play corporate history, and you would like to format the company milestone timetable like a Word table.

1   Be sure that LESSN13.PPT appears on your screen.

2   Switch to Slide 4, "History and Organization."

| Layout... |

3   In the lower-right corner of the window, click the Layout button.

The Slide Layout dialog box appears.

4   Select the Table layout, which is the last layout shown.

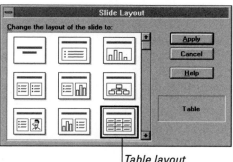

Table layout

Another method for embedding a Word table is to click the Insert Microsoft Word Table button on the Standard toolbar. Then drag to define the table size.

5   Choose the Apply button.

The slide changes from the Bulleted List layout to the Table layout.

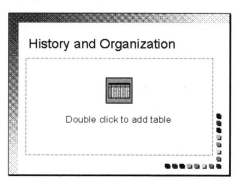

6   Double-click the table icon.

The Insert Word Table dialog box appears.

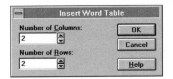

7   Leave Number Of Columns at 2. Under Number Of Rows, select any existing text, and type **4**. Choose the OK button.

A blank Word table is embedded and opened within your slide. The PowerPoint menu and toolbars change to the Word menu and toolbars. Your screen should look similar to the following illustration.

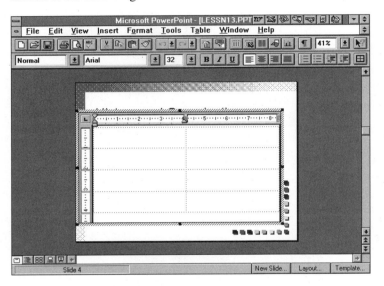

8   Type the following information into the embedded Word table.

November 1982	**Childs Play is founded.**
August 1985	**Childs Play is incorporated.**
May 1990	**Childs Play goes public.**
January 1995	**You join Childs Play to help continue its success!**

9   Click outside the Word object editing window.

The Word menu and toolbars return to those of PowerPoint. Your slide should look similar to the following illustration.

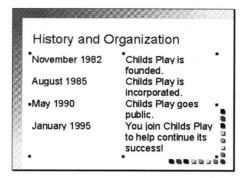

Edit a Word table embedded in a PowerPoint slide

You've decided that you would like the table to look more polished. Use Word's formatting tools to enhance the table embedded in PowerPoint.

1 In Slide 4, double-click the embedded Word table.

The table opens and your PowerPoint menu and toolbars change to those of Word.

2 Select all the text in the table.

3 On the Formatting toolbar, use the Font Size box to change the font size to 28 points.

4 Select the word "You" in the last cell.

Bold

5 Click the Bold and the Italic buttons on the Formatting toolbar to make the selected word bold and italic.

6 Click outside the Word object frame.

Italic

The Word object editing window closes and the menu and toolbars return to those of PowerPoint. Your slide should look similar to the following illustration.

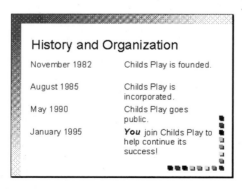

Save

7 On the Standard toolbar, click the Save button.

One Step Further

If you are working on a network and are running Microsoft Mail version 3.0 or later, you can switch to Microsoft Mail, write a note, attach the PowerPoint file, and send them to another user on your network.

Attach your presentation to a mail message

The director of your division wants to see the orientation presentation slides. In Microsoft Mail, write an introductory message, and attach the presentation file to the message.

Microsoft Mail

1   On the Office Manager toolbar, click the Microsoft Mail button.

The Microsoft Mail window appears.

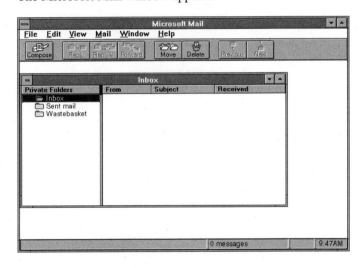

2   Click the Compose button.

3   In the To box, type the mail user name of one or more users on your network. Also type your own user name.

4   In the Subject box, type **Microsoft Office Test**

5   In the Message area, type **This is a test**, or any other message you prefer, and then click the Attach button.

The Attach dialog box appears.

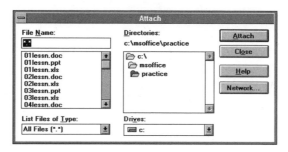

6   From the PRACTICE directory, select LESSN13.PPT, and then choose the Attach button.

7   Choose the Close button.

The attached file appears in your message as a PowerPoint icon.

8   Choose the Send button.

The document and your message are sent to the users you specified, and they will be in your mailbox as well. If the recipients have PowerPoint installed on their computers, they will be able to double-click the icon to view the presentation.

9   From the File menu, choose Exit.

End the Lesson

1   To continue to the next lesson, from the File menu in PowerPoint, choose Close. To quit for now, from the File menu in PowerPoint, choose Exit.

If you see the Save dialog box, click Yes.

Microsoft Word

2   Hold down ALT and, on the Office Manager toolbar, click the Microsoft Word button.

If you see the Save dialog box, click Yes.

Lesson Summary

To	Do this	Button
Import a Word outline to a new PowerPoint presentation file	On the Standard toolbar in PowerPoint, click the Open button. In the List Files Of Type list, select Outlines. Select the Word document file, and then choose the OK button.	
Insert a Word document outline into an existing PowerPoint presentation file	In PowerPoint, display the slide after which the new slide will be inserted. From the Insert menu, choose Slides From Outline. Select the Word document file, and then choose the OK button.	
Link Word information to a PowerPoint slide	In Word, select the text you want to link. On the Standard toolbar, click the Copy button. In PowerPoint, select the location where you want the linked text to be inserted. From the Edit menu, choose Paste Special. Click the Paste Link option button, and then choose the OK button.	
Embed a new Word table in a PowerPoint slide	In PowerPoint, select the location where the table should be placed, and then click the Layout button. Select the Table layout, and then choose the Apply button. Double-click the table icon, and then specify the number of columns and rows you want in the table. Choose the OK button. Enter your information into the table. When finished, click outside the Word object editing window to return to PowerPoint.	Layout...

For more information on	See in *Microsoft Office Getting Started*
Linking and embedding information between applications	Chapter 4, "How Office Applications Work Together"

For more information on	See in *Microsoft Office Getting Started*
Inserting information from other applications into PowerPoint	Chapter 5, "Using Microsoft Office"
Importing and exporting documents with different file formats into PowerPoint format	Chapter 6, "Sharing Information with Others"
Attaching a PowerPoint presentation file to a mail message	Chapter 6, "Sharing Information with Others"

For online information about	Choose <u>S</u>earch For Help On from the <u>H</u>elp menu of
Exporting a Word outline to a new PowerPoint presentation file	Microsoft Word, and then type **exporting documents**
Importing a Word outline to a new PowerPoint presentation file	Microsoft PowerPoint, and then type **import outline**
Inserting a Word document outline into an existing PowerPoint presentation file	Microsoft PowerPoint, and then type **import outline**
Linking Word information to a PowerPoint slide	Microsoft PowerPoint, and then type **link** *or* Microsoft Word, and then type **linking**
Embedding a new Word table in a PowerPoint slide	Microsoft PowerPoint, and then type **table**

Preview of the Next Lesson

In the next lesson, you'll learn how to bring Microsoft Excel information into a PowerPoint presentation and then automatically update the information. You'll also insert Microsoft Excel worksheets and charts into a PowerPoint slide.

Creating Slides with Microsoft Excel

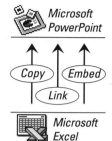

Microsoft
PowerPoint

Copy   Embed
    Link

Microsoft
Excel

You can use cells or charts from a Microsoft Excel workbook in a PowerPoint presentation. For example, you might do this if you have a workbook that charts student test scores, and you're giving a presentation on student performance. Or perhaps you have Microsoft Excel charts on investment results, and you want to include them in a presentation to potential investors.

In this lesson, you'll add information generated in Microsoft Excel to the Childs Play new employee orientation presentation in PowerPoint. You'll copy cells and charts from Microsoft Excel to PowerPoint, link information from Microsoft Excel to PowerPoint for automatic updates, and insert new Microsoft Excel information into a presentation slide.

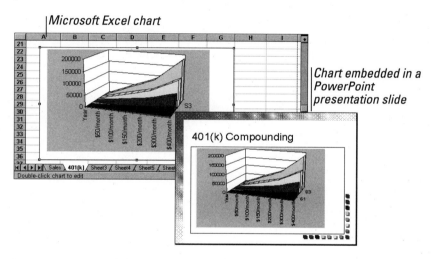

Microsoft Excel chart

Chart embedded in a PowerPoint presentation slide

You will learn how to:

- Copy Microsoft Excel information for use in a PowerPoint presentation.
- Link Microsoft Excel data and charts to a PowerPoint presentation.
- Embed Microsoft Excel data and charts in a PowerPoint presentation.

Estimated lesson time: 35 minutes

Start the lesson

Start PowerPoint and open 14LESSN.PPT. Start Microsoft Excel and open 14LESSN.XLS.

Microsoft PowerPoint

1 On the Office Manager toolbar, click the Microsoft PowerPoint button. If the Tip Of The Day dialog box appears, choose the OK button.

2 From your PRACTICE directory, open 14LESSN.PPT.

This is the presentation file for the new employee orientation. Be sure that both the PowerPoint window and the presentation window are maximized.

3 Save the presentation as **lessn14.ppt**. If the Summary Info dialog box appears, choose the OK button.

4 On the Office Manager toolbar, click the Microsoft Excel button.

Microsoft Excel

5 From your PRACTICE directory, open 14LESSN.XLS.

This workbook contains sales information and 401(k) computations that you will use in different sections of your orientation presentation. Be sure that both the Microsoft Excel window and the workbook window are maximized.

6 Save the workbook as **lessn14.xls**

Copying Microsoft Excel Data to a Presentation

You can insert information from Microsoft Excel into a PowerPoint slide. This can be useful when you want to include calculations or charts created in Microsoft Excel in a presentation you're giving on the topic.

One way to do this is to copy Microsoft Excel cells and charts and then paste them into a PowerPoint slide. You can paste the contents of cells as either text or a picture. When you paste cells as text into PowerPoint, the text acts as if you originally typed the information into PowerPoint. When you paste cells as a picture into PowerPoint, the image is similar to a piece of clip art that you can size or move on the slide.

Note When you copy a Microsoft Excel chart into a PowerPoint slide, it is always pasted as a picture. However, if you copy and embed the chart, you can then edit the chart. See "One Step Further" later in this lesson for the specific procedure.

Copying and pasting Microsoft Excel cells as text in PowerPoint is the best technique to use when you need to edit or format the Excel information in PowerPoint.

Copying and pasting Microsoft Excel cells or charts as pictures in PowerPoint is the best technique to use when you need to use the Microsoft Excel information in PowerPoint as a one-time snapshot of the information, and you will not need to update, edit, or format the information further.

You paste information from Microsoft Excel into PowerPoint by using the Paste Special command in PowerPoint.

Copy Microsoft Excel cells as text into PowerPoint

You have annual sales data in Microsoft Excel workbook cells that you want to copy into the Childs Play employee orientation presentation being developed in PowerPoint. Copy the cells as text so you can edit and format the information later.

1 In the LESSN14.XLS file in Microsoft Excel, be sure that the Sales sheet is the active sheet.

2 Select cells A4 through G8.

Copy

3 On the Standard toolbar, click the Copy button.

4 On the Office Manager toolbar, click the Microsoft PowerPoint button.

PowerPoint and the LESSN14.PPT presentation file appear.

5 Use the navigation buttons in the lower-right corner of the window to switch to Slide 2, entitled "Sales Performance - 1994."

This is the slide on which you want to paste the Microsoft Excel sales information.

6 From the Edit menu, choose Paste Special.

The Paste Special dialog box appears.

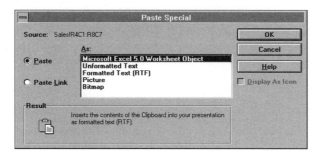

If you choose Unformatted Text instead of Formatted Text (RTF), the font and any other formatting are disregarded, and the text is pasted with a generic font and all normal styles.

7 In the Paste Special dialog box, select Formatted Text (RTF), and then choose the OK button.

PowerPoint creates a new text object on the slide, and the copied cells are pasted into the object as text formatted as it was in Microsoft Excel, including the font, bold, italic, and so forth. Your screen should look similar to the following illustration.

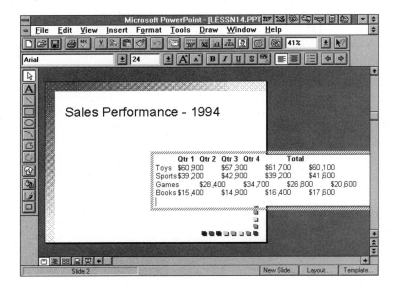

You can now select, edit, and format the individual text as if you had originally typed the information in PowerPoint.

Note You can also paste cells copied from Microsoft Excel as a picture. In this case, the information is pasted as a single unit, like clip art, and you cannot edit the text or numbers individually.

Move and format the copied workbook information

Now select, move, and format the Childs Play sales information to make it look appropriate for the slide.

1   Still in Slide 2, drag the new text object frame to the left edge of the slide.

2   Select all the text in the new text object by dragging across it.

3   On the Formatting toolbar, use the Font Size box to change the font size to 18 points.

Your slide should now look similar to the following illustration.

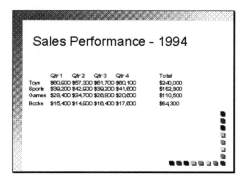

Save

4 On the Standard toolbar, click the Save button.

Copy a Microsoft Excel chart as a picture into PowerPoint

You have 401(k) information in a Microsoft Excel chart that you will include in the Childs Play employee orientation presentation. Copy the chart and paste it into a PowerPoint slide.

Microsoft Excel

1 On the Office Manager toolbar, click the Microsoft Excel button, and then click the 401(k) sheet to make it the active sheet.

2 Scroll downward to row 22, where the 401(k) compounding chart begins, and then click the chart to select it.

3 On the Standard toolbar in Microsoft Excel, click the Copy button.

Copy

4 On the Office Manager toolbar, click the Microsoft PowerPoint button.

5 Switch to Slide 6, entitled "401(k) Compounding."

6 From the Edit menu in PowerPoint, choose Paste Special.

*Microsoft
PowerPoint*

7 In the Paste Special dialog box, select Picture, and then choose the OK button.

PowerPoint creates a new graphic object on the current slide, and the copied chart is pasted into the object as a picture.

*Selecting Microsoft
Excel 5.0 Object or
simply clicking the
Paste button inserts
the chart as an
embedded object.
Embed the object
when you want to
edit the workbook
later.*

8 Drag the object frame's sizing boxes to enlarge it. If necessary, drag the object frame to the left edge of the slide.

The slide should look similar to the following illustration.

If you double-click the picture object, you can convert the picture into a series of PowerPoint drawing objects that you can then manipulate and edit individually.

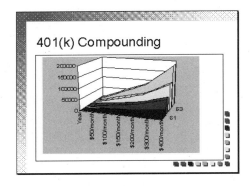

Save

9   On the Standard toolbar, click the Save button.

Linking Microsoft Excel Data to a Presentation

You might want to insert Microsoft Excel information that is subject to periodic updates into a PowerPoint slide. Because this information is going to be updated in Microsoft Excel, you also want the same information to be updated automatically in the slide.

You can copy and *link* Microsoft Excel cells or charts to a PowerPoint presentation. Whenever the *source* file in Microsoft Excel is edited, the changes are automatically updated in the *destination* file in PowerPoint.

Linking information from Microsoft Excel to PowerPoint is the best technique to use when your project meets all of the following criteria:

- You have workbook information that you want to use in a presentation slide.

- The workbook information is subject to change.

- You want the information in the presentation to be automatically updated when the workbook information is edited.

To link a Microsoft Excel object, you use the Paste Special command in PowerPoint. To edit the linked object, you double-click the object in PowerPoint. This opens the source file in Microsoft Excel so you can make the necessary changes.

Link Microsoft Excel cells to a PowerPoint presentation

You have a Microsoft Excel workbook on sales projections for the next fiscal year. These projections are still under development, and are therefore being edited frequently as new information comes in. You will use this information in the employee orientation presentation, and as information changes in the workbook, you want the information in your presentation slide to be automatically updated as well. Link selected workbook cells to your presentation.

Microsoft Excel

1   On the Office Manager toolbar, click the Microsoft Excel button, and then click the Sales sheet to make it the active sheet.

Copy

*Microsoft
PowerPoint*

2 Select cells A20 through G25.

3 On the Standard toolbar, click the Copy button.

4 On the Office Manager toolbar, click the Microsoft PowerPoint button.

5 Switch to Slide 3, entitled "Sales Projections -1995."

6 From the Edit menu, choose Paste Special.

7 In the Paste Special dialog box, select the Paste Link option button, be sure that Microsoft Excel 5.0 Worksheet Object is selected, and then choose the OK button.

PowerPoint creates a new object on the current slide, and the copied cells are pasted and linked to the object. Now, whenever the information from the Microsoft Excel workbook changes, the linked information in this slide will be updated automatically.

8 Drag the object frame's sizing boxes to enlarge it.

The slide should look similar to the following illustration.

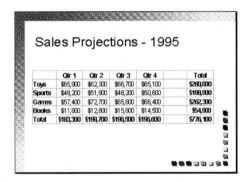

9 On the Standard toolbar, click the Save button.

Edit the linked Microsoft Excel cells

You've just received new information from Accounting that affects the company's sales projections for the toys and book categories. Edit the linked information in the source file in Microsoft Excel, and observe that the information is automatically updated in the destination file in PowerPoint.

1 Still in Slide 3, double-click the linked Microsoft Excel workbook object.

The source file in Microsoft Excel appears.

2 In cell D21, type **70,000** to change the Quarter 3 projection for Toys.

3 In cell E24, type **16,000** to change the Quarter 4 projection for Books.

Notice that the totals in column G and in row 25 change automatically, because those figures are based on formulas.

Save

Microsoft PowerPoint

4 On the Standard toolbar in Microsoft Excel, click the Save button.

5 On the Office Manager toolbar, click the Microsoft PowerPoint button.

In Slide 3, notice that the changes you made in the source file in Microsoft Excel are reflected automatically in your PowerPoint slide.

6 On the Standard toolbar in PowerPoint, click the Save button.

Link a Microsoft Excel chart to a PowerPoint presentation

In addition to the Sales Projections workbook cells, you want to include the corresponding column chart for this data in the employee orientation presentation. Just as with the workbook cells, you want the chart in your presentation slide to be automatically updated as soon as the workbook information changes. Link the workbook chart to your presentation.

Microsoft Excel

1 On the Office Manager toolbar, click the Microsoft Excel button, and be sure that the Sales sheet is the active sheet.

2 Scroll to cell I20, where the 1995 Sales Projections chart begins.

3 Click the chart to select it.

Copy

4 On the Standard toolbar in Microsoft Excel, click the Copy button.

5 On the Office Manager toolbar, click the Microsoft PowerPoint button. Be sure that Slide 3 is the current slide.

6 From the Edit menu in PowerPoint, choose Paste Special.

7 In the Paste Special dialog box, select the Paste Link option button, be sure that Microsoft Excel 5.0 Chart Object is selected, and then choose the OK button.

PowerPoint creates a new object in the current slide, and the copied chart is pasted and linked to the object.

8 Drag the chart object until it is positioned below the object containing the linked cells.

9 Drag the object frame's sizing boxes to enlarge it.

The slide should look similar to the following illustration.

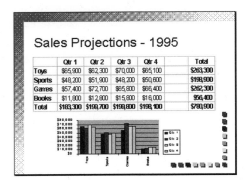

Now, whenever the Microsoft Excel chart changes, the linked chart in this slide will be updated automatically.

Edit the linked Microsoft Excel chart

You've decided that the information in the Microsoft Excel column chart could be better presented and more clearly understood as a bar chart. Make this change to the chart in the source file in Microsoft Excel, and observe that the chart is automatically updated in the destination file in PowerPoint.

1   Still in Slide 3, double-click the linked Microsoft Excel chart object.

The source file in Microsoft Excel appears. If necessary, maximize the workbook window.

2   Double-click the sales projection chart, which starts at cell I20.

The chart opens for editing and formatting.

3   From the Format menu in Microsoft Excel, choose Chart Type.

The Chart Type dialog box appears.

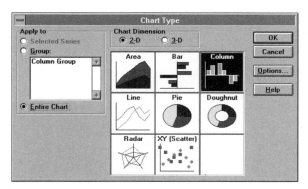

4   Select the Bar illustration, and then choose the OK button.

The chart changes from a column chart to a bar chart.

5   Click outside the chart window.

6   On the Standard toolbar, click the Save button.

7   On the Office Manager toolbar, click the Microsoft PowerPoint button.

In Slide 3, notice that the changes you made in the Microsoft Excel source document are reflected automatically in your PowerPoint slide.

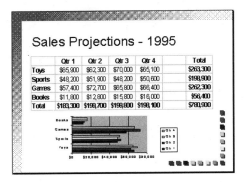

8   On the Standard toolbar in PowerPoint, click the Save button.

Embedding Microsoft Excel Data in a Presentation

Suppose you want to create a new Microsoft Excel workbook file within an existing PowerPoint slide. This can be useful if you have new information you want to present in rows and columns or in a chart form, or if calculations or other mathematical functions need to be performed.

You can create and *embed* a new Microsoft Excel workbook within an existing PowerPoint slide. The workbook exists as a Microsoft Excel file entirely within the PowerPoint file.

Embedding a new Microsoft Excel workbook in a PowerPoint slide is the best technique to use when your project meets all of the following criteria:

- You want to insert new information into your PowerPoint slide that requires Microsoft Excel resources such as columns and rows, calculating, or charts.

- The information does not need to be in a separate file by itself.

- You might need to edit the workbook later on.

- You'll want to use Microsoft Excel tools to edit or format the information.

There are two ways to embed a new Microsoft Excel workbook in PowerPoint. The easiest way is to click the Insert Microsoft Excel Worksheet button on the Standard toolbar in PowerPoint. The other way is to choose the Object command from the Insert menu.

You edit an embedded Microsoft Excel workbook by double-clicking the workbook object in the slide. The PowerPoint menu and toolbars change to those of Microsoft Excel. You can use Microsoft Excel functions, commands, and other resources to make any necessary changes. When you are finished editing the embedded object, you click outside the object frame. The menu and toolbars return to those of PowerPoint.

Embed a new Microsoft Excel workbook in a presentation

You are creating slides in your PowerPoint presentation having to do with 401(k) investment information. You would like to lay out and format information as you would a Microsoft Excel workbook. Embed a new workbook in your presentation.

1   In PowerPoint, switch to Slide 5, entitled "401(k) Contributions."

*Insert Microsoft
Excel Worksheet*

2   On the Standard toolbar, click the Insert Microsoft Excel Worksheet button.

A worksheet grid appears.

3   Drag in the worksheet grid to define a worksheet of five rows by five columns.

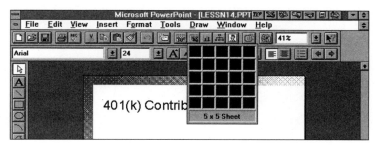

A blank Microsoft Excel workbook is embedded and opened for editing within the current slide. The PowerPoint menu and toolbars also change to those of Microsoft Excel. Your screen should look similar to the following illustration.

*Another method for
embedding a
Microsoft Excel
workbook is to
choose the Object
command from the
Insert menu. Be sure
that the Create New
option button is
selected. Select
Microsoft Excel 5.0
Worksheet, and then
choose the OK
button.*

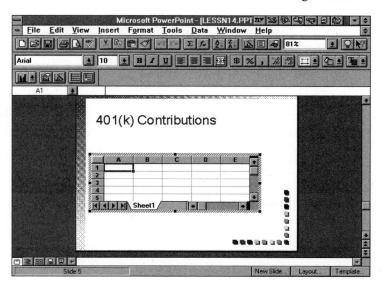

4   Type the following information into the first four rows of the Microsoft Excel workbook object.

Percent	$15,000	$25,000	$35,000
2%	$25/month	$42/month	$58/month
4%	$50/month	$83/month	$117/month
6%	$75/month	$125/month	$175/month

5 Adjust the column widths so that all the text fits properly. To do this, double-click the column edges or, from the Format menu, choose Column, and then choose Autofit Selection.

6 Click outside the Microsoft Excel object frame.

The Microsoft Excel menu and toolbars return to those of PowerPoint.

7 Drag the sizing boxes on the Microsoft Excel object frame to size the object to fit the slide properly and with the correct proportions. If necessary, drag the object frame to a better position on the slide. Your slide should look similar to the following illustration.

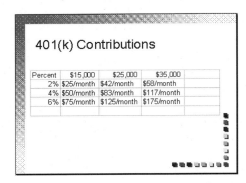

Save

8 On the Standard toolbar in PowerPoint, click the Save button.

Edit Microsoft Excel cells embedded in a presentation

In your embedded Microsoft Excel workbook, you want to add another row, showing the deduction amounts at 8%. Double-click the workbook object to edit it and make this change.

1 In Slide 5, double-click the embedded Microsoft Excel workbook object.

The workbook opens and your PowerPoint menu and toolbars change to those of Microsoft Excel. You can now use Microsoft Excel commands to edit and format the table.

2 In row 5, type the following figures:

8% $100/month $167/month $233/month

Bold

3 Select cells A1 through D1 and then, on the Formatting toolbar, click the Bold button.

Align Right

4 Select cells A2 through D5 and then, on the Formatting toolbar, click the Align Right button.

5 Click outside the Microsoft Excel object frame. Adjust the position of the object in the slide as necessary.

The Microsoft Excel object editing window closes and the menu and toolbars return to those of PowerPoint. Your slide should look similar to the following illustration.

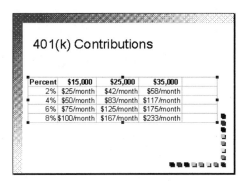

6 On the Standard toolbar in PowerPoint, click the Save button.

One Step Further

You already know how to copy a Microsoft Excel chart into a PowerPoint slide as a picture. However, if you think you might want to insert a chart and have it available for editing later, you might prefer to embed it as an editable object, rather than inserting it as a picture.

You can select an existing Microsoft Excel chart and embed it in a PowerPoint slide.

Embedding existing Microsoft Excel information in a PowerPoint slide is the best technique to use when your project meets all of the following criteria:

■ You want to insert existing Microsoft Excel information in your PowerPoint slide.

■ You want the Microsoft Excel information in the slide to be independent of the original information, rather than linked.

■ You'll want to use Microsoft Excel tools to edit or format the information later on.

You embed specific Microsoft Excel information by selecting the information (chart or cells) and then using the Copy command. Then, in PowerPoint, you use the Paste command. When you use the Paste command with copied Microsoft Excel information, the object is embedded in the current slide, instead of simply pasted as a static object. As with any embedded object, you can then double-click the object to edit it using Microsoft Excel resources.

Embed an existing Microsoft Excel chart in a presentation

You want to insert the 1994 Sales Performance chart into an orientation presentation slide that depicts Childs Play sales history. Embed the chart so that you can use Microsoft Excel resources to edit the embedded chart later without changing the original chart in the source file.

Microsoft Excel

1   On the Office Manager toolbar, click the Microsoft Excel button, and be sure that the Sales sheet is the active sheet.

You might need to click outside of the chart to see the sheet names.

2   Scroll to cell I10, where the 1994 Sales Performance chart begins, and then click the chart to select it.

Copy

3   On the Standard toolbar in Microsoft Excel, click the Copy button.

4   On the Office Manager toolbar, click the Microsoft PowerPoint button.

5   Switch to Slide 2, entitled "Sales Performance - 1994."

*Microsoft
PowerPoint*

6   On the Standard toolbar in PowerPoint, click the Paste button.

PowerPoint creates a new object in the current slide, and the copied chart is pasted and embedded in the object.

Paste

7   Drag the chart object until it is positioned below the table.

8   Drag the sizing boxes of the object frame to enlarge it.

The slide should look similar to the following illustration.

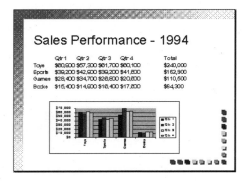

Now, whenever you double-click the chart object, you will be able to edit and format the chart using Microsoft Excel menus, toolbars, and other resources.

9   On the Standard toolbar, click the Save button.

End the Lesson

1 To continue to the next lesson, from the File menu in PowerPoint, choose Close. To quit for now, from the File menu in PowerPoint, choose Exit.

If you see the Save dialog box, click Yes.

2 Hold down ALT and, on the Office Manager toolbar, click the Microsoft Excel button.

If you see the Save dialog box, click Yes.

Lesson Summary

To	Do this
Copy Microsoft Excel cells as text into PowerPoint	In Microsoft Excel, select the cells, and then click the Copy button on the Standard toolbar. In PowerPoint, switch to the slide you want, and then from the Edit menu, choose Paste Special. Select Formatted Text (RTF) or Unformatted Text, and then choose the OK button.
Copy Microsoft Excel cells or a chart as a picture into PowerPoint	In Microsoft Excel, select the cells or chart, and then click the Copy button on the Standard toolbar. In PowerPoint, switch to the slide you want, and then from the Edit menu, choose Paste Special. Select Picture, and then choose the OK button.
Link Microsoft Excel cells or a chart to PowerPoint for automatic updates	In Microsoft Excel, select the cells or chart, and then click the Copy button on the Standard toolbar. In PowerPoint, switch to the slide you want, and then from the Edit menu, choose Paste Special. Select the Paste Link option button. If you are linking cells, be sure that Microsoft Excel 5.0 Worksheet Object is selected. If you are linking a chart, be sure that Microsoft Excel 5.0 Chart Object is selected. Then choose the OK button.
Edit a linked Microsoft Excel object in a PowerPoint slide	Double-click the Microsoft Excel object in PowerPoint. Microsoft Excel and the source file appear. You can now edit the source file.

To	Do this	Button
Embed new Microsoft Excel information in PowerPoint	In PowerPoint, switch to the slide you want. On the Standard toolbar, click the Insert Microsoft Excel Worksheet button. Drag in the worksheet grid to define the size of the worksheet. Type your information into the new workbook. When finished, click outside the workbook object editing window.	

For more information on	See in *Microsoft Office Getting Started*
Copying, linking, and embedding information between applications	Chapter 4, "How Office Applications Work Together"
Inserting information from other applications into PowerPoint	Chapter 5, "Using Microsoft Office"

For online information about	Choose <u>S</u>earch For Help On from the <u>H</u>elp menu of
Copying Microsoft Excel information into PowerPoint	PowerPoint, and then type **excel** *or* Microsoft Excel, and then type **copying, to other applications**
Linking to and editing linked Microsoft Excel information in PowerPoint for automatic updates	PowerPoint, and then type **link** *or* Microsoft Excel, and then type **linking, source worksheets to dependent documents**
Embedding Microsoft Excel information in PowerPoint	PowerPoint, and then type **embedded object** *or* Microsoft Excel, and then type **embedding**

Preview of the Next Lessons

In Part 5, you'll learn how to create a compound Microsoft Access database using the different integration techniques. In the next lesson, you'll create a Microsoft Access database table using text from Word.

Review & Practice

In the lessons in Part 4, you learned how to use information from different applications to create and enhance PowerPoint presentations. If you want to practice these skills and test your understanding before you proceed with the lessons in Part 5, you can work through the Review & Practice section following this lesson.

Part 4   Review & Practice

In Part 4, you learned how to create and enhance PowerPoint presentations by bringing information in from other applications. You can practice these skills by working through the steps in this Review & Practice section. You will create a presentation by copying, linking, embedding, and importing information from Word and Microsoft Excel.

Scenario

You are scheduled to give a series of presentations on the proposed Childs Play marketing strategy. You will use PowerPoint to create presentation slides for the series. You have a strategy document in Word that you will use as a source document for the presentation. You also have a Microsoft Excel workbook that includes marketing costs and sales projections that you will use. When the presentation is complete, you will use Microsoft Mail to send it to your manager for review.

You will review and practice how to:

- Import a Word outline to create a new PowerPoint presentation.
- Embed existing Word information in an existing PowerPoint presentation.
- Link Microsoft Excel information to a PowerPoint slide for automatic updates.
- Copy Microsoft Excel information for use in a PowerPoint presentation.
- Embed a Word table in a PowerPoint slide.
- Send the presentation to another user in your workgroup with Microsoft Mail.

Estimated practice time: 35 minutes

Step 1: Import a Word Outline into a New Presentation

To create the majority of your presentation, you will use the outline of the marketing strategy report in Word. From PowerPoint, import the Word document outline into PowerPoint format.

1 In PowerPoint, import the outline P4AREV.DOC from your PRACTICE directory. (Tip: Use the Open command from the File menu.)

2 Switch from Outline view to Slide view, and page through the slides.

3 Save the new presentation file as **reviewp4.ppt** in your PRACTICE directory.

For more information on	See
Importing a file from one application into another	Lesson 4
Importing and exporting information from Word into PowerPoint	Lesson 13

Step 2: Insert New Slides from a Word Outline

A second Word document has additional information for the marketing presentation. Insert the document outline as a new slide within your existing presentation.

1 In the PowerPoint REVIEWP4.PPT presentation file, switch to Slide 6, entitled "Marketing Methods—Other."

2 Insert the P4BREV.DOC document outline as a new slide after Slide 6. (Tip: Use the Slides From Outline command from the Insert menu.)

3 View the new Slide 7, entitled "Budget," along with the rest of the presentation.

4 Save the presentation.

For more information on	See
Importing a file from one application into another	Lesson 4
Inserting new PowerPoint slides from existing Word information	Lesson 13

Step 3: Link Workbook Data to a Slide

Every week, you edit information in a Microsoft Excel workbook on sales performance. You want to use this information in your marketing presentation, and have it automatically updated there. Copy and link the Microsoft Excel information to the presentation slide.

1 In Microsoft Excel, open the file P4REVIEW.XLS and save it as **reviewp4.xls**

2 In the Weekly Sales sheet, copy the information in cells A4 through O11.

3 In the PowerPoint REVIEWP4.PPT presentation file, link the copied information to Slide 8, entitled "Current Sales." (Tip: Use the Paste Special command from the Edit menu.)

4 Size and move the object as necessary to fit the proportions and layout of the slide.

5 Switch to the Microsoft Excel Weekly Sales sheet containing the linked information. (Tip: Double-click the linked object in PowerPoint.)

6 Type **39,200**, **32,000**, **22,000**, and **11,000** in the column for week 5.

7 In PowerPoint, see that the changes you made in the workbook are automatically reflected in the linked information in your presentation.

8   Save the presentation.

For more information on	See
Linking information from one application to another	Lesson 3
Linking Microsoft Excel data to a presentation	Lesson 14

Step 4: Copy a Workbook Chart into a Slide

You have a Microsoft Excel chart that illustrates projected sales performance based on the new marketing strategy. Copy the chart and paste it into your presentation.

1   In the Microsoft Excel REVIEWP4.XLS workbook, switch to the Sales Chart sheet, and then copy the column chart there.

2   Switch to the PowerPoint REVIEWP4.PPT presentation, and then paste the copied chart as a picture in Slide 9, entitled "Projected Sales." (Tip: Use the Paste Special command from the Edit menu.)

3   Size and move the chart as necessary to fit the proportions and layout of the slide.

4   Save the presentation.

5   Exit Microsoft Excel.

For more information on	See
Copying information from one application into another	Lesson 2
Copying Microsoft Excel information into a PowerPoint presentation	Lesson 14

Step 5: Embed a New Word Table in a Slide

In your presentation, you are including new information on marketing methods. You feel that the information will be conveyed most effectively if you format the information like a Word table. Embed and create a new Word table within an existing PowerPoint slide.

1   In Slide 3 ("Marketing Methods") of the REVIEWP4.PPT presentation, embed a new table consisting of three columns by five rows. (Tip: Use the Layout button in the lower-right corner of the window.)

2   Enter the following information into the embedded table.

Method	Quantity	Production $
Magazine Display Ads	4 ads	$1000 per ad
Newspaper Display Ads	12 ads	$600 per ad
Television Commercials	4 commercials	$5000 per commercial
Radio Commercials	3 commercials	$2500 per commercial

3   Click outside the Word table object frame, and then size and move the embedded table as necessary to fit the proportions and layout of the slide.

4   Save the presentation.

For more information on	See
Embedding information from one application in another	Lesson 3
Embedding a new Word table in a PowerPoint slide	Lesson 13

Step 6: Mail a Presentation

Now that the presentation is complete, you want to have your manager review it and provide you with feedback. If you are working on a network and are running Microsoft Mail, attach the presentation file to a mail message to your manager.

1   Switch to Microsoft Mail.

2   Compose a test mail message to another user on your network.

3   Attach the REVIEWP4.PPT presentation file to the mail message, and then send the message.

4   Exit Microsoft Mail.

For more information on	See
Attaching a file to a Microsoft Mail message	Lesson 3
Attaching a PowerPoint presentation file to a Microsoft Mail message	Lesson 13

End the Lesson

▶   Exit the PowerPoint application.

If you see the Save dialog box, click Yes.

5 Creating Databases in Microsoft Access Using Integrated Information

Microsoft Access is a relational database application that you can use to organize lists of information on employees, customers, inventory, contacts, and so forth. You store such information in database tables. Based on the information in these tables, you can build queries to find specific information stored in the tables, create forms to facilitate quick data entry into the table records, and generate reports that summarize data from the tables.

In this part, you'll learn how to use Microsoft Access as the base application for incorporating information that originates from Word and Microsoft Excel. Using various integration techniques, you'll bring Word tables and Microsoft Excel workbook data into Microsoft Access tables and databases.

Bringing Text from Word into a Database

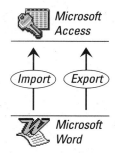

Microsoft Access

Import Export

Microsoft Word

You can use tabular information from a Word document in a Microsoft Access database. For example, you might have an inventory list in Word that you'd like to add to a Microsoft Access inventory database so you can sort records, query specific information, and generate summary reports. Or, perhaps a colleague has a list of vendor names and addresses in a Word document that you want to use in a database table.

In this lesson, you'll take Childs Play employee information listed in a Word document and bring it into a Microsoft Access database for inclusion in an employee database.

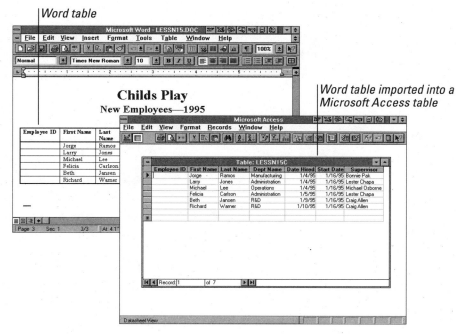

Word table

Word table imported into a Microsoft Access table

You will learn how to:

- Import delimited Word text into a Microsoft Access table.

- Convert a Word table into delimited text, and import it into a Microsoft Access table.

Estimated lesson time: 40 minutes

Start the lesson

Start Microsoft Access and open SBSDATA.MDB. Copy and paste the tables you will use with new names so the original tables will remain intact. Start Word and open 15LESSN.DOC.

Microsoft Access

1   On the Office Manager toolbar, click the Microsoft Access button. If the Welcome message appears, double-click the Control-menu box to close it.

2   From your PRACTICE directory, open SBSDATA.MDB.

This is the Childs Play employee database.

3   In the Database window, select the 15-Employees table, but do not open it.

This is a portion of the Childs Play employee list.

4   From the Edit menu, choose Copy, and then from the Edit menu, choose Paste.

By copying and pasting the table, you can work with a new copy of the table while leaving the original intact.

5   In the Paste Table As dialog box, type **Employees-15**, and then choose the OK button.

6   Click the Form button, and then select the 15-Detailed Employee Info form.

This is a Childs Play employee information form used by Human Resources personnel to enter employee data into the database.

7   From the Edit menu, choose Copy, and then from the Edit menu, choose Paste.

8   In the Paste As dialog box, type **Employees-15**, and then choose the OK button.

This will be the version of the form that you will work with in this lesson, while the original form will remain intact.

Microsoft Word

9   On the Office Manager toolbar, click the Microsoft Word button. If the Tip Of The Day dialog box appears, choose the OK button.

10 From your PRACTICE directory, open 15LESSN.DOC. Be sure that both the Word window and the document window are maximized.

This file contains employee information that you will use in the Microsoft Access database.

11 Save the document as **lessn15.doc**

Importing Information from Delimited Word Data

Bringing tabular information from Word into a database table in Microsoft Access is useful when you have information listed in Word and you want to use this information in a new or existing database.

You convert the Word data by saving, or *exporting*, the Word data to a *file format* that Microsoft Access can interpret. You then open, or *import*, the converted file into the

Microsoft Access database. The imported Word data appears as if you had originally typed the information in Microsoft Access.

Importing tabular data from Word into Microsoft Access is the best technique to use when your project meets all of the following criteria:

- You have tabular data in Word.

- You want to use this data in a new or existing Microsoft Access table.

- The fields of the listed Word information are separated by tabs, commas, or another separating character.

When the Word information is separated by tabs, commas, semicolons, or another separating character, it is called a *delimited* table. (This is not the same as a table in Word containing rows and columns, which is covered in the next major section, "Importing Information from a Word Table.") The following illustration shows two examples of delimited tables in Word.

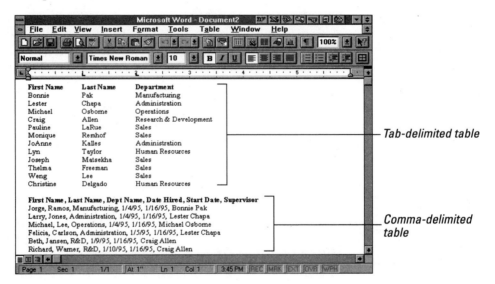

Tab-delimited table

Comma-delimited table

A Microsoft Access database table is the basic building block for all database activities. The information is stored in *fields* and *records* in a column-and-row format in a database table. From this table, you can then create queries to find specific records or types of records. You can create forms to enter data quickly into the table. And you can design and generate reports that summarize the different types of information in the table.

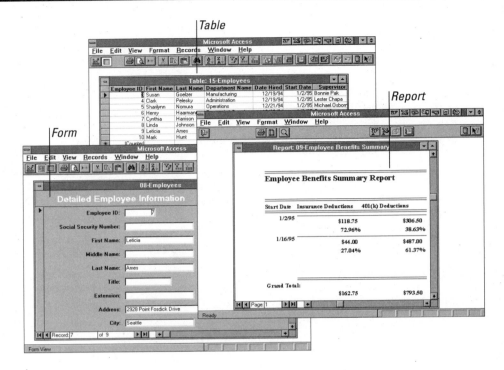

Table

Form

Report

You can bring tabular information from Word into either a new Microsoft Access table or an existing table. Which method you use depends on the information you already have in your database. If you're just starting to set up your database, you bring the Word information into a new table. If you have a related table already set up, you can integrate the Word information with that existing table.

You have existing Childs Play employee information that is listed in a Word document. In the following exercises, you will use this information to create a new table in the employee database you're starting to build in Microsoft Access. The Word information is set up in a simple table built with tabs.

Copy the delimited Word information to a separate file

When you export information, the entire file is exported. Because the Word document contains other information besides the delimited table, copy the table to a separate document file so that only the table, and not the surrounding information, is exported.

1 In page 2 of the LESSN15.DOC document file, select the entire table by dragging across it, selecting all data from "First Name" through "Operations."

2 On the Standard toolbar in Word, click the Copy button.

3 On the Standard toolbar, click the New button.

A new blank document appears.

Copy

New

Paste

4   On the Standard toolbar of the new document, click the Paste button.

The copied table is pasted into the new document.

Export the Word file

Export the file containing the delimited employee information to a file format that Microsoft Access can interpret.

1   From the File menu, choose Save As.

2   In the Save File As Type list, select Text Only With Line Breaks.

This option exports the Word document file into a simpler text format that can be imported and interpreted by Microsoft Access in a database table.

3   In the File Name box, type **lessn15a**, and then choose the OK button.

The document file is converted and saved as a text file with the filename LESSN15A.TXT. It is now ready for importing into Microsoft Access.

You must close the file before you can import it into Microsoft Access.

4   From the File menu, choose Close.

A message asks if you want to save LESSN15A.TXT.

5   Choose the No button, because you've already saved the file.

Import the Word file into a new database table

Now import the converted employee information file into a new Microsoft Access table in the Childs Play employee database.

Microsoft Access

1   On the Office Manager toolbar, click the Microsoft Access button.

Be sure that the Database window is active.

2   From the File menu, choose Import.

The Import dialog box appears.

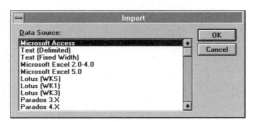

3   In the Data Source list box, select Text (Delimited), and then choose the OK button.

The Select File dialog box appears.

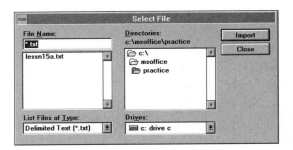

4 Select LESSN15A.TXT, and then choose the Import button.

The Import Text Options dialog box appears.

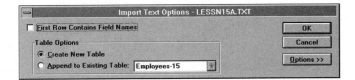

5 Select the First Row Contains Field Names check box. Be sure that the Create New Table option button is selected.

The column titles in the first row of your delimited table become the field names at the top of a new database table.

6 Choose the Options button.

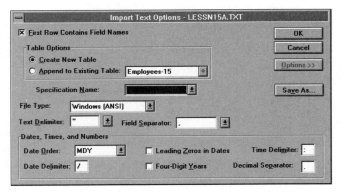

If the text fields in the imported file are each enclosed in quotes or apostrophes, select that as the text delimiter.

7 In the Text Delimiter list, select {None}; in the Field Separator box, select {Tab}; and then choose the OK button.

You select {None} because there are no quotation marks or other characters surrounding each field in the table. You select {Tab} because each field in the Word file is separated with a tab. Microsoft Access imports the text file from

Word and creates a new database table from the information. A message confirms that the import is successful.

8 Choose the OK button, and then choose the Close button in the Select File dialog box.

In the Database window, be sure that the Table tab is selected. You'll see a new table in the list named LESSN15A.

9 Select the LESSN15A table, and then choose the Open button.

The imported LESSN15A table appears. If you choose, you can now manipulate the table, sort the information, create queries, generate reports, or perform other database functions on the table information.

10 From the File menu, choose Close.

Importing Information from a Word Table

You can bring a *formatted* Word table (in a rows-and-column format) into a new or existing database table in Microsoft Access. You do this when you have a Word table that contains information you want to use in a database.

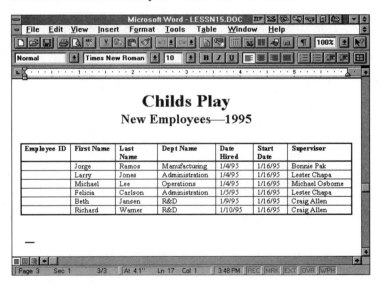

Because Microsoft Access cannot directly import a Word table in its original table format, you must first convert the table to a delimited text format to prepare it for importing.

When you import and append Word information into an existing database table, you must first prepare the Word table to meet the following conditions:

- Each field must have the same data type (such as numbers, dates, text, or currency) as the corresponding field in the destination Microsoft Access table.

- If you are not using the first row of the Word table as field names, each field must be in the same order as the fields in the destination Microsoft Access table. This ensures that the data will flow into the appropriate places in the order of the database table.

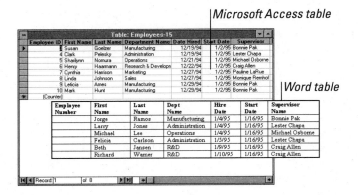

- If you are using the first row of the Word table as field names, the field names must match exactly. (The field name might be different from the field caption shown as the column title in the database table. Review the Microsoft Access Table Design view to be sure that you are using the correct field names.) The matching field names ensure that the data will flow into the correct fields in the database table, even if the fields are in a different order.

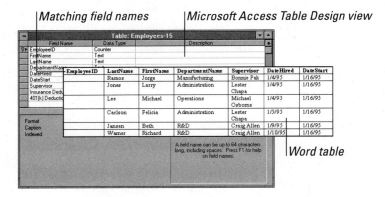

You've been maintaining new employee information in a Word table. In the following exercises, you will append this information to an existing table in an employee database you're building with Microsoft Access.

Copy the Word table to a separate file

When you export information, the entire file is exported. Because the Word document contains other information besides the table, copy the table into a separate document file so that only the table, and not the surrounding information, is exported.

1   In the Microsoft Access Database window, select the Employees-15 table, and then choose the Open button.

   The table appears.

2   Review the table's field order and field names to see how you can make the Word table compatible.

   You can then make any necessary changes to the Word table to either match the field order or the field names. This ensures that you can successfully import and append records.

3   From the File menu in Microsoft Access, choose Close.

4   On the Office Manager toolbar, click the Microsoft Word button.

Microsoft Word

5   In page 3 of the LESSN15.DOC document file, click anywhere within the table and then, from the Table menu, choose Select Table.

   Notice that the Word table fields are in the same order as the destination table in Microsoft Access, but the field names are slightly different. In this case, it's easier to delete the first row rather than match the field names.

6   On the Standard toolbar in Word, click the Copy button.

Copy

7   On the Standard toolbar, click the New button.

   A new blank document appears.

New

8   On the Standard toolbar of the new document, click the Paste button.

   The copied table is pasted into the new document.

Paste

9   Select the first row of the table, which contains the field names and then, from the Standard toolbar, click the Cut button.

   Because the field names do not match but the field order does match between the Word table and the Microsoft Access table, you simply delete the field names to prepare the table for importing.

Cut

Convert the Word table to delimited text

Because Microsoft Access does not import formatted Word tables, convert the employee table to delimited text.

1   Select the entire Word table in the new document.

2   From the Table menu, choose Convert Table To Text.

   The Convert Table To Text dialog box appears.

3   Be sure that the Tabs option button is selected, and then choose the OK button.

The table is converted to text, with tabs instead of cells to separate the text. Your screen should look similar to the following illustration.

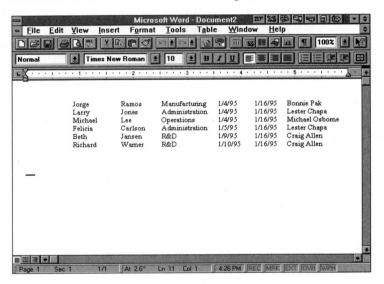

The file is now ready to be exported.

Export the Word file

Export the file containing the delimited employee information to a file format that Microsoft Access can interpret.

1   From the File menu in Word, choose Save As.

2   In the Save File As Type list, select Text Only With Line Breaks.

This exports the Word document file to another file format that can be imported and interpreted by Microsoft Access in a database table.

3   In the File Name box, type **lessn15b**, and then choose the OK button.

The document file is converted and saved as a text file named LESSN15B.TXT. It is now ready for importing into Microsoft Access.

4 From the File menu, choose Close.

You must close the file before you can import it into Microsoft Access. A message asks if you want to save LESSN15B.TXT.

5 Choose the No button, because you've already saved the file.

Import the Word file into an existing database table

Now import the converted employee information file into an existing Microsoft Access table in the Childs Play employee database. This database table already contains information on another set of new employees.

Microsoft Access

1 On the Office Manager toolbar, click the Microsoft Access button.

Be sure that the Database window is active.

2 From the File menu, choose Import.

The Import dialog box appears.

3 In the Data Source list box, select Text (Delimited), and then choose the OK button.

The Select File dialog box appears.

4 Select LESSN15B.TXT, and then choose the Import button.

The Import Text Options dialog box appears.

5 Select the Append To Existing Table option button, and be sure that Employees-15 is selected in the list of existing tables.

6 Choose the Options button.

You can use this process to convert a Word merge data source document that might have names, addresses, or other data, into a new or existing Microsoft Access database.

7 In the Text Delimiter list, select {None}; in the Field Separator box, select {Tab}; and then choose the OK button.

You select {None} because there are no quotation marks or other characters surrounding each field in the table. You select {Tab} because each field in the Word file is separated with a tab. Microsoft Access imports the text file from Word and appends the records to the Employees-15 database table. A message confirms that the import is successful.

8 Choose the OK button, and then choose the Close button in the Select File dialog box.

In the Database window, be sure that the Table tab is selected.

9 Select the Employees-15 table, and then choose the Open button.

The Employees-15 table appears and displays the seven records you appended.

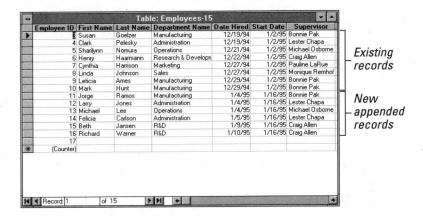

Employee ID	First Name	Last Name	Department Name	Date Hired	Start Date	Supervisor
3	Susan	Goelzer	Manufacturing	12/19/94	1/2/95	Bonnie Pak
4	Clark	Pelesky	Administration	12/19/94	1/2/95	Lester Chapa
5	Sharilynn	Nomura	Operations	12/21/94	1/2/95	Michael Osborne
6	Henry	Haarmann	Research & Developn	12/22/94	1/2/95	Craig Allen
7	Cynthia	Harrison	Marketing	12/27/94	1/2/95	Pauline LaRue
8	Linda	Johnson	Sales	12/27/94	1/2/95	Monique Remhof
9	Leticia	Ames	Manufacturing	12/29/94	1/2/95	Bonnie Pak
10	Mark	Hunt	Manufacturing	12/29/94	1/2/95	Bonnie Pak
11	Jorge	Ramos	Manufacturing	1/4/95	1/16/95	Bonnie Pak
12	Larry	Jones	Administration	1/4/95	1/16/95	Lester Chapa
13	Michael	Lee	Operations	1/4/95	1/16/95	Michael Osborne
14	Felicia	Carlson	Administration	1/5/95	1/16/95	Lester Chapa
15	Beth	Jansen	R&D	1/9/95	1/16/95	Craig Allen
16	Richard	Warner	R&D	1/10/95	1/16/95	Craig Allen
17						
(Counter)						

Existing records

New appended records

Record: 1   of 15

If you choose, you can now manipulate the table, sort the information, create queries or reports, or perform other database functions on the information in the table.

10   From the File menu, choose Close.

One Step Further

You can *link* text from a Word document to a form. This is useful if you have special information for users of the form that is subject to change.

Link Word text to a Microsoft Access form when your project meets all of the following criteria:

- You have information in an existing Word file that you want to use in a form.

- The Word information is edited on a regular basis.

- You want the information in the form to be automatically updated as soon as the corresponding information in the Word file changes.

To link text from Word, the *source application*, to a form in Microsoft Access, the *destination application*, you use the Paste Special command from the Edit menu.

Link Word information to a Microsoft Access form

You have designed a form in your employee database. This form will be used by various members of the Human Resources department when they enter information about new employees into the database. You also have important information in a Word document that you update each week. You want this information to be included in the database form and automatically updated whenever you change the Word document.

Microsoft Word

1   On the Office Manager toolbar, click the Microsoft Word button.

2   On page 1 of the LESSN15.DOC document, select the second paragraph, which begins with "New employees" and ends with "1/2/95."

Copy

Microsoft Access

3   On the Standard toolbar, click the Copy button.

4   On the Office Manager toolbar, click the Microsoft Access button.

5   In the Database window, click the Form tab.

6   Select the 15-Detailed Employee Info form, and then choose the Design button.

7   From the Edit menu, choose Paste Special, and then select the Paste Link option button.

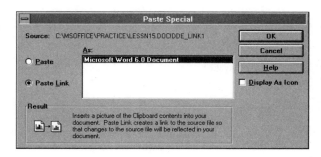

8   Choose the OK button.

The information is linked as an object on the form design.

9   Drag the sizing boxes on the object frame to fit the frame just around the text. Then move the object frame to the area to the right of the Employee ID field.

Your form design should look similar to the following illustration.

Linked object from Word

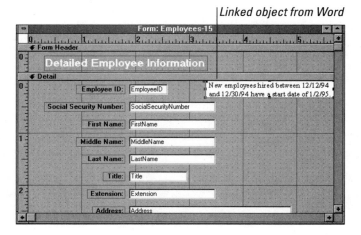

Now, whenever the information changes in Word, the linked information in the Microsoft Access form will be automatically updated.

Edit the linked information in the form

You need to update the linked information in the Word document to indicate the hire and start dates of the most recent group of new employees.

Microsoft Word

1   On the Office Manager toolbar, click the Microsoft Word button.

2   On page 1 of the LESSN15.DOC document, change the dates in the second paragraph to **1/2/95**, **1/13/95**, and **1/16/95**

Microsoft Access

3   On the Office Manager toolbar, click the Microsoft Access button.

You'll notice that the changes you made in the Word text are automatically updated in the linked object in the Microsoft Access form.

4   From the File menu, choose Save.

5   From the File menu, choose Close.

Note   You can also embed existing Word text in a Microsoft Access form. Select the Word information and then from the Standard toolbar, click the Copy button. In the Microsoft Access form, switch to Form Design view. From the Edit menu, choose Paste. Once the information has been embedded, you can move and size the object box as needed. To edit embedded text, double-click the object.

End the Lesson

1   If you want to continue to the next lesson, leave the Microsoft Access SBSDATA.MDB database file open. If you want to quit for now, from the File menu in Microsoft Access, choose Exit.

If you see the Save dialog box, click Yes.

2   Hold down ALT and, on the Office Manager toolbar, click the Microsoft Word button.

If you see the Save dialog box, click Yes.

Lesson Summary

To	Do this
Convert a Word table to delimited text	Select the entire Word table, and then from the Table menu, choose Convert Table To Text. Select the Tabs or Commas option button to indicate the text separator you want to use, and then choose the OK button.

To	Do this
Export a delimited Word text file to Microsoft Access	From the File menu in Word, choose Save As. In the Save File As Type list, select Text Only With Line Breaks. Name the file, and then choose the OK button.
Import a delimited Word text file into a Microsoft Access table	In the Microsoft Access Database window, choose Import from the File menu. Select Text (Delimited), and then choose the OK button. Select the file to be imported, and then choose the Import button. Select either the Create New Table or Append To Existing Table option button, as appropriate. Choose the Options button and then, in the Text Delimiter list, select {None}. Be sure that the Field Separator box reflects the separator used in the exported file. Choose the OK button, and then choose the Close button.

For more information about	See in *Microsoft Office Getting Started*
Copying, linking, and embedding information between applications	Chapter 4, "How Office Applications Work Together"
Inserting information from other applications into Microsoft Access	Chapter 5, "Using Microsoft Office"
Importing and exporting files between different applications	Chapter 6, "Sharing Information with Others"

For online information about	From the <u>H</u>elp menu of
Converting a Word table to delimited text	Word, choose <u>S</u>earch For Help On, and then type **converting tables to text**
Exporting a delimited Word text file to Microsoft Access	Word, choose <u>S</u>earch For Help On, and then type **exporting documents**
Importing a delimited Word text file into a Microsoft Access table	Microsoft Access, choose <u>S</u>earch, and then type **importing data: basics**

For online information about	**From the Help menu of**
Embedding Word information in a Microsoft Access form	Microsoft Access, choose Search, and then type **embedding OLE objects** *or* Word, choose Search For Help On, and then type **embedding**
Copying and linking Word information to a Microsoft Access form	Microsoft Access, choose Search, and then type **link: OLE objects** *or* Word, choose Search For Help On, and then type **linking**

Preview of the Next Lesson

In the next lesson, you'll learn how to use Microsoft Excel worksheets to create Microsoft Access tables. You'll learn how to use an entire worksheet, and how to specify ranges within a worksheet for use in database tables.

Using Workbook Data in a Database

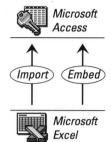

Microsoft Access

↑ Import   ↑ Embed

Microsoft Excel

You can use information that is listed in a Microsoft Excel workbook more effectively in a database. For example, you might have product records in Microsoft Excel that you'd like to use in a Microsoft Access product database. Or, maybe you have a customer contact list including names, addresses, and communication history. In either case, if you move the information into a Microsoft Access database, you can run detailed queries, create data forms, and generate sophisticated reports based on the information.

In this lesson, you'll take Childs Play employee information from a Microsoft Excel workbook and bring it into a Microsoft Access employee database. You'll also insert Microsoft Excel workbook and chart information into database tables and forms.

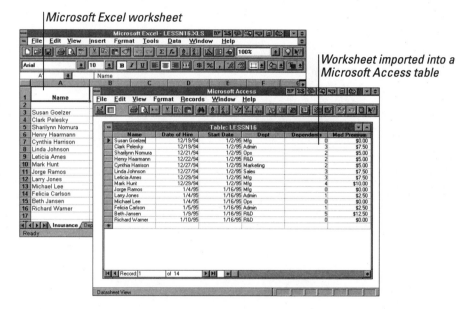

Microsoft Excel worksheet

Worksheet imported into a Microsoft Access table

You will learn how to:

- Import Microsoft Excel workbook data into a new Microsoft Access table.
- Append Microsoft Excel workbook data to an existing Microsoft Access table.
- Embed Microsoft Excel workbook information in a Microsoft Access table.
- Insert Microsoft Excel workbook information into a Microsoft Access form.

Estimated lesson time: 45 minutes

Start the lesson

Start Microsoft Access and open SBSDATA.MDB. Start Microsoft Excel, and open LESSN16.XLS.

Microsoft Excel

1 On the Office Manager toolbar, click the Microsoft Excel button.

2 From your PRACTICE directory, open 16LESSN.XLS.

This workbook contains employee information to be used in the Microsoft Access employee database. Be sure that both the Microsoft Excel window and the workbook window are maximized.

3 Save the document as **lessn16.xls**

4 From the File menu of the LESSN16.XLS workbook, choose Close.

Microsoft Access

5 On the Office Manager toolbar, click the Microsoft Access button. If the Welcome message appears, double-click the Control-menu box to close it.

6 From your PRACTICE directory, open SBSDATA.MDB, if it is not already open.

This is the Childs Play employee database.

Importing Data from a Workbook into a Database

Bringing information from a Microsoft Excel workbook into a Microsoft Access database table is useful when you want to perform sophisticated database functions on lists of items that you have previously maintained in a workbook.

You convert Microsoft Excel worksheet information by *importing* the workbook file into the Microsoft Access database. The imported Microsoft Excel worksheet appears as if you had originally typed the information into the Microsoft Access table.

When importing workbook information into a database table, you can:

■ Import information from Microsoft Excel into a new Microsoft Access table.

■ Append information to an existing Microsoft Access table.

■ Import an entire worksheet.

■ Import a cell range on a worksheet.

■ Import a named range on a worksheet.

Importing worksheet information from Microsoft Excel into a Microsoft Access table is the best technique to use when your project meets any of the following criteria:

■ You want to sort records.

■ You need to create data forms or build reports.

■ You have specific information you need to query.

■ You want to perform other database functions on the information.

In Microsoft Access, you use the Import command from the File menu to convert and open a Microsoft Excel sheet as a database table. You can import the worksheet into either a new or existing table in the database.

Importing Workbook Data into a New Table

Importing a Microsoft Excel sheet into a new table is best when you are creating a new database table based on the imported information from Microsoft Excel.

You import Microsoft Excel data into a new Microsoft Access table by using the Create New Table option in the Import Spreadsheet Options dialog box. You can import an entire sheet from the workbook, or you can specify a range of cells to be imported.

Import an entire sheet into a new database table

You have detailed Childs Play employee information listed in a Microsoft Excel workbook, and you want to bring this information into an employee database you're building with Microsoft Access.

1   From the File menu in Microsoft Access, choose Import.

The Import dialog box appears.

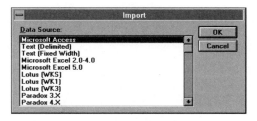

2   Select Microsoft Excel 5.0, and then choose the OK button.

The Select File dialog box appears.

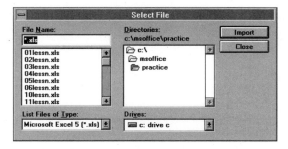

3   Select LESSN16.XLS, and then choose the Import button.

The Import Spreadsheet Options dialog box appears.

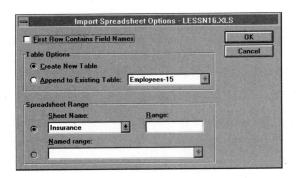

4 Select the First Row Contains Field Names check box. Be sure that the Create New Table option button is selected. Also be sure that the "Insurance" sheet is selected in the Sheet Name box.

The column titles in the first row of your sheet become the field names at the top of the new database table.

5 Choose the OK button.

Microsoft Access imports the specified sheet from Microsoft Excel and creates a new database table from the information. A message confirms that the import is successful.

6 Choose the OK button, and then choose the Close button in the Select File dialog box.

In the Database window, you'll see a new table named LESSN16.

7 Select the LESSN16 table, and then choose the Open button.

The imported LESSN16 table appears, as shown in the following illustration.

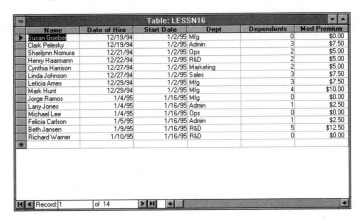

You can now manipulate the table, sort the information, create queries, generate reports, or perform other database functions on the table information.

8 From the File menu, choose Close.

Note Using a similar procedure, you can import a cell range rather than the entire sheet from a Microsoft Excel workbook. In the Import Spreadsheet Options dialog box, type the cell range you want to import in the Range Text box under Spreadsheet Range. Also be sure that the First Row Contains Field Names check box is clear.

Appending Workbook Data to an Existing Table

Appending a workbook file to an existing table is best when you already have related information in your database to which you want to add the imported workbook data.

When you want to append Microsoft Excel data to an existing Microsoft Access table, you first arrange the information in Microsoft Excel into the proper format so that upon importing, the data will flow into the appropriate places.

Prepare the Microsoft Excel sheet to meet the following conditions:

■ Each field must have the same data type (such as numbers, dates, text, or currency) as the corresponding field in the destination Microsoft Access table.

■ If you are not using the first row of the sheet as field names, each field must be in the same order as the fields in the destination Microsoft Access table. This ensures that the data will flow into the appropriate places in the order of the database table.

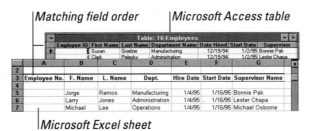

Matching field order   *Microsoft Access table*

Microsoft Excel sheet

■ If you are using the first row of the sheet as field names, the field names must match exactly. (The field name might be different from the field caption shown as the column title in the database table. Review the Table Design view to be sure you are using the correct field names.) The matching field names ensure that the data will flow into the correct fields in the database table, even if the fields are in a different order.

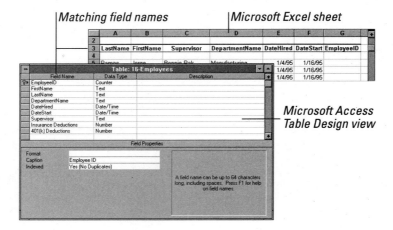

Matching field names   *Microsoft Excel sheet*

Microsoft Access Table Design view

You append imported data by using the Append To Existing Table option in the Import Spreadsheet Options dialog box. You then select the name of the table to which you want to append the data.

Copy the database table

Copy and paste the Childs Play employee database table, so you can work with a new copy of the table while leaving the original intact.

1   In the Database window, select the 16-Employees table but don't open it.

2   From the Edit menu, choose Copy

3   From the Edit menu again, choose Paste.

4   In the Paste Table As dialog box, type **Employees-16**, and then choose the OK button.

Compare the database table to the workbook data

Review the Microsoft Access table and the Microsoft Excel sheet that you'll be importing. Review the field order and the field names. This will help you decide how the sheet being imported needs to be modified.

1   In the Database window, select the Employees-16 table, and then choose the Open button.

The Employees-16 table appears.

2   Maximize the table window.

Microsoft Excel

3   Hold down SHIFT and, on the Office Manager toolbar, click the Microsoft Excel button.

The Microsoft Excel and Microsoft Access windows are tiled together on the screen.

4   In the Microsoft Excel window, open LESSN16.XLS.

5   Click the Dept sheet tab to make it the active sheet.

Your screen should look similar to the following illustration.

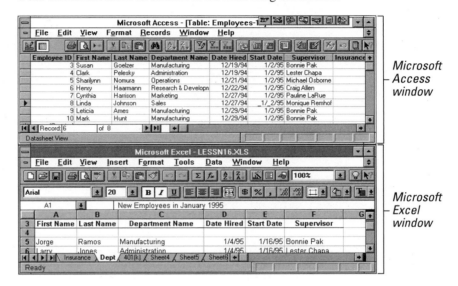

Microsoft Access window

Microsoft Excel window

6   Review the order of the fields to see how it compares with the structure of the Microsoft Access table.

You'll notice that the Microsoft Access table has a few more fields than the Dept sheet.

Design View

7   From the Table Datasheet toolbar in the Microsoft Access window, click the Design View button.

The table switches to Design view.

8   Click in the FirstName field under Field Name.

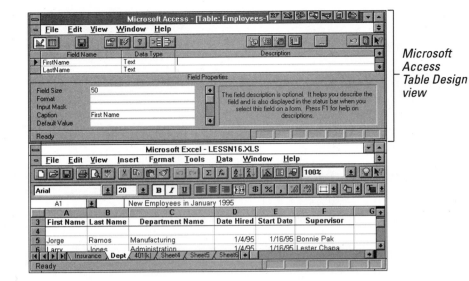

Microsoft Access Table Design view

9 Review the field names of the Microsoft Excel sheet to see how they compare with the field names in the Microsoft Access table.

While the Microsoft Access table has more fields than the Microsoft Excel sheet, the field names are close enough to be easily modified.

Modify the sheet to match the database table

Make the necessary changes to the field names. This will ensure that your information is imported successfully.

1 Make the following changes to the Microsoft Excel field names in the column titles:

Change	To
First Name	**FirstName**
Last Name	**LastName**
Department Name	**DepartmentName**
Date Hired	**DateHired**
Start Date	**DateStart**

If it's easier to change the field order than edit the field names, select the column you want to move, and then use the Cut and Paste buttons on the Standard toolbar.

Your modified sheet should look similar to the following illustration.

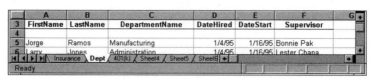

2   From the File menu in Microsoft Access, choose Close.

The table closes and the Database window appears again.

3   In the Microsoft Excel window, click the Maximize button. Note the range of cells that are to be imported: A3 through F10.

Save

4   On the Standard toolbar, click the Save button.

5   From the File menu, choose Close.

You must close the file before you can import it.

You're now ready to import and append the worksheet data.

Append worksheet data to an existing database table

Append the Childs Play new employee data from LESSN16.XLS to the Employees-16 table in Microsoft Access.

Microsoft Access

1   On the Office Manager toolbar, click the Microsoft Access button. If necessary, maximize the Microsoft Access window, and then restore the Database window to its original size.

2   From the File menu in Microsoft Access, choose Import.

The Import dialog box appears.

3   Select Microsoft Excel 5.0, and then choose the OK button.

The Select File dialog box appears.

4   Select LESSN16.XLS, and then choose the Import button.

The Import Spreadsheet Options dialog box appears.

5   Select the First Row Contains Field Names check box.

6   Select the Append To Existing Table option button, and then select Employees-16 from the list of tables.

7   In the Sheet Name list, select Dept and then, in the Range text box, type **A3:F10** to indicate the specific cell range to be imported and appended.

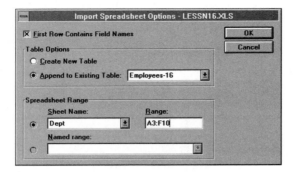

8 Choose the OK button.

Microsoft Access imports the cell range from the Microsoft Excel workbook sheet and appends the contents of that cell range as new records at the end of the Employees-16 table. A message confirms that the import is successful.

9 Choose the OK button, and then choose the Close button in the Select File dialog box.

You can now view the modified table with the appended records and perform any database manipulations that you want.

Open the database table with the appended records

Open and view the Childs Play employee database table containing the appended records.

1 In the Database window, select the Employees-16 table, and then choose the Open button.

The table appears, showing the newly appended information—records 11 through 16—imported from the Microsoft Excel sheet. The table should look similar to the following illustration.

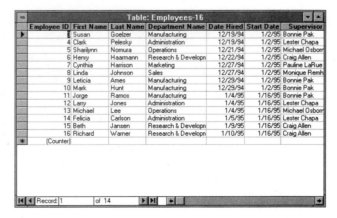

If you choose, you can now manipulate the table, sort the information, create queries or reports, or perform other database functions on the table information.

2 From the File menu, choose Close.

Inserting Workbook Information into a Database

You can insert a Microsoft Excel chart or sheet into a Microsoft Access database by *embedding* it as an *object*. This is useful when you want to include an entire workbook file in a database table, form, or report. With embedding, you always have the workbook and Microsoft Excel commands and tools available to you from within the database.

When you embed, you can:

- Create and embed an entirely new workbook object in your database.
- Embed an existing workbook file as an object in your database.

When you want to embed workbook information in a database, first you create a field in the database table that is set up to accept *OLE* objects. Then you can select and insert the workbook file. At this point, you choose whether you want the file to be embedded or linked.

Embedding an Existing Workbook in a Table

You can embed an existing workbook in a database table record. The embedded workbook is then attached to that particular record. This is useful when you have detailed information in a Microsoft Excel workbook that you want to include as part of the database record. You can then open the embedded file to view the information when you need it.

When you embed an existing workbook, you're making a copy of the entire file and inserting it into the database table record. You can open and edit this file to make changes that apply only to the copy of the workbook attached to that selected record. Any other copies of the workbook remain unchanged. You can embed different workbooks in different records in a single table.

Because embedding inserts an entire file, this can significantly increase the size of your database file.

Embedding existing Microsoft Excel information in a Microsoft Access table, form, or report is the best technique to use when your project meets all of the following criteria:

- You want to use Microsoft Excel resources to enter, analyze, calculate, or chart numbers and other data in a database.
- You might want to update the workbook at a later time.
- You want the workbook to be separate from the source file, and separate from other versions of the workbook in other records in the database.
- You want the workbook to be an integral part of the database file.

Review the workbook

You have a workbook that includes a basic format for 401(k) investment choices. You want to include this workbook as a part of the Childs Play employee database, and adapt it for each employee, reflecting each individual's investment choices. First review the workbook to ensure that the proper sheet is open.

Microsoft Excel

1   From the Office Manager toolbar, click the Microsoft Excel button.

2   From your PRACTICE directory, open LESSN16.XLS.

3   Click the 401(k) sheet tab.

This makes the 401(k) sheet the active sheet. When you embed the workbook in Microsoft Access, the current sheet will appear when you open the embedded object. The other sheets in the workbook will be available as well.

Save

4   On the Standard toolbar, click the Save button.

The workbook is now ready to be embedded in the Microsoft Access table.

Copy and open the table

Copy the Childs Play employee database table, so you can work with a new copy of the table while leaving the original intact.

Microsoft Access

1   From the Office Manager toolbar, click the Microsoft Access button.

2   In the Database window of Microsoft Access, select the 16-Investments table.

3   From the Edit menu, choose Copy.

4   From the Edit menu, choose Paste.

5   In the Paste Table As dialog box, type **Investments-16**, and then choose the OK button.

6   In the Database window, select Investments-16 and then choose the Open button.

Add an OLE Object field in the Microsoft Access table

Before you insert existing Microsoft Excel information into a Microsoft Access table or form, specify an OLE Object field in the table. This provides a place for the Microsoft Excel information, and it also identifies the data type as an OLE object.

Design View

1   On the Table Datasheet toolbar, click the Design View button.

The table switches to Table Design view.

2   Select the next available blank Field Name field (after the Deductions field), and type **401(k)** into the field.

This adds "401(k)" as a new field in the table.

3   Move to the Data Type field, and then click the down arrow. Select OLE Object from the list of data types.

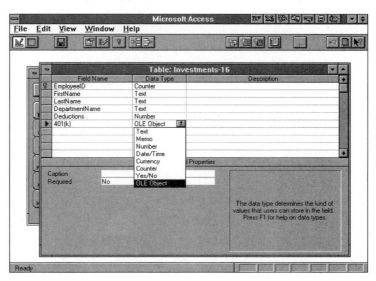

This indicates that the new field will contain OLE objects—that is, objects either embedded or linked from another application.

4   Under Field Properties, type **401(k) Investment Choices** in the Caption field.

This will be the field name appearing in Datasheet view.

Datasheet View

5   On the Table Design toolbar, click the Datasheet View button, and then choose the OK button to save the table.

The table datasheet appears, showing the new field you just added.

6   Drag the right edge of the 401(k) Investment Choices column so that all the text is visible.

Your screen should look similar to the following illustration.

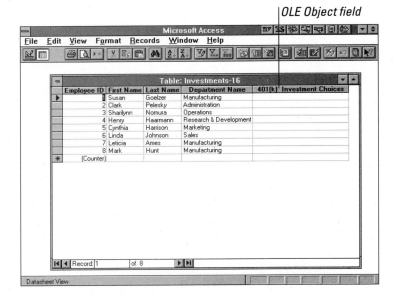

You're now ready to embed the workbook object in the table records.

Embed the workbook object in a Microsoft Access table

Embed the 401(k) sheet from the LESSN16.XLS workbook in several records of the employee database table.

1   Click the 401(k) field for record 1.

2   From the Edit menu, choose Insert Object.

The Insert Object dialog box appears.

You can also create and embed a new workbook object. Select the Create New option button, select Microsoft Excel 5.0 Worksheet, and then choose the OK button.

3   Click the Create From File option button.

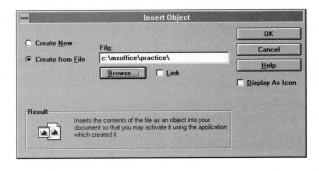

4 In the File box, type **lessn16.xls** after the path, and then choose the OK button.

"Microsoft Excel 5.0 Worksheet" appears in the current field, indicating that the workbook has been embedded for that record.

Copy

5 With the 401(k) field for record 1 still selected, click the Copy button on the Table Datasheet toolbar.

The embedded workbook object is copied.

6 Click the 401(k) field for record 2.

7 On the Table Datasheet toolbar, click the Paste button.

Paste

The embedded workbook object is pasted into record 2.

8 Click the 401(k) field for record 3, and paste the object again.

With the Microsoft Excel workbook objects inserted into the OLE Object fields, you can now open and edit the objects. You can also view the objects in a form.

Note   Another method for embedding is to select any portion of the Microsoft Excel workbook and choose Copy. Switch back to Microsoft Access, click the OLE Object field where you want to embed the object, and then choose Paste. The entire workbook is embedded in the field.

If you copy and paste information from Microsoft Excel into a Microsoft Access Text field, the selected text is simply inserted into the field.

Open and edit the embedded workbook object

Modify the embedded workbook object in each record to reflect each individual's choices.

1 Double-click the embedded workbook object in record 1.

The embedded workbook opens in a Microsoft Excel window, as shown in the following illustration.

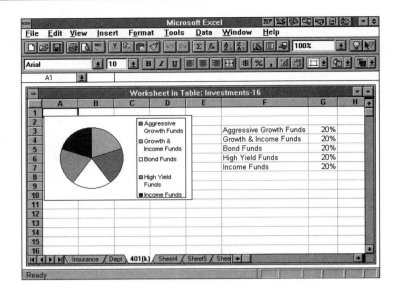

2   In column G, change the investment percentages as follows. Be sure to type the percent sign (%) after the number.

From	To
20%	**40%**
20%	**10%**
20%	**10%**
20%	**15%**
20%	**25%**

Notice that the chart adjusts with each change you make.

Save

3   On the Standard toolbar in Microsoft Excel, click the Save button.

4   From the File menu in Microsoft Excel, choose Close.

The database table appears again.

5   Double-click the embedded object in record 2.

6   In column G of the Microsoft Excel sheet, change the investment percentages as follows. Be sure to type the percent sign (%) after each number.

From	To
20%	10%
20%	15%
20%	20%
20%	25%
20%	30%

Save

7   On the Standard toolbar in Microsoft Excel, click the Save button.

8   From the File menu in Microsoft Excel, choose Close.

The database table appears again. You have now modified two separate versions of the embedded workbook, leaving the third one intact. Embedded objects are copies of the source file, and are not linked to them. Instead, they are separate and independent files within the three table records.

Creating a Form with Workbook Information

You can create a form that displays the embedded information from the table on which the form is based. You can also open the embedded object and edit the information.

Because there is a separate embedded object for each record, Microsoft Access displays a different object for each individual record in the form. Each embedded object is tied, or *bound*, to the specific field and record in the database table on which the form is based. Therefore, these objects are called *bound objects*.

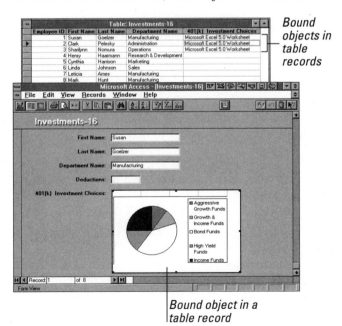

Bound objects in table records

Bound object in a table record

The easiest way to create a form based on the current table is to use the New Form button on the Table Datasheet toolbar.

Create a form from a table including embedded objects

You want to create a form based on the Investments-16 table that will make data entry easier for your colleagues in Human Resources. You also want this form to display the information embedded in the 401(k) field.

New Form

1   With the Investments-16 table open, click the New Form button on the Table Datasheet toolbar.

The New Form dialog box appears.

2   Click the Form Wizards button.

The Form Wizards dialog box appears.

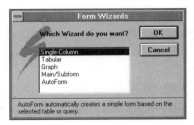

3   Select AutoForm, and then choose the OK button.

Microsoft Access creates and opens a form based on the Investments-16 table. It includes all fields in the table, including the 401(k) OLE Object field.

Open and edit the embedded object in the form

Some employees have changed their 401(k) investment choices, and you want to enter the new information quickly and easily through the database form.

1   In record 1 of the form, double-click the 401(k) Investment Choices object. You might need to scroll downward to bring it into view.

A Microsoft Excel object editing window opens on the form. The Microsoft Excel Standard and Formatting toolbars also appear.

2 Drag the sizing boxes of the object editing window to make it fill the space available for the object on the form.

Your screen should look similar to the following illustration.

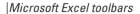

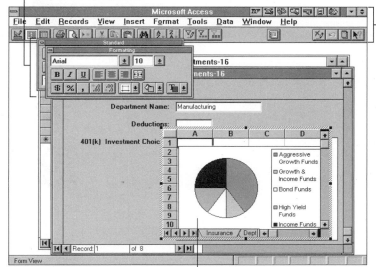

Microsoft Excel toolbars

Microsoft Access menu and toolbar

Microsoft Excel object editing window

3 Use the arrow keys to move to and view the data to the right of the chart.

4 Change cell G3 from 40% to **10%,** and then change cell G5 from 10% to **40%**

5 Press HOME to bring the chart into view again.

The chart reflects the changes you just made.

6 Click outside the embedded Microsoft Excel object frame.

7 Use the form navigation buttons on the lower edge of the form window to page through the other records.

Notice that the charts are different in records 1 through 3, because you changed the information for the first two records. Also notice that while records 4 through 8 each have object frames, they're blank, because objects have not been embedded in them yet.

Add a new embedded object to a form

While you can insert an object in a table's OLE Object field, you can also insert and view an object in a form's object frame.

You can also click the Browse button to select the directory and filename of the file you want to embed in your form.

1   Switch to record 4 in the Investments-16 form, and click the object frame to make it active.

2   From the Edit menu, choose Insert Object.

3   In the Insert Object dialog box, select the Create From File option button.

4   Type **lessn16.xls** after the path, and then choose the OK button.

The workbook is embedded in the object frame of record 4. If you choose, you can now double-click the object to open and edit it.

One Step Further

You can link information from a Microsoft Excel workbook to a Microsoft Access form or report, and have it automatically updated whenever the source data changes.

You can link a Microsoft Excel sheet or chart as an *unbound object* in a database form or report. An unbound object is like a label control in that it is identical in each form, and is independent of specific field information in the table on which the form is based. An unbound object can make your forms and reports more attractive or easy to use. Or, as in this case, the unbound object can provide general information in all the records.

Linking a Microsoft Excel workbook object to a Microsoft Access table, form, or report is the best technique to use when your project meets all of the following criteria:

- You want to use Microsoft Excel resources to enter, analyze, calculate, or chart numbers and other data in a database.

- You think you might want to update the workbook at a later time.

- You want all the changes taking place in the *source file* in Microsoft Excel to be reflected automatically in the *destination file* in Microsoft Access.

Insert a Microsoft Excel sheet or chart as an unbound object in a form when you want identical information to appear in each record of the form.

You can link an unbound object by using either the Insert Object or the Paste Special command from the Edit menu of Form Design view.

Link an unbound chart object to a form

In your employee database form, you want to show another pie chart of total investment choices for all Childs Play employees. This pie chart shows company-wide totals, and the chart will be updated every month as new employees join the company, and as current employees change their investment mixes. You want the summary pie chart in your form to be updated automatically as soon as the source chart changes, and you want the chart to appear in each record of the form.

1   On the Form View toolbar, click the Design View button.

Design View

Object Frame

2 On the Toolbox toolbar in Form Design view, click the Object Frame button.

With this button, you can create an unbound object in the form.

3 Move the mouse pointer into the Detail section of the form design.

The mouse pointer changes to a crosshairs shape.

4 Drag a box on the left side of the form design, to the left of the bound object frame.

The Insert Object dialog box appears.

5 Select the Create From File option button.

6 Type **lessn16.xls** after the path, select the Link check box, and then choose the OK button.

The workbook is linked to the unbound object frame of the Investments-16 form. This workbook will appear in each record of the form. Furthermore, whenever the workbook information changes, the linked object in the form will be automatically updated.

7 If necessary, use the sizing boxes on the object frame to fit the chart on the form.

You don't need to include the legend in the frame—only the chart itself. Your form design should look similar to the following illustration.

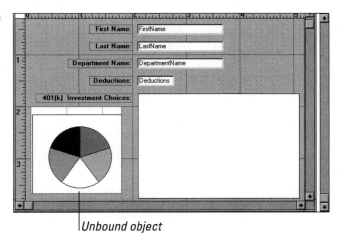

Unbound object

Form View

8 On the Form Design toolbar, click the Form View button.

9 Use the navigation buttons at the bottom of the form window to page through the records. You'll see that the unbound object frame and its linked workbook object appear the same in each record.

Note   Another method for linking is to select the portion of the Microsoft Excel workbook you want to link, and then choose Copy. Switch to Microsoft Access, and select the OLE object field or object frame to which you want to link the object. From the Edit menu, choose Paste Special. In the Paste Special dialog box, select the Paste Link option button, and then choose the OK button.

End the Lesson

1   From the File menu of Form view, choose Save Form.

2   In the Save Form dialog box, type **Investments-16** and then choose the OK button.

3   From the File menu, choose Close.

4   From the File menu of Table view, choose Close.

   If you see the Save dialog box, click Yes.

5   To continue to the Review & Practice, leave the Microsoft Access SBSDATA.MDB database file open. To quit for now, from the File menu in Microsoft Access, choose Exit.

Microsoft Excel

6   Hold down ALT and, on the Office Manager toolbar, click the Microsoft Excel button.

   If you see the Save dialog box, click Yes.

Lesson Summary

To	Do this
Import a Microsoft Excel sheet or cell range to a new Microsoft Access table	From the File menu in Microsoft Access, choose Import. Select Microsoft Excel 5.0, and then choose the OK button. Select the workbook file containing the sheet or cell range to be imported, and then choose the Import button. Be sure that the Create New Table option button is selected. Specify the sheet name and spreadsheet range if necessary. Choose the OK button. Choose OK in the confirmation box, and then choose Close.

To	Do this
Append a Microsoft Excel sheet or cell range to an existing Microsoft Access table	Be sure that the field order and/or the field names of the workbook sheet or cell range being imported match those of the database table. From the File menu in Microsoft Access, choose Import. Select Microsoft Excel 5.0, and then choose the OK button. Select the workbook file containing the sheet or cell range to be imported, and then choose the Import button. Select the Append To Existing Table option button, and select the table. Specify the sheet name and spreadsheet range if necessary. Choose the OK button.
Create an OLE Object field in a table	In Design view, select a blank field and type the field name. In the Data Type field, click the down arrow, and select OLE Object. Under Field Properties, type a field name in the Caption field. On the Table Design toolbar, click the Datasheet View button, and then choose the OK button.
Embed an existing Microsoft Excel workbook object in a Microsoft Access table	In Microsoft Access, create an OLE Object field type in the table where you want to embed the workbook. Select the OLE Object field, and then from the Edit menu, choose Insert Object. Select the Create From File option button, type the filename, and then choose the OK button.
Embed a Microsoft Excel workbook object as a bound object in a Microsoft Access form	In the Microsoft Access form, be sure that there is an object frame defined for the record. Click the object frame, and then from the Edit menu, choose Insert Object. Select the Create From File option, type the filename of the file to embed, and then choose the OK button.

For more information on	See in *Microsoft Office Getting Started*
Copying, linking, and embedding information between applications	Chapter 4, "How Office Applications Work Together"
Inserting information from other applications into Microsoft Access	Chapter 5, "Using Microsoft Office"
Importing and exporting files between different applications	Chapter 6, "Sharing Information with Others"

For online information about	From the <u>H</u>elp menu of
Importing a Microsoft Excel sheet or cell range into a Microsoft Access table	Microsoft Access, choose <u>S</u>earch, and then type **importing data: basics** and **spreadsheets**
Embedding a Microsoft Excel workbook object in a Microsoft Access table or form	Microsoft Access, choose <u>S</u>earch, and then type **embedding OLE objects** *or* Microsoft Excel, choose <u>S</u>earch For Help On, and then type **embedding**
Embedding a Microsoft Excel workbook object as a bound object in a Microsoft Access form or report	Microsoft Access, choose <u>S</u>earch, and then type **bound OLE objects** *or* Microsoft Excel, choose <u>S</u>earch For Help On, and then type **embedding**

Review & Practice

In the lessons in Part 5, you learned how to use information from different applications to create and enhance a Microsoft Access database. If you want to practice these skills and test your understanding of these techniques, you can work through the Review & Practice section following this lesson.

Part 5   Review & Practice

In Part 5, you learned how to build Microsoft Access database tables and forms by bringing information in from other applications. You can practice these skills by working through the steps in this Review & Practice section. You will enhance a Microsoft Access database by exporting, importing, embedding, and linking information from Word and Microsoft Excel.

Scenario

You have begun to build a marketing database using Microsoft Access. But you still have assorted sets of information in different sources in Word and Microsoft Excel. Colleagues throughout the company are also providing you with Word and Microsoft Excel information, to help make the database comprehensive and complete.

You will review and practice how to:

- Convert and import a Word table into a new Microsoft Access table.

- Embed new Word information in a Microsoft Access form.

- Append a range of cells and an entire workbook to a Microsoft Access table.

- Link an existing Microsoft Excel chart to a Microsoft Access form.

Estimated practice time: 45 minutes

Step 1: Import a Word Table into a Database Table

You have a table in Word that includes details on the various marketing methods used by Childs Play to publicize and sell its products. Export the table to a text-only format, and then import the table into a new Microsoft Access table.

1   In Word, open the file P5REVIEW.DOC and save it as **reviewp5.doc**

2   Select and copy just the Word table to a new file.

3   Convert the Word table to text. (Tip: Use the Convert Table To Text command from the Table menu, and use either tabs or commas as the text separator.)

4   Export the Word table as a text-only file with line breaks, and name the file **reviewp5.txt** (Tip: Use the Save As command from the File menu.)

5   Close the Word files and exit Word.

6   In Microsoft Access, open SBSDATA.MDB, if it is not already open.

7   Import the REVIEWP5.TXT delimited Word text into a new Microsoft Access database table. (Tip: Use the Import command on the File menu.)

In the Import Text Options dialog box, make selections to import the Word table into a new database table, using the first row as the field names. (Tip: Set the Text Delimiter and Field Separator fields to match the information in the Word file.)

8   Open and view the imported REVIEWP5 table.

For more information on	See
Importing and exporting a file from one application to another	Lesson 4
Importing and exporting information from Word to Microsoft Access	Lesson 15

Step 2: Embed Word Text in a Database Form

Now that you have a marketing methods table in your marketing database, you want to create a form based on this table to provide for easier maintenance and updating of the information. Because others in Marketing will be using this database, you want to be sure that they know who to contact for questions. Create a form based on the table. Embed new Word text that includes your name and telephone extension in such a way that it appears in each record of the form.

1   In the REVIEWP5 table, create a new form. (Tip: Click the New Form button on the Table Datasheet toolbar, click the Form Wizards button, and then select AutoForm.)

2   In the new form, switch to Form Design view.

3   Maximize the form window in Design view, and then drag the lower border of the form detail section to add more space for the form. Create, position, and size a new object frame along the bottom of the form, under the 1996 Budget field. (Tip: Click the Object Frame button on the Toolbox toolbar.)

4   In the Insert Object dialog box, specify that you want to create a new Microsoft Word 6.0 Document object.

5   In the Word object, type **For help or further information, please call Denise at x629, between 7:30am and 4:30pm. Or, send email to deniseni. Thank you!** Make any formatting changes you want to the text.

6   Close the Word object and return to the form.

7   Switch back to Form view to see your embedded Word object in the form records.

8   Restore the form view to its original size. Page through the form to see the Word object in each record.

9   Save the form as Methods-P5, and then close the form. Close the REVIEWP5 table.

For more information on	See
Embedding information from one application in another	Lesson 3
Embedding Word text in a Microsoft Access form	Lesson 15
Creating a database form based on a table	Lesson 16

Step 3: Append a Cell Range to a Database Table

As another part of your Microsoft Access marketing database, you have started a Childs Play customer representative table. To this table you want to add cells from a Microsoft Excel workbook that contains a detailed list of additional customer representatives. Import and append the cell range containing the records for the customer representatives you don't already have in your table.

1   In the Microsoft Access SBSDATA.MDB file, copy the P5-Customer Reps table and paste it as **Reps-P5**. (Tip: Use the Copy and Paste commands from the Edit menu.)

2   Open the Reps-P5 table, and review the field order and field names. (Tip: Switch to Table Design view to see the field names.) Close the table.

3   In Microsoft Excel, open the file P5AREV.XLS and save it as **revp5a.xls**

4   In the Reps sheet, review the order of the fields and review the field names to see how they compare to those of the Microsoft Access Reps-P5 table. Change either the field order or the field names to match the database table to which this sheet will be appended. (Tip: When comparing, tile the Microsoft Excel and Microsoft Access windows to view them both at the same time.)

5   Note the range of cells to be imported. (Tip: If you're matching the field order, the range is A6 through F12. If you're matching field names, the range is B5 through F12.)

6   Save and close REVP5A.XLS.

7   In Microsoft Access, begin importing the Microsoft Excel REVP5A.XLS workbook. (Tip: Use the Import command on the File menu.)

8   In the Import Text Options dialog box, select the appropriate specifications to append the identified Microsoft Excel cell range to the existing Reps-P5 database table. (Tip: Type the cell range in the Range box.)

9   Open the Reps-P5 table, and view the appended cell range in records 11 through 17.

For more information on	See
Importing a file from one application to another	Lesson 4
Appending a Microsoft Excel cell range to an existing Microsoft Access table	Lesson 16

Step 4: Embed a Workbook in a Database Table

You want to add a new field to the Reps-P5 database table that will include detailed sales performance information for each individual customer representative. To do this, you've decided to insert a separate workbook into the record for each representative. Add an OLE Object field to the Reps-P5 table, embed workbook objects in the field, and then modify the objects to reflect the individual representative information.

1   In Microsoft Excel, open the file P5BREV.XLS, save it as **revp5b.xls**, and then close the file.

2   In the Microsoft Access Reps-P5 table, switch to Table Design view.

3   Type **Sales** into the next available field name field, and then identify the data type for the field as OLE Object.

4   Under Field Properties, type **Sales Performance** as the caption for the field.

5   Save the table design and switch to the datasheet view.

6   Drag the right edge of the Sales Performance field so that all the text is visible.

7   Embed the workbook file REVP5B.XLS as objects in the first four records. (Tip: For the first record, choose Insert Object from the Edit menu. For the other three, use the Copy and Paste buttons.)

8   Open and edit the embedded workbook objects as follows. (Tip: Double-click the field. When you are finished editing, save and close the file, and then go on to the next record.)

Record	Name	Qtr 1	Qtr 2	Qtr 3	Qtr 4
1	Garcia	**1000**	**1500**	**2500**	**3000**
2	Kanarowski	**1890**	**1350**	**1540**	**2060**
3	Wilson	**2500**	**2700**	**2200**	**2630**
4	Jacoby	**900**	**1020**	**1490**	**1210**

9   Save and close the table.

For more information on	See
Embedding information from one application in another	Lesson 3
Embedding Microsoft Excel information in a Microsoft Access table	Lesson 16

Step 5: Link a Workbook Chart to a Database Form

You have a form based on the customer representatives table, and it displays the embedded Microsoft Excel object. In this form, you also want to include a chart that shows the overall company sales on an ongoing basis. This will help you compare the sales performance of individual representatives to the overall performance. Copy and link the sales chart to the form.

1 In the Database window, switch to the Forms list. Copy the P5-Customer Reps form and paste it as **Reps-P5**. (Tip: Use the Copy and Paste commands from the Edit menu.)

2 Open the Reps-P5 form in Form Design view.

3 Switch to Microsoft Excel and open the REVP5A.XLS workbook. Switch to the Chart sheet. Select and copy the chart.

4 Close the workbook and exit Microsoft Excel.

5 In the Reps-P5 form, link the copied chart to the form design. (Tip: Choose Paste Special from the Edit menu, and then select Paste Link.)

6 Position the frame until it's to the right of the first six fields. If necessary, size the object frame to make it fit properly.

7 Switch to Form view.

8 Page through the form to see the linked chart in each record.

9 Save and close the form.

For more information on	See
Embedding information from one application in another	Lesson 3
Linking Microsoft Excel information to a Microsoft Access form	Lesson 15
Creating a database form based on a table	Lesson 16

End the Lesson

▶ Close the Microsoft Access application, along with the SBSDATA.MDB database file.

If you see the Save dialog box, click Yes.

Appendixes

In the Appendixes, you can find information that will help you to use both Microsoft Office and this Step by Step book more effectively. In Appendix A, you can read about installing Microsoft Office and about optimizing your computer system to enhance the performance of Microsoft Office. In Appendix B, you can find a complete list of the Step by Step practice files that are used throughout this book with their names, the lessons they are used in, and descriptions of the files.

Optimizing Microsoft Office

This appendix describes some of the issues associated with using Microsoft Office successfully, including installation and system optimization. For further assistance with installation and system questions, contact Microsoft Product Support. You can find Product Support phone numbers in the user guides for the individual applications of Microsoft Office.

Microsoft Office Installation

This section covers the issues associated with using the different components of Microsoft Office successfully with the lessons in this book. For specific installation procedures, see *Microsoft Office Getting Started*, which comes with Microsoft Office.

Installing Microsoft Office

Microsoft Office contains four applications, along with a variety of tools and modules that can be used with the four applications. To completely and effectively use the lessons in this book with Microsoft Office, you need to install the following components:

- Microsoft Word
- Microsoft Excel
- Microsoft PowerPoint
- Microsoft Access (if you have Microsoft Office Professional)
- Help for all applications, including Cue Cards where applicable
- ClipArt Gallery
- Microsoft Graph
- WordArt
- PowerPoint Viewer

If you like, you can also install the Equation Editor and Organization Chart. These are referred to in the lessons, but are not directly used in the exercises.

During installation, you are presented with a number of installation choices. For best results in working with this book, and in working in general on a day-to-day basis, install Microsoft Office as follows.

- Choose a complete installation.
- Choose automatic startup of Office in Windows.

- Have all applications, files, and resources stored centrally in subdirectories under the MSOFFICE directory.

If You Have an Earlier Version of Microsoft Office

If you're upgrading from an earlier version of Microsoft Office, simply run the Microsoft Office Setup program. The earlier versions of the program files will be replaced by the new versions. Your data files from the earlier version will remain intact, and you will be able to open them with the new version.

If you have any problems with upgrading from an earlier version of Microsoft Office, you might consider deleting all the Microsoft Office program files from the earlier version, as well as the directory that held them, before you install the new version. However, be careful not to delete any of your data files.

If You Have Individual Microsoft Office Applications

You might be installing Microsoft Office for the first time but already have individual applications installed that are part of Microsoft Office (for example, Microsoft Excel or Word).

If the currently installed version is the same as the one in your version of Microsoft Office, you can choose not to install it again. Choose Complete/Custom installation, and select only those applications and tools that you don't already have.

If the currently installed version of the application is earlier than the one in your version of Microsoft Office, install the new version along with the rest of the Microsoft Office applications and tools. The Setup program will detect that you have an earlier version of the application, and will replace those program files with the new ones, while leaving any data files intact.

When you want to install only some of the Microsoft Office applications, note the following.

- Be sure that the files for the Microsoft Office applications you already have are centrally stored under the MSOFFICE directory.

- Choose the Complete/Custom installation option, and then select the individual applications you want to install.

- Be sure to store the applications that you are installing under the MSOFFICE directory.

Installing Individual Resources

You can install individual tools and resources if you previously did a typical or minimum installation and you now need other resources that were not included as part of that installation.

You might also need to install resources individually if you ask for a resource, such as Help or ClipArt, and a message indicates that the resource is not available. With ClipArt in particular, if you see a different set of clip art illustrations in the ClipArt Gallery than the ones called out in the lessons, this might indicate that you have another application that includes a different set of clip art. You can install the Microsoft Office ClipArt, which will add those illustrations to your existing set of clip art in the ClipArt Gallery.

When you install individual tools or resources, do the following:

- Be sure that the files for the resources you already have are stored in a subdirectory within the MSOFFICE directory.

- Run the Microsoft Office Setup program.

- Choose the Complete/Custom installation option, and then select the individual tools or resources you want to install.

- Be sure that the files for the resources you are installing are stored in the same subdirectory within the MSOFFICE directory as the resources you already have installed.

Enhancing System Performance

Microsoft Office is a collection of powerful and comprehensive applications. Because of this, using the different applications at the same time can consume your computer's system resources and you might experience slower performance. There are three basic strategies to enhance your system's performance:

- Be sure that your computer system meets the recommended system configuration for running Microsoft Office successfully.

- Optimize the memory you have.

- Upgrade your system to augment your current resources.

This section describes these three approaches to helping you use Microsoft Office most efficiently with your system configuration.

System Requirements

The components needed for your computer system depend on whether you have Microsoft Office Standard or Microsoft Office Professional.

For more information, refer to the manual that came with your computer equipment. Or, call Microsoft Product Support.

System Requirements for Microsoft Office Standard

To run Microsoft Office Standard, your computer system must have the following components:

- MS-DOS operating system version 3.1 or later

- Microsoft Windows, Windows for Workgroups, or Windows NT operating system version 3.1 or later

- Personal computer using a 386 or higher microprocessor

- 6 MB of memory (8 MB recommended when running multiple programs)
- Hard disk space required for a typical installation: 49 MB (the minimum installation requires 21 MB, and the maximum installation of all files requires 68 MB)
- One 3.5" or 5.25" high-density disk drive
- VGA or higher resolution video adapter compatible with Microsoft Windows version 3.1

System Requirements for Microsoft Office Professional

To run Microsoft Office Professional, which adds Microsoft Access to the set of applications provided by Microsoft Office Standard, your computer system must have the following components.

- MS-DOS operating system version 3.1 or later
- Microsoft Windows, Windows for Workgroups, or Windows NT operating system version 3.1 or later
- Personal computer using a 386 or higher microprocessor
- 6 MB of memory (8 MB recommended)
- Hard disk space required for typical installation: 58 MB (the minimum installation requires 29 MB, and the maximum installation of all files requires 82 MB)
- One 3.5" or 5.25" high-density disk drive
- VGA or higher resolution video adapter compatible with Microsoft Windows version 3.1

Optimizing System Memory

With each application you open, more memory is used up. When your system's memory is consumed by the applications, your system spends more time getting information from your hard disk. This can make your system performance slower than you might expect. However, the following sections describe solutions for maximizing your system's memory management.

Working Habits

If your system has minimal memory or speed, consider the following guidelines to working as efficiently as possible.

- Open only those applications you need for the task at hand. Close an application when you're finished with it.
- If you've been working with one or more applications for a while and the system performance seems to be degrading, close the applications, close Windows, and then start them up again.

- If you want to check how much memory is being used, from the Help menu in Program Manager, choose About Program Manager. In the About dialog box, you'll see statistics on the percentage of memory currently being used.

System Setup

Many variables in an individual system setup can affect the performance of your system with Microsoft Office. The following is a list of common items that you might investigate if you're experiencing poor system performance.

- Memory resident programs, such as disk compression programs and virus checkers, might take memory resources from Microsoft Office applications and make the system run more slowly.

- Turning on virtual memory can improve performance.

- Optimizing your memory management parameters can improve performance.

- Be sure that the system unit's turbo button is on, to use the maximum speed at which your system's processor can work.

For more information about memory management issues, consult your MS-DOS or Windows user's guide. You can also contact Microsoft Office Product Support for ideas on improving your memory management.

System Resource Upgrades

Speed is the major performance issue with powerful applications, especially when using more than one application at a time, as is often the case with Microsoft Office applications. If you find that you are continually stretching the limits of your system's performance, and you've already tried the various optimization techniques described earlier in this Appendix, you might consider upgrading different components.

- Add memory. Besides optimizing the memory management parameters, adding RAM chips to your system unit is probably one of the easiest and most affordable methods for optimizing your system performance. If you're using a 386 computer, you can upgrade to up to 8 MB of RAM. If you're using a 486 computer, you can upgrade to up to 64 MB of RAM.

- Add speed. The only way you can increase the speed of your microprocessor is to obtain a faster microprocessor chip. For the 386, your typical choices are 16 megaHertz (MHz), 25 MHz, or 33 MHz. You can obtain 486 microprocessors at speeds of 25 MHz, 33 MHz, and 66 MHz.

- Upgrade the microprocessor. If you're running a 386 computer, consider upgrading to a 486 or Pentium computer to maximize system performance. Because this is the most expensive option, however, consider it as a last resort. You should be able to do enough with memory management and adding RAM to meet your performance needs for Microsoft Office, even with a 386 computer.

For more information on system resource upgrades, you can contact Microsoft Product Support, or talk with your local computer dealer.

Practice File List

Here's a list of the files on the Practice Files disk, the lessons in which each file is used, and a description of each file:

Filename	Lesson	Description
01LESSN.DOC	Lesson 1	Word letter to new employees
01LESSN.PPT	Lesson 1	PowerPoint presentation for the new employee orientation
01LESSN.XLS	Lesson 1	Microsoft Excel workbook containing new employee information
02LESSN.DOC	Lesson 2	Word document on employee benefits
02LESSN.XLS	Lesson 2	Microsoft Excel workbook containing employee benefits information
03LESSN.PPT	Lesson 3	PowerPoint presentation for the new employee orientation
03LESSN.XLS	Lesson 3	Microsoft Excel workbook containing current sales figures
04LESSN.DOC	Lesson 4	Word document consisting of a portion of the new employee orientation packet
04LESSN.XLS	Lesson 4	Microsoft Excel workbook containing new employee information
05LESSN.DOC	Lesson 5	Word document with information for the new employee orientation packet
05LESSN.XLS	Lesson 5	Microsoft Excel workbook containing 401(k) information
06LESSN.DOC	Lesson 6	Word report to management regarding new employee statistics
06LESSN.XLS	Lesson 6	Microsoft Excel workbook containing a list of new employees and their benefits information
07LESSN.DOC	Lesson 7	Word memo regarding a review of the PowerPoint presentation
07LESSN.PPT	Lesson 7	PowerPoint presentation for the new employee orientation
08LESSN.DOC	Lesson 8	Word form letter to new employees

Filename	Lesson	Description
09LESSN.DOC	Lesson 9	Word report to upper management regarding new employee statistics
10LESSN.DOC	Lesson 10	Word document regarding employee retirement benefits
10LESSN.XLS	Lesson 10	Microsoft Excel workbook containing retirement benefits calculations
11LESSN.PPT	Lesson 11	PowerPoint presentation for the new employee orientation
11LESSN.XLS	Lesson 11	Microsoft Excel workbook containing new employee orientation information
13ALESSN.DOC	Lesson 13	Word document containing an outline for the new employee orientation packet
13BLESSN.DOC	Lesson 13	Word document and outline of a portion of the new employee orientation packet
13CLESSN.DOC	Lesson 13	Word document containing information for the new employee orientation presentation
14LESSN.PPT	Lesson 14	PowerPoint new employee orientation presentation
14LESSN.XLS	Lesson 14	Microsoft Excel workbook containing sales information and 401(k) computations
15LESSN.DOC	Lesson 15	Word document containing listed employee information
16LESSN.XLS	Lesson 16	Microsoft Excel workbook containing employee information
P1REVIEW.DOC	Review & Practice Part 1	Word report on marketing strategy proposal
P1REVIEW.XLS	Review & Practice Part 1	Microsoft Excel workbook containing marketing method cost data
P2AREV.DOC	Review & Practice Part 2	Word memo to contain the marketing presentation for review
P2CREV.DOC	Review & Practice Part 2	Word marketing strategy proposal

Filename	Lesson	Description
P2DREV.DOC	Review & Practice Part 2	Word marketing status report
P2EREV.DOC	Review & Practice Part 2	Word form letters to customer representatives
P2REVIEW.PPT	Review & Practice Part 2	PowerPoint presentation on the marketing strategy proposal
P2REVIEW.XLS	Review & Practice Part 2	Microsoft Excel workbook containing information on projected marketing costs and projected sales revenues
P3REVIEW.DOC	Review & Practice Part 3	Word document including marketing information to be used in a workbook
P3REVIEW.PPT	Review & Practice Part 3	PowerPoint marketing strategy presentation
P4AREV.DOC	Review & Practice Part 4	Word report and outline on the marketing strategy proposal
P4BREV.DOC	Review & Practice Part 4	Word document and outline on marketing costs
P4REVIEW.XLS	Review & Practice Part 4	Microsoft Excel workbook containing sales performance data
P5AREV.XLS	Review & Practice Part 5	Microsoft Excel workbook containing a list of customer representatives
P5BREV.XLS	Review & Practice Part 5	Microsoft Excel workbook containing sales information
P5REVIEW.DOC	Review & Practice Part 5	Word marketing methods table

Filename	Lesson	Description
SBSDATA.MDB	Lesson 8, 9, 12, 15, and 16 Review & Practice for Parts 2, 3, and 5	Microsoft Access company database

Glossary

application   A computer software program, such as a word processor, spreadsheet, presentation designer, or relational database, that is designed to do a specific type of work.

attach   The Microsoft Mail function you can use to send an entire file along with an electronic mail message.

bound object   A linked or embedded object that is associated with a specific field and record in a database. *See also* unbound object.

clip art   Electronic illustrations that you can copy or embed into a file of any Microsoft Office application.

ClipArt Gallery   A collection of approximately 1000 pieces of clip art that you can view from any Microsoft Office application. From the ClipArt Gallery, you can preview, select, and insert a clip art illustration into your current file.

Clipboard   A temporary holding area in Microsoft Windows that stores the last set of information that was copied or cut.

comma delimited   A file format in which fields of data are separated by commas.

comma separated values (CSV)   Another term for a comma-delimited file format.

copy   To duplicate information from one location to another, either within a file, to another file, or to a file in another application.

data source   A file that contains the specific information to be merged into a main document to create form letters or other merged documents. *See also* main document.

database   A type of application that you can use to organize and manipulate detailed lists of information.

database form   A database component based on a table that consists of controls for each field, including a blank for quick data entry.

database query   A database component based on a table that you can use to filter and review selected categories of information from the table.

database report   A database component based on a table that summarizes and categorizes certain types of information from the table in a report form.

database table   The database component in which data records and fields are stored in a row and column format.

destination application   The application receiving a set of information that was originally generated in another application.

destination file   The file containing a set of information that was originally generated in another application.

document   A Microsoft Word file in which you can enter, edit, and format multiple pages of text. Sometimes used to refer to a generic data file in other applications.

drag-and-drop editing   A mouse technique for directly moving or copying a set of information from one location to another.

embed   To insert an object from a source application into a destination document. When you double-click the object in the destination document, the source application is opened and the object can be edited.

embedded object   The set of information in a source application that can be opened and edited using the full resources of that application while it is in the destination document.

Equation Editor   A mathematical expression editor that you can use to correctly and automatically format expressions such as fractions, exponents, and integers in any Microsoft Office application.

export   The process of converting and saving a file to be used in another application. *See also* import.

field separator   The character that separates one data field from another, often a tab, comma, or semi-colon.

file format   The specific manner in which an application codes the information you enter into it.

form   *See* database form.

import   The process of converting and opening a file that was created in a different application. *See also* export.

link   To copy information from one application to another so that there is a dependent relationship between the object and its source file. Whenever the original information in the source file changes, the information in the linked object is automatically updated.

linked object   The set of information that originated in another application and maintains a connection to the source file.

mail merge   A process by which you can merge specific information in a data source (either a Word table or a Microsoft Access database) into a standard form letter to personalize each letter. *See also* data source.

main document   The mail merge document that contains the form letter into which the personalized information will be merged. *See also* data source.

merge fields   Locations within a main document that indicate where specific information from the data source is to be placed in the main document.

Microsoft Access   A relational database application that you can use to organize lists of information on employees, customers, inventory, contacts, and so forth. You can store the information in database tables, and then build queries to find specific information, create forms to facilitate quick data entry, and generate reports that summarize data.

Microsoft Excel   A spreadsheet application that you can use to store, manipulate, and analyze numerical information. You can enter data into a column and row format, perform calculations, and create charts.

Microsoft Graph   A simple graphing resource that you can use to create a variety of charts from tables of numeric data in any Microsoft Office application.

Microsoft Mail   An electronic mail application that you can use to send messages and files to other users in your network.

Microsoft Office   An integrated family of business applications. Microsoft Office Standard 4.2 includes Microsoft Word, Microsoft Excel, Microsoft PowerPoint, and the Microsoft Mail Workstation License. Microsoft Office Professional (version 4.3) adds Microsoft Access to this package.

Microsoft Office Manager   A utility that allows you to integrate Microsoft Office applications.

Microsoft Organization Chart   A tool that you can use to quickly create an organization chart in any Microsoft Office application.

Microsoft PowerPoint   A presentation application designed to bring text, graphics, and other resources together in unique combinations to create attractive presentation slides for meetings, training sessions, speeches, and other group talks.

Microsoft Word   A word processing application that you can use to enter, edit, and format text.

move   To transfer information from one location to another, either within a file, to another file, or to a file in another application.

object   The OLE component that contains information (such as text or graphics) created in the source application to be used the destination application.

Office Manager menu   The list of commands you can use to control Microsoft Office, get help on Microsoft Office, and customize Microsoft Office.

Office Manager toolbar   The toolbar displayed on the Windows desktop whenever Microsoft Office is open. The buttons on the toolbar represent each of the Microsoft Office applications you have installed on your computer.

OLE   The protocol that you can use to link or embed objects between different applications.

paste   To insert copied or moved information into a selected location in a file.

pivot table   A table in Microsoft Excel in which you can display two-dimensional summaries of selected data from a database in different combinations.

PowerPoint Viewer   A resource that you can use to view slide presentations on your computer, on other computers, and within files from other applications, regardless of whether PowerPoint is installed.

presentation   The Microsoft PowerPoint file in which you can create and design multiple slides or overhead foils for group talks.

query   *See* database query.

report   *See* database report.

Rich Text Format (RTF)   A file format that converts not only text but also formatting codes across different applications.

Route   The Microsoft Mail function that is available from the File menu of the Microsoft Office applications. With the Route command, you can send the current file to several other users sequentially or all at once.

sheet   *See* worksheet.

slide   A single page in a presentation file, consisting of text, graphics, a bulleted list, or other elements. Each slide can become a separate overhead foil, a photographic slide, or page in an audience handout.

source application   The application in which an original object is created and is then used in another (destination) application.

source file   The file that stores the original object that is being used in the destination application.

tab delimited   A file format in which fields of data are separated by tabs.

table   *See* database table.

text delimiter   The characters that separate text in a data field, such as apostrophes, commas, or quotation marks.

text only   A file format that converts text for use in other applications, but strips out any formatting codes.

tiling   A screen arrangement that displays two windows side by side or one on top of the other, so you can view the contents of both windows at the same time.

unbound object   A linked or embedded object that is common to all records in a database. Unbound objects are often used in database forms and reports to provide common information for all records.

WordArt   A special effects resource that you can use to apply creative font effects such as stretching, shadowing, shaping, and aligning to letters, words, and phrases.

workbook   The Microsoft Excel file in which you can store multiple sheets, charts, and modules.

worksheet   The set of rows, columns, and cells in which you store and manipulate Microsoft Excel data. There can be multiple worksheets in one workbook. Also called sheet.

Index

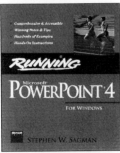

More from the Step by Step Series

The *Step by Step* books are the perfect self-paced training solution for Microsoft Office users. Each book comes with disk-based practice files. By using the practice files and following instructions in the book, you can learn by doing, which means you can start applying what you've learned to business situations right away. If you're too busy to attend a class or if classroom training doesn't make sense for you or your office, you can build the computer skills you need with the *Step by Step* books from Microsoft Press.

Microsoft® Word 6 for Windows™
Step by Step
Catapult, Inc.
336 pages, softcover with one 3.5-inch disk
$29.95 ($39.95 Canada)   ISBN 1-55615-576-X

Microsoft® Excel 5 for Windows™
Step by Step
Catapult, Inc.
368 pages, softcover with one 3.5-inch disk
$29.95 ($39.95 Canada)   ISBN 1-55615-587-5

Microsoft® PowerPoint® 4 for Windows™
Step by Step
Perspection, Inc.
350 pages, softcover with one 3.5-inch disk
$29.95 ($39.95 Canada)   ISBN 1-55615-622-7

Microsoft Access® 2 for Windows™
Step by Step
Catapult, Inc.
344 pages, softcover with one 3.5-inch disk
$29.95 ($39.95 Canada)   ISBN 1-55615-593-X

Microsoft Press.

IMPORTANT — READ CAREFULLY BEFORE OPENING SOFTWARE PACKET(S).
By opening the sealed packet(s) containing the software, you indicate your acceptance
of the following Microsoft License Agreement.

Microsoft License Agreement

MICROSOFT LICENSE AGREEMENT
Microsoft Press Step by Step
(Single User Products)

This is a legal agreement between you (either an individual or an entity) and Microsoft Corporation. By opening the sealed software packet(s) you are agreeing to be bound by the terms of this agreement. If you do not agree to the terms of this agreement, promptly return the book, including the unopened software packet(s), to the place you obtained it for a full refund.

MICROSOFT SOFTWARE LICENSE

1. GRANT OF LICENSE. Microsoft grants to you the right to use one copy of the Microsoft software program included with this book (the "SOFTWARE") on a single terminal connected to a single computer. The SOFTWARE is in "use" on a computer when it is loaded into temporary memory (i.e., RAM) or installed into permanent memory (e.g., hard disk, CD-ROM, or other storage device) of that computer. You may not network the SOFTWARE or otherwise use it on more than one computer or computer terminal at the same time.

2. COPYRIGHT. The SOFTWARE is owned by Microsoft or its suppliers and is protected by United States copyright laws and international treaty provisions. Therefore, you must treat the SOFTWARE like any other copyrighted material (e.g., a book or musical recording) except that you may either (a) make one copy of the SOFTWARE solely for backup or archival purposes, or (b) transfer the SOFTWARE to a single hard disk provided you keep the original solely for backup or archival purposes. You may not copy the written materials accompanying the SOFTWARE.

3. OTHER RESTRICTIONS. You may not rent or lease the SOFTWARE, but you may transfer the SOFTWARE and accompanying written materials on a permanent basis provided you retain no copies and the recipient agrees to the terms of this Agreement. You may not reverse engineer, decompile, or disassemble the SOFTWARE. If the SOFTWARE is an update or has been updated, any transfer must include the most recent update and all prior versions.

4. DUAL MEDIA SOFTWARE. If the SOFTWARE package contains both 3.5" and 5.25" disks, then you may use only the disks appropriate for your single-user computer. You may not use the other disks on another computer or loan, rent, lease, or transfer them to another user except as part of the permanent transfer (as provided above) of all SOFTWARE and written materials.

5. LANGUAGE SOFTWARE. If the SOFTWARE is a Microsoft language product, then you have a royalty-free right to reproduce and distribute executable files created using the SOFTWARE. If the language product is a Basic or COBOL product, then Microsoft grants you a royalty-free right to reproduce and distribute the run-time modules of the SOFTWARE provided that you: (a) distribute the run-time modules only in conjunction with and as a part of your software product; (b) do not use Microsoft's name, logo, or trademarks to market your software product; (c) include a valid copyright notice on your software product; and (d) agree to indemnify, hold harmless, and defend Microsoft and its suppliers from and against any claims or lawsuits, including attorneys' fees, that arise or result from the use or distribution of your software product. The "run-time modules" are those files in the SOFTWARE that are identified in the accompanying written materials as required during execution of your software program. The run-time modules are limited to run-time files, install files, and ISAM and REBUILD files. If required in the SOFTWARE documentation, you agree to display the designated patent notices on the packaging and in the README file of your software product.

LIMITED WARRANTY

LIMITED WARRANTY. Microsoft warrants that (a) the SOFTWARE will perform substantially in accordance with the accompanying written materials for a period of ninety (90) days from the date of receipt, and (b) any hardware accompanying the SOFTWARE will be free from defects in materials and workmanship under normal use and service for a period of one (1) year from the date of receipt. Any implied warranties on the SOFTWARE and hardware are limited to ninety (90) days and one (1) year, respectively. Some states/countries do not allow limitations on duration of an implied warranty, so the above limitation may not apply to you.

CUSTOMER REMEDIES. Microsoft's and its suppliers' entire liability and your exclusive remedy shall be, at Microsoft's option, either (a) return of the price paid, or (b) repair or replacement of the SOFTWARE or hardware that does not meet Microsoft's Limited Warranty and which is returned to Microsoft with a copy of your receipt. This Limited Warranty is void if failure of the SOFTWARE or hardware has resulted from accident, abuse, or misapplication. Any replacement SOFTWARE or hardware will be warranted for the remainder of the original warranty period or thirty (30) days, whichever is longer. Outside the United States, these remedies are not available without proof of purchase from an authorized non-U.S. source.

NO OTHER WARRANTIES. Microsoft and its suppliers disclaim all other warranties, either express or implied, including, but not limited to implied warranties of merchantability and fitness for a particular purpose, with regard to the SOFTWARE, the accompanying written materials, and any accompanying hardware. This limited warranty gives you specific legal rights. You may have others which vary from state/country to state/country.

NO LIABILITY FOR CONSEQUENTIAL DAMAGES. In no event shall Microsoft or its suppliers be liable for any damages whatsoever (including without limitation, damages for loss of business profits, business interruption, loss of business information, or any other pecuniary loss) arising out of the use of or inability to use this Microsoft product, even if Microsoft has been advised of the possibility of such damages. Because some states/countries do not allow the exclusion or limitation of liability for consequential or incidental damages, the above limitation may not apply to you.

U.S. GOVERNMENT RESTRICTED RIGHTS

The SOFTWARE and documentation are provided with RESTRICTED RIGHTS. Use, duplication, or disclosure by the Government is subject to restrictions as set forth in subparagraph (c)(1)(ii) of The Rights in Technical Data and Computer Software clause at DFARS 252.227-7013 or subparagraphs (c)(1) and (2) of the Commercial Computer Software — Restricted Rights 48 CFR 52.227-19, as applicable. Manufacturer is Microsoft Corporation, One Microsoft Way, Redmond, WA 98052-6399. This Agreement is governed by the laws of the State of Washington.

Should you have any questions concerning this Agreement, or if you desire to contact Microsoft for any reason, please write: Microsoft Sales and Service, One Microsoft Way, Redmond, WA 98052-6399.

CORPORATE ORDERS

If you're placing a large-volume corporate
order for additional copies of this
Step by Step title, or for any other
Microsoft Press book, you may be eligible
for our corporate discount.

Call **1-800-888-3303, ext. 61659,** for details.

097-000-681

The Step by Step Practice Files Disk

The enclosed 3.5-inch disk contains timesaving, ready-to-use practice files that complement the lessons in this book. To use the practice files, you'll need MS-DOS® operating system version 3.1 or later, Microsoft® Windows™ version 3.1 or later, and Microsoft Office for Windows version 4.2 or 4.3.

Each *Step by Step* lesson uses practice files from the disk. Before you begin the *Step by Step* lessons, read the "Getting Ready" section of the book for easy instructions telling how to install the files on your computer's hard disk. As you work through each lesson, be sure to follow the instructions for renaming the practice files so that you can go through a lesson more than once if you need to.

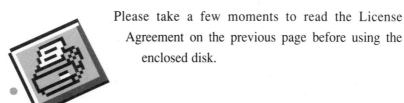

Please take a few moments to read the License Agreement on the previous page before using the enclosed disk.

Register your Microsoft Press® book today, and let us know what you think.

At Microsoft Press, we listen to our customers. We update our books as new releases of software are issued, and we'd like you to tell us the kinds of additional information you'd find most useful in these updates. Your feedback will be considered when we prepare a future edition; plus, when you become a registered owner, you'll get Microsoft Press catalogs and exclusive offers on specially priced books. Thanks!

I used this book as
❏ A way to learn the software
❏ A reference when I needed it
❏ A way to find out about
   advanced features
❏ Other _____

I purchased this book from
❏ A bookstore ❏ A software store
❏ A direct mail offer
❏ Other _____

I consider myself
❏ A beginning or an occasional computer user
❏ An intermediate-level user with a pretty
   good grasp of the basics
❏ An advanced user who helps and provides solutions
   for others
❏ Other _____

I will buy the next edition of the book when it's updated
❏ Definitely ❏ Probably
❏ I will not buy the next edition

The next edition of this book should include the following additional information:
1) _____
2) _____
3) _____

The most useful things about this book are _____
_____
_____

This book would be more helpful if _____
_____
_____

My general impressions of this book are _____
_____

May we contact you regarding your comments? ❏ Yes   ❏ No
Would you like to receive a Microsoft Press catalog regularly? ❏ Yes   ❏ No

Name _____

Company (if applicable) _____

Address _____

City _____ State _____ Zip _____

Daytime phone number (optional) (_____) _____

(1-55615-648-0A Microsoft Office for Windows Step by Step)

Please mail back your feedback form—postage free! Fold this form into an envelope, or fax this sheet to:

Microsoft Press, Attn: Marketing Department, Fax 206-936-7329

Microsoft Press.

NO POSTAGE
NECESSARY
IF MAILED
IN THE
UNITED STATES

BUSINESS REPLY MAIL

FIRST-CLASS MAIL   PERMIT NO. 108   REDMOND, WA

POSTAGE WILL BE PAID BY ADDRESSEE

ATTN: MARKETING DEPT
MICROSOFT PRESS
ONE MICROSOFT WAY
REDMOND WA   98052-9953